CONTENTS

To get around Manhattan use the subway and bus maps folded into the guide.

CONVENTIONAL SYMBOLS

★★★ Very highly recommended	**THE CLOISTERS**	Interstate Highway
★★ Recommended	**LEVER HOUSE**	① U.S. Highway
★ Interesting	**CITY HALL**	㉔ State Highway
See if possible	**BRYANT PARK**	

General maps		Detailed maps (pp. 34 to 114)
	## Urban Street System	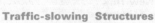
	Divided highway, Elevated highway	
	Divided scenic highway	
	Main cross-town street	
	Other cross-town street	
	Sightseeing route and recommended direction	
	Tree-lined street	
	No entry or street closed to traffic	
	Steps	

Traffic-slowing Structures

Underpass
Overpass or bridge
Interchange or junction
Railroad
Elevated rapid transit

Miscellaneous Symbols

Start of sightseeing tour — **START**
Church or building described
Church or building described
in a different walk
Church or building mentioned
Church, chapel (landmark)
Building (landmark)
University
Castle described
Isolated point of interest
Panoramic view; partial view
Height
Park
Park described
Cemetery
Cemetery described
Monument or statue
Fountain
Hospital
Synagogue
Factory
Gas tank
Airport

AZ **B** Reference letters locating points of interest

Visiting New York

You will find on pp. 16 to 19 two suggested programs for visiting New York in two or four days if you are pressed for time.

If you have more time available or if you want to plan your own visit, you should consult the map of the walks and principal sights (pp. 9 to 12) and use the descriptive texts of the guide (pp. 34 to 144).

PRACTICAL INFORMATION

WHEN TO VISIT NEW YORK

The Seasons. – The best season to visit New York is certainly the **fall** ; in early fall, between late September and early November, nature explodes in a blaze of color, Indian Summer has arrived. Warm temperatures, the clear transparency of the air and the brilliant colors of the trees, especially the reds and oranges of the maples, are typical of this favored season.

In the **summer,** temperatures may rise into the 90's however, practically all buildings and many buses and subway cars are air conditioned.

Although quite cold in **winter** (often around 32°F), New York's climate is fairly dry and brisk. The sky is usually a clear bright blue, which may suddenly be covered over with clouds bearing a rain or snowstorm, snarling traffic temporarily. **Spring** is a brief and uncertain season.

HOW TO GET AROUND NEW YORK

On foot

In the center of town, where traffic moves slowly at rush hours and "No Parking" signs abound, the best way to get around is on foot. A pleasant pastime during the day, walking by oneself is less safe at night in certain areas, especially for women : reasonable precautions should be taken. In general, it is wise to avoid the parks after nightfall.

By car

It is farily easy to get around by car, but not to park. Traffic moves smoothly except during the morning and afternoon rush hours.

Renting a car. – It is very easy to rent a car in New York if you hold one of the many credit cards. Compact model rentals are about $16 a day plus 24 cents a mile or $139 weekly (for 700 free miles ; after that 21 cents per mile). A chauffeur-driven limousine costs about $20 an hour up or 75 cents per mile, plus tips.

Hiring a taxi. – Taxis are identifiable by their color, yellow. There are very few taxi stands : one has to take one's chances on hailing a cab which is not always easy, especially at rush hours and on rainy days.

A cab ride costs 75 cents for the first 1/7 mile and 10 cents for each additional 1/7 mile. A minimum tip should be 20 cents on the dollar.

BUSES

There are more than 200 bus routes in the City over which some 4,500 buses operate. The bus system is a supplement to the subway system. In Manhattan, buses run north and south (uptown and downtown) on most avenues and east and west (crosstown) on principal crosstown, streets.

The route number and destination is indicated on the front of each bus. Buses stop frequently, about every two blocks. Passengers board the front of the bus and deposit 50 cents *(exact fare required)* or a subway token. Most of the lines run all night with reduced service after midnight.

THE SUBWAY

The subway system is the most popular means of transportation in New York and certainly the most practical for traveling long distances and for avoiding congested street traffic. Comfort has increased with the introduction of a new type of subway car which is larger, quieter and air-conditioned and makes for smoother riding.

Some 4 million passengers daily ride over 230 miles of track. The subway system never closes.

On Sunday travelers pay half fare on subways and buses.

Originally, some of the tracks were elevated (hence the nickname, "the El"). Now they are underground, except on some suburban lines.

A subway token costs 50 cents for a ride. You must deposit a token in the turnstile. Tokens may be purchased at any change-booth.

Our map shows only the subway system in Manhattan, all other details are to be found on the official map, obtainable on request at the stations free of charge.

Stations. – There are 460 stations in all. Many stations have signs above the platform that indicate what trains stop here. Some stations, especially the small local stops, have separate entrances for the uptown and downtown trains. Be sure to read the sign carefully before entering.

Trains. – There are express trains, which stop only at the most important stations, and local trains, which make all stops.

Before boarding, check the letter or number (i.e. the line) and the destination which appear on the front of the train and the sides of each car, since trains for several different points often use the same track.

Changing trains. – Any possibility of transfer is indicated on our map. The same station may have different names on different lines or different lines may have different stations with similar names.

STAYING IN NEW YORK

This section includes pratical information intended to facilitate your stay in New York (see map pp. 5-8).

HOTELS

Most hotels are in Manhattan, however some of the larger ones are near the airports. In Manhattan, most of the hotels are located in the midtown area. The most luxurious are on or near Fifth, Park and Madison Avenues ; others, with more modest rates, but stil offering hundreds of rooms, can be found in the theater district around Broadway.

Visitors who seek a less bustling atmosphere may prefer hotels in the Washington Square or Gramercy Park area, or near the Metropolitan Museum, on upper Fifth Avenue.

There are two main types of hotel in New York : the more or less commercial and usually ultra-modern, such as the Americana or the New York Hilton, with their extensive convention facilities ; and the continental type hotels, more intimate and luxurious in a slightly old-fashioned manner, such as the Pierre, the St. Regis and the Plaza.

Low-cost accomodations can be provided to students by the New York Student Center located at Hotel Empire 63rd Street and Broadway ; 695-0291.

Further information can be obtained from the Hotel Association of New York City, 141 West 51st Street, telephone : CL 7-0805.

USEFUL ADDRESSES

Unless otherwise indicated all telephone numbers listed have the area code 212.

Airports, heliports, airline and ship terminals. — For their location and main routes of access, see p. 21. For detailed information on flights contact the airline concerned (see map pp. 5-8).

Kennedy International Airport : Jamaica, Queens, New York ; 656-4444
La Guardia Airport : Flushing, Queens, New York ; 476-5001
Newark Airport : Newark, New Jersey ; (201) 961-2015
34th Street East Heliport : 34th Street at East River ; 895-5372
Pan Am Metroport : 60th Street at East River Drive ; 973-3528
Port Authority Downtown Heliport : Wall Street, Pier 6 ; 248-7240
East Side Terminal : First Avenue at 37th Street ; 697-3374
Passenger Ship Terminal : 711 12th Avenue at 52nd Street ; 466-7974.
Manhattan Air Terminal : 100 East 42nd Street ; 986-0888

American	661-4242	National	697-9000
Braniff	687-8200	Pan American	973-4000
Delta	239-0700	TWA	695-6000
Eastern	986-5000	United	867-3000

Information Bureaus. — New York Convention and Visitors Bureau, 90 East 42nd Street (across from Grand Central) ; 687-1300.

Spirit of New York Information Center 42nd Street and Broadway ; 221-9869.

Places of Worship. — A list is posted in most hotel lobbies. It gives their addresses and hours of services. Among them, we have chosen the best known.

Roman Catholic Churches : St. Patrick's Cathedral, Fifth Avenue at 51st Street ; 753-2261.
Notre-Dame, Morningside Drive at 114st Street ; UN 6-1500.
St. Vincent-Ferrer, Lexington Avenue at 66th Street ; 744-2080.
St. Vincent-de-Paul, 120 West 24th Street ; CH 3-4727.
Greek Orthodox Church : St. Nicholas, 155 Cedar Street ; BA 7-0773.
Baptist Church : Calvary Baptist, 123 W. 57th Street ; 975-0170.
Episcopal Churches : Cathedral of St. John the Divine, Amsterdam Avenue at 112th Street ; 678-6888.
St. Bartholomew's, Park Avenue at 51st Street ; PL 1-1616.
St. Thomas, Fifth Avenue at W. 53rd Street ; 397-1660.
Trinity, Broadway at Wall Street ; 285-0800.
Lutheran Churches : Gustavus Adolphus, 155 East 22nd Street ; OR 4-0739.
Holy Trinity, Central Park West at 65th Street ; TR 7-6815.
Methodist Churches : Christ Church Methodist, 520 Park Avenue ; TE 8-3036.
John Street, 44 John Street ; BO 9-0014.
Presbyterian Churches : Fifth Avenue, at 55th Street ; CI 7-0490.
Rutgers, 236 West 73rd Street ; TR 7-8227.
Synagogues : Temples Emanu-El, Fifth Avenue at 65th Street ; 744-1400.
Congregation B'Nai Jeshurun, 270 West 89th Street ; SU 7-7600.
Spanish and Portuguese Synagogue (Congregation Shearith Israel), 8 West 70th Street, 873-0300.

Miscellaneous information

U.S. General Post Offices : West Side : Eighth Avenue at 33rd Street.
East Side : Lexington Avenue at 45th Street.
Foreign Newspapers : Hotalings, 142 West 42nd Street. 279-5064.
Baby Sitters : Baby Sitters Guild ; 751-8730.
Part-time Child Care ; TR 9-4343.
Lost and Found : taxi, 87 Beaver Street ; 374-5084.
Subway or bus, 370 Jay Street, Brooklyn ; 625-6200.
Weather forecast ; WE 6-1212.
Exact time : 936-1616.
Car trouble : Police Emergency, 911.
New York County Medical Society : 582-1462.
Transit Authority : 330-1234.
Fire ; Police ; Ambulance : 911.

ENTERTAINMENT IN NEW YORK

New York, and especially Broadway, exerts a powerful attraction on out-of-towners in search of amusement, but the "New Yorkers" are also assiduous pleasure-seekers.

There is so much to do that the tourist could no doubt spend every evening out at a different "spot" for several months. Since such hardy souls are rare, we shall merely give some general information on entertainment.

For details you should consult a newspaper, or the weekly Cue, the New Yorker or New York magazines. Or call the Park Department Events : telephone 755-4100 for festivities in New York parks.

In many museums, libraries and other institutions, there are musical evenings, lectures, or film shows. In addition each borough has a cultural center of its own.

Opera and concerts. – A temple of the vocal art, the Metropolitan Opera moved in 1966 to Lincoln Center *(see p. 102)*.

The opera season is extremely popular, due to the quality of the troupe as well as the star performers. The season lasts from November to March. There are many regular subscribers, and tickets may be difficult to obtain.

At the New York State Theater, also in Lincoln Center, the New York City Opera Company gives excellent performances, although with less lavish means. Tickets are relatively moderately priced and easier to obtain than seats at the Met.

The most famous concert halls, presenting internationally known artists and orchestras, are Carnegie Hall (154 West 57th Street) *(see p. 121)* and Avery Fisher Hall at Lincoln Center.

The New York City Ballet dances at the New York State Theater, across the mall.

Legitimate Theaters. – The Broadway theater district in the Times Square area *(see p. 41)* has the greatest concentration of legitimate theaters in the world, presenting musical comedies, dramas and comedies. Hit plays are often sold out for months in advance. If you cannot obtain tickets at the box office, you can try a ticket agent or the entertainment desk at your hotel or by telephone order with the use of accepted credit cards, or by mail order.

"Off-Broadway" theater, centered in Greenwich Village, Upper East and West Sides, presents new and experimental plays and revivals of the classics in smaller playhouses.

"Off-Off Broadway" theaters offer a wide spectrum of theatrical material from avant-garde to classical revivals with an experimental approach. Presented usually in small intimate houses located throughout town, Off-Broadway theaters include play readings, workshops and full-scale productions, emphasizing audience involvement. For information on current events call 757-4473 or consult the *Village Voice*.

In the summer, open-air theater is quite popular : Shakespeare played in the evenings in Central Park *(free of charge)* draws so many enthusiasts that one has to line up more than an hour in advance.

Movie Theaters. – Many first-run movie houses are now located on the upper East Side. Most of these have continuous shows from noon to midnight. A great variety of films are shown in the Times Square area.

Some movie houses midtown and in Greenwich Village specialize in revivals.

Art and experimental films and special film series are programmed by the Museum of Modern Art and the Whitney Museum.

'New York by Night'. – In New York you will find everything from the students' dive in Greenwich Village, with whimsical or macabre decoration, through supper clubs to nightclubs with elaborate floor shows. Many of the latter are in large hotels.

Some clubs specialize in rock or jazz, others in satire of soft music. It is wise to reserve in the elegant establishments.

Sports. – The two most popular sports are football and baseball *(see p. 98)*. Basketball and boxing are also avidly followed. Football and baseball games often take place during the week.

The football season lasts from September to December ; baseball is played from April to October. Many games are played at night to avoid the heat, at Yankee Stadium *(see p. 125)* or Shea Stadium *(advance booking recommended)*. The Giant's Stadium, part of the Meadowlands complex in New Jersey, will be the home of the Giants football team.

Madison Square Garden *(see p. 97)* is the center of high quality sporting events : the famous horse show, rodeos, ice hockey, basketball and boxing in particular.

There is horse racing almost all year round : thoroughbred racing at the Aqueduct and Belmont race tracks, and harness racing at the Roosevelt and Yonkers Raceways, at the Meadowlands Racetrack, East Rutherford New Jersey both thoroughbred and harness racing occur.

SUGGESTED PROGRAMS FOR A SHORT VISIT

You will find in the pages of this guide all necessary historical and practical information on museums and monuments, as well as maps to direct you during your visit.

Guided tours. – The Museum of the City of New York organizes guided walking tours of the monuments and neighborhoods of New York. Each tour lasts about 2 hours ; information at the Museum, 1220 Fifth Avenue, New York 10029 ; telephone : LE 4-1672.

Other associations also organize guided tours ; consult a newspaper or specialized magazine (*Cue*, etc.).

Sightseeing by Helicopter. – Helicopter tours available every day all year round at Island Helicopters 34th Street East Heliport, 34th Street at East River : for further information call 895-5372. Reservations recommended.

Culture Bus Loops. – The New York City Transit Authority organizes two sightseeing tours which run on Saturdays, Sundays and holidays. The tickets valid for one day allow the tourist to get on and off at any of the scheduled stops, but do not include the admission price to any points of interest. The exact fare is required when boarding the bus at one of the stops or tickets can be bought, during the hours of Culture Bus Operation at subway change booths, Grand Central Terminal, Penn Station, Port Authority Bus Terminal and Times Square for Loops I and II ; Brooklyn Borough Hall and Atlantic Avenue for Loop II.

The **M41 Culture Bus Loop I** covering midtown and upper Manhattan, going in a clockwise direction has 22 scheduled stops. Included are such places of interest as Lincoln Center, the Metropolitan Museum of Art, Rockefeller Center, United Nations and the Empire State Building. Buses run from 10 AM to 6 PM every 20 minutes in July and August and every 30 minutes the rest of the year.

The **B88 Culture Bus Loop II** serves Brooklyn and lower Manhattan and has 32 stops along the route. Among the places of interest on this circuit are Brooklyn Heights, Prospect Park, Brooklyn Museum, Brooklyn Botanic Garden, Chinatown, Little Italy, United Nations, Greenwich Village, Battery Park and the South Street Seaport. Every 30 minutes from 9 AM to 6 PM.

The Transit Authority also organizes the Shoppers' Special, a daily ticket which for 75 cents allows unlimited rides at non-rush hours, within the midtown rectangle bounded by 59th and 32nd Streets and Third and Eighth Avenues. The Night on the Town Bus Ticket (75 cents) allows unlimited riding for the night on any Manhattan bus, except express buses from 6 PM to 2 AM.

PROGRAM FOR TWO DAYS

First Day   **Getting acquainted with New York**

Morning

A guided bus tour, such as the 4-1/2 hour Gray Line Grand Tour★★★, will introduce you to the City.

Departure 9:00 AM from terminal 900 Eighth Avenue at 53rd Street. Independent subway "D" or "E" train to Seventh Avenue/53rd Street station. Adults $9.50, children $6.50. Information 397-2600.

Lunch

Midtown west (ethnic restaurants in the Clinton area).

Afternoon

Three-hour Circle Line Boat Tour around Manhattan Island★★★ from pier 83, West 43rd Street.

Frequent sailings end of March through mid-November, from 9:45 AM on. Adults $6.00, children $3.00. Information 563-3200. Westbound crosstown buses to pier : No. 106 on 42nd Street or No. 27 on 49th Street.

The trip offers spectacular views of Manhattan's skyline, the great bridges of New York and the Statue of Liberty. Refreshments available on boat.
or
Sightseeing by Helicopter *(see above)*.

Dinner and Evening

Dinner and a show in the Broadway Theater District★★ (for ticket information see p. 15 and p. 42).

Second Day   **From Rockefeller Center to Greenwich Village**

Morning

Rockefeller Center★★★ *(p. 34)* will strike you as a remarkable example of contemporary architecture and urban design.

Take a Fifth Avenue bus to 34th Street. Enjoy a magnificent panoramic view of the New York area from the Observatory of the Empire State Building★★★ *(p. 44)*.

Walk east to Park Avenue, take bus No. 1 to the Financial District★★★ *(p. 87)*. Historic and modern landmarks combine to make Lower Manhattan one of the most interesting walking districts in town.

Lunch

In Lower Manhattan.

Afternoon

Take IRT subway uptown to Grand Central Station. Walk east along 42nd Street★★ *(p. 68)* to the United Nations★★★ *(p. 65)*.

Leaving the United Nations, walk along 49th or 50th Streets to Park Avenue★★★ *(p. 71)*.

Dinner and Evening

Spend the rest of the afternoon and the evening in Greenwich Village★★, a center of cultural and recreational attractions *(p. 78)*.

Independent subway "E" or "F" train from 5th Avenue/53rd Street station to East 4th Street or Fifth Avenue buses Nos. 1, 2, 3, 5, to Washington Square or thereabouts.

For an extra day see p. 18.

PROGRAM
FOR TWO DAYS

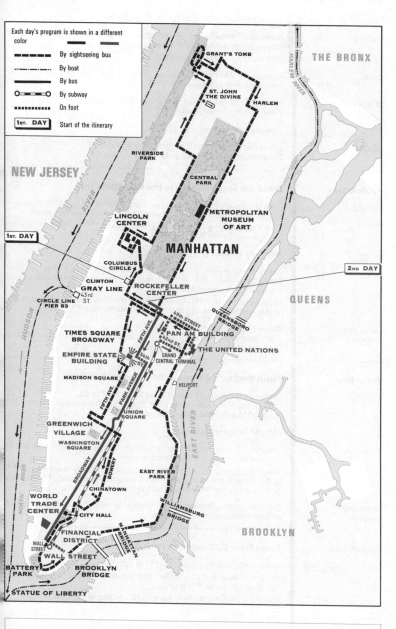

Airports - Heliports - Airline Terminals

*For location of facilities refer to
page 21 : the map of "FEEDER ROADS AND THROUGH ROADS".*

Name	Location	Telephone	Distance to Midtown
Airports			
Kennedy International Airport	Jamaica, Queens, New York	(212) 656-4444	15 miles
La Guardia Airport	Flushing, Queens, New York	(212) 476-5001	8 miles
Newark Airport	Newark, N.J.	(201) 961-2015	16 miles
Heliports			
Pan Am Metroport	60th Street at East River Drive	(212) 973-3528	
Port Authority Downtown Heliport	Wall Street, Pier 6	(212) 248-7240	
34th Street East Heliport	34th Street at East River	(212) 895-5372	
Airline Terminals			
East Side Terminal	First Ave at 37th Street	(212) 697-3374	
Manhattan Air Terminal	100 East 42nd Street	(212) 986-0888	

PROGRAM
FOR FOUR DAYS

First Day — From Rockefeller Center to Broadway

Morning

Rockefeller Center★★★ *(p. 34)* will strike you as a remarkable example of contemporary architecture and urban design.
Visit the Museum of Modern Art★★★ *(p. 38)*.

Lunch

Museum of Modern Art Garden Restaurant or Midtown west (ethnic restaurants in the Clinton area).

Afternoon

Three-hour Circle Line Boat Tour around Manhattan Island★★★ from pier 83, West 43rd Street *(see details p. 16)*
or
Sightseeing by Helicopter *(p. 16)*.

Evening

Dinner and a show in the Broadway Theater District★★.
Ticket information p. 15 and p. 42.

Second Day — From the Empire State to the RCA Building

Morning

From the Observatory of the Empire State Building★★★ *(p. 44)*, Fifth Avenue at 34th Street, you will enjoy a panoramic view of the New York area.
Take a leisurely stroll on cosmopolitan Fifth Avenue★★★ *(p. 43)* as far as 59th Street where Central Park★ begins *(p. 99)*.

Lunch

Near Central Park.

Afternoon

Take a Madison Avenue bus to 82nd Street, walk one block west ; visit the Metropolitan Museum of Art★★★ *(see p. 54)* ; plan to devote enough time to the area of your special interest.
Before returning to midtown on a Fifth Avenue bus, catch a glimpse of the unique snail-like silhouette of the Guggenheim Museum★★ *(p. 64)*.

Dinner and Evening

Dinner Midtown west
The Observation Roof of the RCA Building★★★ *(p. 35)* commands a breathtaking view of New York by night.

Third Day — From the United Nations to Greenwich Village

Morning

Begin your morning tour at the United Nations★★★ *(p. 65)*.
Leaving the U.N., walk along 42nd Street★★ *(p. 68)* towards the Pan Am Building★★★ and Grand Central Station★.

Lunch

Midtown or Lower Manhattan.

Afternoon

Historic and modern landmarks combine to make Lower Manhattan one of the most interesting walking districts in town.
Take IRT Express No. 4 to Wall Street, visit the World Trade Center★★★ *(p. 87)*. Other sights nearby are Chase Manhattan Bank Building★★ and Plaza *(p. 92)* and City Hall★★ *(p. 84)*, as well as Chinatown★★ *(p. 83)*.

Dinner and Evening

Enjoy the artistic atmosphere of Greenwich Village★★ *(p. 78)*, a center of cultural and recreational attractions.

Fourth Day — From Frick Collection to Park Avenue

Morning

Visit the exquisite Frick Collection★★★ *(p. 52)*.
At Fifth Avenue and 67th Street, take crosstown bus 29 through Central Park to Lincoln Center★★★ *(p. 102)*.
Take the guided tour of the famous music and theater complex.

Lunch

Near Lincoln Center.

Afternoon

At 66th Street/Broadway, take IRT subway downtown one stop to Columbus Circle, change to uptown Independent "A" train to 190th Street. Walk through Fort Tryon Park★★ *(p. 109)*. Visit the Cloisters★★★ *(p. 110)*, a museum of medieval art housed in reconstructed European monasteries.
Return to midtown on bus No. 4.
On Park Avenue★★★ *(p. 71)*, you may view some of New York's most beautiful modern buildings.

Evening

Dine in one of the elegant hotels or supper clubs near Park Avenue.

FINAL DAY

If you have an extra day or even a morning, visit the highlights of one of the other boroughs. A selection of their main sights is briefly described at the end of the guide : the Bronx *(pp. 123-126)* Brooklyn *(pp. 127 to 132)*, Queens *(pp. 133 to 135)*, and Staten Island *(pp. 136 to 137)*.

To find the description a point of interest which you already know by name, please consult the **index,** pp. 145 to 148.

Each day's program is shown in a different color

- - - - - By boat
———— By bus
o—o—o By subway
■■■■■■■■ On foot
| 1ST. DAY | Start of the itinerary

THE CLOISTERS
FORT TRYON PARK
190 ST. FT. WASH. AV.

WASHINGTON BRIDGE

THE BRONX

NEW JERSEY

HUDSON RIVER

RIVERSIDE PARK

HARLEM

MANHATTAN

CENTRAL PARK

1ST. DAY

METROPOLITAN MUSEUM OF ART   GUGGENHEIM MUSEUM

LINCOLN CENTER

42nd ST.

FIFTH AVENUE

MADISON AVE.

FRICK COLLECTION

4TH DAY

COLUMBUS CIRCLE
MUSEUM OF MODERN ART
CLINTON
ROCKEFELLER CENTER

CIRCLE LINE PIER 83

42nd ST.

R C A BUILDING

GRAND ARMY PLAZA

QUEENSBORO BRIDGE

QUEENS

PARK AVENUE

TIMES SQUARE BROADWAY

FIFTH AVE.

PAN AM BUILDING

2ND DAY

GRAND CENTRAL TERMINAL

42nd ST.

THE UNITED NATIONS

34th STREET

EMPIRE STATE BUILDING

HELIPORT

3RD DAY

GREENWICH VILLAGE

WASHINGTON SQUARE

EAST RIVER

CITY HALL

WORLD TRADE CENTER

CHINATOWN

WILLIAMSBURG BRIDGE

NORTH RIVER

FINANCIAL DISTRICT

BROOKLYN

WALL STREET

CHASE MANHATTAN BANK

MANHATTAN BRIDGE

WALL STREET
BROOKLYN BRIDGE

STATUE OF LIBERTY

NEW YORK : A BRIEF SKETCH

THE CITY AND THE STATE OF NEW YORK

A magnet for much of the northeastern United States, the city of New York is a world unto itself because of its size, the density and diversity of its population its dynamic economic activity and its vibrant cultural life.

Location. – On the east coast of the United States, New York is bathed by the Atlantic Ocean ; the nearby Labrador current chills its waters, but not the summer temperatures in the city. The location of the Port of New York is unique *(details, p. 26)* ; the Hudson River and the East River (in fact an estuary, like the Harlem River) are two relatively protected waterways, ideal for ocean-going vessels.

New York Bay is also protected by two islands to the south. The Narrows lead out to the open sea from one of the largest and safest bays in the world.

New York City is located at 40° north latitude and 74° west longitude. Its height above sea level varies from 5 feet (Battery Park) to 400 feet (Washington Heights). The climate is of the continental type *(see details on the seasons, p. 13)*, with predominating westerly winds, although one can frequently enjoy a sea breeze.

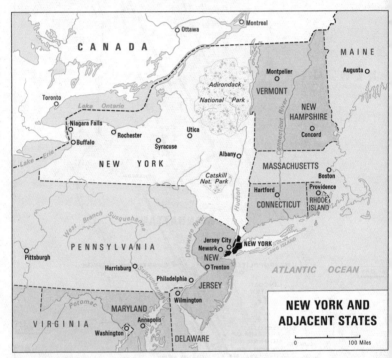

**NEW YORK AND
ADJACENT STATES**

0 _____ 100 Miles

Size and population. – The total area of the five boroughs *(see below)* which make up New York City is about 300 square miles ; the longest distance beween its boundaries, from the northeast to the southwest, is about 35 miles.

The total population of New York City is 7,454,000 inhabitants, of whom 20 % are Manhattanites. If we add the daily commuters it raises the total to 10,000,000. Only London and Tokyo can rival these imposing figures. The population is of various origins, a result of successive waves of immigration *(see p. 24)*.

The five boroughs. – New York City, limited to the borough of Manhattan until 1898, has since then incorporated the other four boroughs ; their boundaries are the same as the counties which previously existed : **Manhattan** (New York County), **Brooklyn** (Kings County), **Queens, the Bronx** and **Staten Island** (Richmond County). These counties correspond to the original colonial administrative divisions : the names of the counties still persist for judicial districts. **Greater New York** includes the five boroughs, plus Nassau and Suffolk (Long Island), Westchester, Rockland and Putnam counties.

The Bronx is the only borough which is a part of the continent, for Manhattan and Richmond are islands, and Brooklyn and Queens are on the western end of Long Island. New York is, indeed, as geographers have pointed out, an archipelago, a city on the water.

The five boroughs are not developed to the same extent. A few open spaces exist on the fringes of Brooklyn and Queens ; Staten Island is still quite countrified. However, it has been developing rapidly since the completion of the Verrazano-Narrows Bridge.

	Manhattan	The Bronx	Queens	Brooklyn	Staten Island
Surface in square miles	22.7	41.2	108	70.3	57.5
Population (1976)	1,417,000	1,343,000	1,967,000	2,398,000	328,000

The New York Metropolitan Area. – This is the name of the economic region of 29 counties around New York City.

Twelve of these counties are in New York State, nine in New Jersey and one in Connecticut *(see map opposite)*.

The region extends over 7,000 square miles and includes about 12,000,000 inhabitants.

In addition to the city of New York itself, the area includes Newark (390,000) and five other cities of over 100,000 in population.

Two organizations are responsible for the expansion of transportation facilities in the Metropolitan Area : the Port Authority of New York and New Jersey, which covers 17 counties in New York State and New Jersey, and the Triborough Bridge and Tunnel Authority *(for details on these two bodies, see p. 27)*.

The State of New York. – The city gave its name to the state, the eleventh of the original 13 states of the Union, which by virtue of its economic expansion and political influence became known as the "Empire State", as Washington had foreseen.

New York State extends from east of the Hudson to the Great Lakes and Niagara Falls ; it borders Canada on the north. It is divided into counties, and its capital is Albany (New York City was the capital from 1784-1797).

The flag of New York City, with its blue, white and orange vertical stripes, was inspired by the flag of the Netherlands in the 17th century.

FEEDER ROADS AND THROUGH ROADS

The map below shows the main roads leading into the city, as well as through roads which cross or bypass it ; it also includes the bridges, tunnels, railroad, bus and ship terminals, airports, heliports and airline terminal which are most used by visitors.

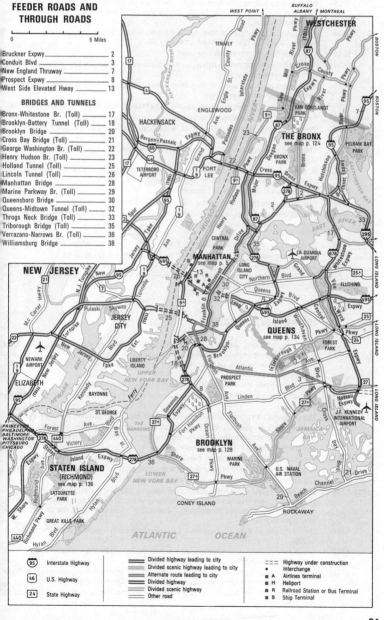

FEEDER ROADS AND THROUGH ROADS

0   5 Miles

Bruckner Expwy	2
Conduit Blvd	3
New England Thruway	7
Prospect Expwy	8
West Side Elevated Hway	13

BRIDGES AND TUNNELS

Bronx-Whitestone Br. (Toll)	17
Brooklyn-Battery Tunnel (Toll)	18
Brooklyn Bridge	20
Cross Bay Bridge (Toll)	21
George Washington Br. (Toll)	22
Henry Hudson Br. (Toll)	23
Holland Tunnel (Toll)	25
Lincoln Tunnel (Toll)	26
Manhattan Bridge	28
Queensboro Bridge	30
Queens-Midtown Tunnel (Toll)	32
Throgs Neck Bridge (Toll)	33
Triborough Bridge (Toll)	35
Verrazano-Narrows Br. (Toll)	36
Williamsburg Bridge	38

(95) Interstate Highway	
(46) U.S. Highway	
(24) State Highway	

═══ Divided highway leading to city	
Divided scenic highway leading to city	
Alternate route leading to city	
Divided highway	
Divided scenic highway	
Other road	

═ ═ ═ Highway under construction	
• Interchange	
■ A Airlines terminal	
■ H Heliport	
■ R Railroad Station or Bus Terminal	
■ S Ship Terminal	

NEW YORK
IN THE PAST

THE INDIANS - NEW AMSTERDAM

In early times the area was peopled by Indians, each tribe with its own specific territory lived a fairly peaceful and settled existence in villages of bark huts, gaining their livelihood from crop planting, hunting, trapping and fishing. The Algonquin tribe was the most numerous in the New York area.

1524 The first European explorer enters the bay. **Giovanni da Verrazano,** an Italian in the service of the French King, Francis I, discovers the island of Manhattan *(p. 93).*

1609 **Henry Hudson** sails up the river which now bears his name, in his ship the *Half Moon,* while on a voyage for the Dutch East India Company looking for the legendary Northwest passage.

1613 The Dutch explorer cum trader, Adriaen Block, is forced to winter on the island when his boat, the *Tiger* burns off Manhattan *(p. 114).*

1614 The name New Netherland is first used.

1619 Arrival of African slaves on American soil in Jamestown and the first in New York City with the first settlement.

1624 A shipload of Dutch settlers, including some Walloons, arrive and settle in various places throughout the province.

1625 First permanent settlement is established. The trading post is named **Nieuw Amsterdam.**

1626 **Peter Minuit** buys Manhattan from the Indians for the equivalent $24.

1628 With the arrival of a regular minister, a member of the Reformed Dutch Church, the island's first church is established.

1639 The Dane, Johannes Bronck settles beyond the Harlem River, in the area now known as the Bronx.

1642 A settlement is made at Maspeth (Queens), but first permanent settlement not established until 1643, at Flushing.

1644 Some slaves are given partial freedom.

1647 **Peter Stuyvesant** becomes Director-General of the community *(p. 81).*

1653 The settlement of Nieuw Amsterdam (New Amsterdam) is recognized as a town and receives a charter. Stuyvesant has a protective wall built on the present location of Wall Street.

1654 First permanent Jewish settlement in the colonies established in New Amsterdam.

1661 First permanent settlement established on Staten Island at Oude Dorp.

1664 As a repercussion of the English and Dutch trading rivalries in Europe, the English take New Amsterdam without a struggle and rename it **New York** after the Duke of York, the brother of the English King, Charles II.

TOWARDS INDEPENDENCE

1667 The Treaty of Breda, ending the second Anglo-Dutch war, confirms the English control over the province of New Netherland, while the Dutch retain Surinam or Dutch Guiana. The town of New York passes under the English system of municipal government. English replaces Dutch as the official language.

1673 The Dutch retake New York without a fight and rename it New Orange.

1674 By the Treaty of Westminster the province of New Netherland becomes permanently English.

1686 The Dongan Charter, the second English charter, is granted carrying the city seal.

1689 A rebellion in England against the Catholic King James II, the former Duke of York, causes him to abdicate and flee the country. Leisler's Rebellion in New York is a rising, led by Jacob Leisler against the English rule.

1725 The first New York newspaper, the *New-York Gazette* is founded by **William Bradford.**

1729 Beaver Street is the site of New York's first synagogue.

1732 The first theater opens in the vicinity of Maiden Lane.

1733-1734 **John Peter Zenger** starts the *New-York Weekly Journal,* in which he attracks the Governor. A year later some of the offending works are publicly burned in the street and Zenger is imprisoned for slander. The acquittal of Zenger marks the beginning of a free press *(p. 87).*

1754 The first college, **King's College** now Columbia University opens behind Trinity Church *(p. 88).*

1763 The Treaty of Paris marks the end of the French and Indian War or Seven Years' War and confirms the English control in the continent.

1765 Meeting of the Stamp Act Congress in New York, where representatives from nine colonies denounce the English colonial policy of taxation without representation.

1766 Repeal of the Stamp Act. A statue is erected to **William Pitt,** the man who did most to obtain the repeal.

1767	**The Townshend Acts,** named after the British Chancellor of the Exchequer, a series of 4 acts which increase taxation and threaten the already established traditions of colonial self-government. The repeal three years later coincided with the Boston Massacre.
1775-1783	The War of Independence, also known as the **American Revolution.**
1776	**Declaration of Independence** *(p. 85)* sets off the American Revolution. The British take control of Long Island after the Battle of Long Island and Washington safely withdraws his forces to Manhattan. From his headquarters at the Morris-Jumel Mansion *(p. 115)* he masterminds his victory at the Battle of Harlem Heights *(p. 106)*. The Americans temporarily repulse the British in the Bronx (Westchester County) in October, but on November 17, Fort Washington falls in northern Manhattan and the British occupy all of the present New York City until 1783.
1783	**The Treaty of Paris** (September 3) ends the U.S. War of Independence and England recognizes Independence for the 13 colonies. The last British troops evacuate New York and Washington returns to the city in triumph before bidding farewell to his troops at Fraunces Tavern on December 4 *(p. 90)*.

NEW YORK AND THE UNION

1784	New York becomes the capital of New York state and a year later is named U.S. Capital under the Articles of Confederation.
1787	The Congress, sitting in New York City, enacts the Northwest Ordinance.
1789	The **Constitution** of the United States is ratified. **Washington** elected first President, takes the oath of office at Federal Hall *(see illustration and p. 91)* in New York City, the first capital under the Constitution.
1790	First official census of the population of Manhattan : 33,000. Federal Capital moves to Philadelphia.
1792	Founding of the forerunner to the New York exchange by the buttonwood tree *(p. 91)* on Wall Street.
1797	Albany becomes the permanent capital of New York State.
1807	**Robert Fulton** tries out his steam-boat, the *Clermont* on the Hudson. The first demonstration had been made on the Collect Pond by John Fitch in 1796.

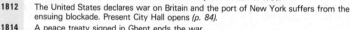

1812	The United States declares war on Britain and the port of New York suffers from the ensuing blockade. Present City Hall opens *(p. 84)*.
1814	A peace treaty signed in Ghent ends the war.
1825	Opening of the **Erie Canal**. New York becomes the gateway to the Great Lakes and the West.
1828	South Street becomes the center of New York's port activities.
1834	City of Brooklyn incorporated.
1835	The Great Fire destroys much of the business area of the town.
1853	World's Fair at the Crystal Palace *(p. 46)*.
1858	Central Park is begun and although parts are open to the public soon thereafter it is not officially completed until 1876.
1861	Start of the **Civil War** with New York on the side of the Union or the 23 Northern States.
1863	Draft Riots : organized insurrection against the avoidance of conscription by payment of $300.
1865	End of the Civil War. Assassination of **Lincoln** *(p. 84)*.
1868	Opening of **the El,** first experimental elevated railway in Lower Manhattan.
1882	Electricity is offered for general use by Thomas Edison's plant in Lower Manhattan.
1883	Opening of **Brooklyn Bridge** *(p. 86)*.
1886	Inauguration of the **Statue of Liberty** *(p. 95)*.
1898	**Greater New York** is created comprising the five boroughs of Manhattan, Brooklyn, the Bronx, Queens and Staten Island. With a population of more than 3 million New York is the world's largest town.

NEW YORK IN THE TWENTIETH CENTURY

1902	Completion of one of the first New York skyscrapers, **Flatiron Building** *(p. 122)*.
1904	Opening of the first underground line of the subway.
1913	**Armory Show,** an international exhibition of modern art.
1927	Ticker tape parade in honor of Charles Lindbergh.
1929	Financial panic of October − the start of the Great Depression.
1931	The **Empire State Building** is completed after two years work *(p. 44)*.
1939-1940	World's Fair at Flushing Meadows attracts over 44 million visitors.
1945	**United Nations** charter is drafted and meetings are held at various locations in New York City until permanent headquarters are ready.
1948	The John F. Kennedy Airport (formerly Idlewild) opens in Queens.
1952	The General Assembly of the United Nations meets for the first time in its new headquarters overlooking East River *(p. 65)*.
1964-1965	World's Fair on the same site as the 1939-1940 Fair.
1969	Ticker Tape Parade : New York gives a triumphal welcome to the first astronauts to land on the moon.
1973	Opening of the World Trade Center in Manhattan.
1975-1976	**American Bicentennial celebrations** (New York City : May 1975 - Nov. 1976).

NEW YORK'S POPULATION

New York has always been known for its cosmopolitanism. The diversity of the population can be traced to the successive waves of immigration to the port of entry into the New World. New York has occasionally been described as "the largest Jewish city" or "the largest Irish town" or "the second largest Italian community" in the world, and the recent influx of Latin Americans and Asians has again changed its physiognomy. It is a tribute to the city that New Yorkers have come to share a common outlook and way of life retaining their ethnic identity and the pride of their cultural heritage.

Population from 1626 to 1976 :

Year	Number of Inhabitants	Events
1626	200	The first boatload of settlers brought by the Dutch to New Amsterdam consists primarily of Protestants of French origin.
1656	1000	The first immigrants are followed by English, Scots, Germans and Scandinavians.
1756	16,000	
1790	33,000	
1800	60,000	Half of New York's population is now of English origin.
1856	630,000	In the middle of the 19th century, Germans and Irish arrive in large numbers.
1880	1,911,700	Beginning in 1880, eastern Europeans and southern Italians immigrate in great waves. This influx will continue until 1924.
1900	3,437,200	This figure includes the five boroughs for the first time.
1920	5,620,000	After the First World War, Negro migration grows, both from the South and from the West Indies.
1924		The immigration law limits foreign immigration.
1930	6,930,500	The rate of growth starts to decline.
1950	7,892,000	After the Second World War, a large Puerto Rican colony settles in New York.
1960	7,782,000	From 1950 to 1960 New York loses more than 100,000 inhabitants. Many New Yorkers have left the city proper for the suburbs.
1970	7,896,000	
1973	7,716,600	
1976	7,454,000	

A population of various origins

In the 19th century and at the beginning of the 20th century, recent immigrants, referred to as "hyphenated citizens", were often denied social status by the "aristocracy" of British and Dutch origin. However, the pyramid of the New York society was not able to withstand the forces of change for long, and today these multi-cultural stands make-up the very fabric of New York's population.

The Italians. – Large-scale Italian immigration only started after 1870. It consisted mainly of laborers and peasants from Southern Italy and Sicily. Many journeyed back to the old country with their first savings, but by far the largest majority brought over their families.

A great number of Italian immigrants started out in the building industry where they worked under the heavy hand of "padroni" (construction bosses), but over the years hard work and enterprise often combined to establish a small family business, especially in the restaurant, contracting and trucking trades.

After generations of economic and social rewards in the New World, Italian-Americans remain deeply attached to the traditions of their family and community life. The colorful atmosphere of their homeland is reflected in "Little Italy".

Russians and Ukrainians. – The massive waves of pre-World War I emigration from the old Russian Empire were not made up of Russians, strangely enough, but mostly of representatives of various minority nationalities – Ukrainians, Poles, Jews, Lithuanians, and others.

At first on the bottom rungs of the American social and economic ladder, like most newly arrived immigrants they tended to congregate in the same neighborhoods as their countrymen.

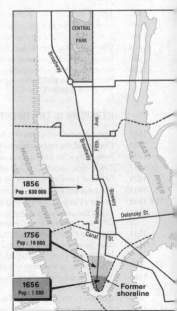

The 1917 Revolution brought only a trickle of so-called White Russians to New York as compared to the large numbers who emigrated to Paris and other European capitals. Many Ukrainians and Russians, however, were among the "displaced persons" who settled in New York in the wake of the Second World War.

The Jews. – Sephardic Jews, originally from Spain and Portugal, had come to New York in the 17th century, mostly via Holland and Latin America. Today, however, the majority of the New York Jews are of Eastern and Central European descent. The Lower East Side was the first home for one-and-a-half million Jews who entered America between 1880 and 1910 ; a great number settled in Brooklyn communities.

New York Jewry has actively participated in all economic and cultural endeavors, and the names of many Jewish individuals and institutions are woven into the history of New York.

The Blacks. – Although there were Blacks among the early inhabitants of New York, it was only in the 20th century that Blacks migrated to the city in large numbers. Today, they total some 2,200,000 or roughly one-fifth of the New York population. Coming mainly from the rural South, Blacks have had to make a difficult adjustment to the urban environnement and the requirements of the industrial economy.

The Black community has richly contributed to the character of the city. It has produced distinguished writers, playwrights and performers, and the influence of Rhythm and Blues and of Jazz is deeply felt on the American musical scene.

The Puerto Ricans. – The growth in the population of Puerto Rican origin has been rapid : only 500 in 1910, they were 77,000 in 1940 but numbered 613,000 in 1960 ; their group is now 812,000. In 1952 Puerto Rico became a commonwealth, but since 1917 its residents have been United States citizens traveling to the continent as they like.

"El Barrio" in East Harlem is host to a large Puerto Rican group, along with parts of the Upper West Side, Brooklyn and the South Bronx.

Just as earlier immigrants, Puerto Ricans had to overcome social and economic barriers, but in roughly one generation they have emerged as a vital community, mindful of their culture, who lend a distinctive Latin flavor to the life of the city.

Germans and Austrians. – This was probably the most rapidly assimilated group, although one of the largest. Composed of conservatives and liberals, craftsmen, laborers, businessmen and intellectuals, they no longer form a very unified group. Leaving behind them in most cases the language of the "old country", they still share a few national traditions.

Germans arrived in great numbers during the 19th century, particularly after the 1848-49 revolution in Germany had failed. They settled mostly around Tompkins Square from where they later moved further uptown. Some German atmosphere can still be found in Yorkville *(see p. 121)*.

The Irish. – Irish immigration dates back to the 17th century, but it was the outbreak of the Irish Potato Famine, in 1846, that touched off the mass exodus from Ireland. In 1890, one-fourth of all New Yorkers were Irish.

From the beginning, the Irish were drawn to public affairs and actively participated in city government. Carrying on the religious tradition of their homeland, they have largely contributed to the influence of the Roman Catholic Church in the United States.

Still a quite homogenous group, Irish-Americans are famous for their exuberant celebration of St. Patrick's Day, March 17, to honor the patron saint of the "ould sod".

The Chinese. – Coming to America after the Civil War, they were mostly from Canton. Today there are more than 70,000 Chinese in New York City with the greatest concentration in Chinatown *(see p. 83)*, the Chinese quarter of New York which is now somewhat Americanized.

Others. – Among those from Eastern Europe, the Polish colony should be noted for the big Polish parade on Fifth Avenue, the first Sunday in October. A sizable Greek community lives in Queens. The recent liberalization of the immigration law has brought an influx of South Americans and Asians.

Terminals

Name and Telephone	Location	Services
Grand Central Terminal . 532-4900 736-4545	East 42nd St., Vanderbilt to Lexington Avenues.	Metropolitan Region, Harlem, Hudson and New Haven Commuter lines. AMTRAK long-distance trains. Grand Central is also a subway stop.
Pennsylvania Station ... 736-6000 739-4200 736-4545	Seventh Avenue from 31st to 33rd St.	New Jersey Commuter lines. L.I.R.R. Long Island Railroad trains. AMTRAK long-distance trains. Pennsylvania Station is also a subway stop.
Port Authority Bus Terminals Midtown .... 564-8484 Uptown 564-1114	Eighth and Ninth Avenues at 41st St. Washington Bridge at 178th St. and Broadway.	Suburban and long line service. Suburban and long line service.

Airports - Heliports - Airline Terminals ..... see p. 17
Toll tunnels and bridges .... see p. 126

NEW YORK'S ECONOMY

Since colonial times, shipping, banking and manufacturing have been the mainstays of economic activity in New York. Other strong sectors are the headquarters activities of most major American corporations, the garment industry, publishing and communications.

The Port. – The first ship berths were built in lower Manhattan on the East River around Fulton Street. The piers originally were extensions of the city streets. As the city grew in the 18th and 19th centuries, wharves and piers were developed along the Hudson River in Manhattan, on the East River in Brooklyn, and in Jersey City and Hoboken, New Jersey.

Today, the port with some 750 miles of shoreline, provides docking space for more than 250 large ships at one time, with specialized facilities to handle any type of cargo. The Manhattan shoreline, ill-suited for modern cargo handling methods is now being developed for commercial, residential and recreational projects (Manhattan Landing on the east side and Battery Park City on the west side) while containerization and other industrial projects are being concentrated on the shorelines of other sections of the harbor. Automated handling of cargo in large steel containers was adopted by major shipping lines and freighters began using specialized new terminals in Brooklyn, Staten Island and in New Jersey. The world's largest and busiest container terminal is operated by the Port Authority in Elizabeth, New Jersey.

Natural Advantages. – They can be listed as follows :
  – a huge and safe harbor which needs little dredging ;
  – a protected anchorage area within the Upper Bay ;
  – channels at least 45 feet deep leading to many pier areas ;
  – proximity to the open sea and freedom from ice ;
  – a climate usually free of fog ;
  – a relatively small (less than five feet) difference between high and low tides.

1976	New York	Rotterdam	Marseilles	London	Yokohama	Genoa
Freight . . . . . . (in metric tons)	117,000,000	280,000,000	103,980,000	48,600,000	113,805,000	49,500,000

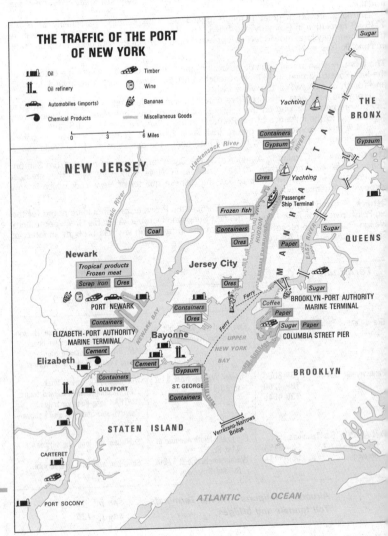

THE TRAFFIC OF THE PORT OF NEW YORK

Oil
Oil refinery
Automobiles (imports)
Chemical Products
Timber
Wine
Bananas
Miscellaneous Goods

0   3   6 Miles

NEW JERSEY

Hackensack River

Passaic River

Newark

Tropical products
Frozen meat
Scrap iron   Ores

PORT NEWARK

Containers

ELIZABETH-PORT AUTHORITY
MARINE TERMINAL

Elizabeth

Cement

Containers   GULFPORT

CARTERET

STATEN ISLAND

PORT SOCONY

Coal

Jersey City

NEWARK BAY

Containers
Ores

Bayonne

Cement

Gypsum

ST. GEORGE

Containers

Ferry

Ferry

UPPER
NEW YORK
BAY

Verrazano-Narrows
Bridge

Sugar

Yachting

Containers
Gypsum

Ores   Yachting

Passenger
Ship Terminal

Frozen fish

Containers
Ores

Ores

Coffee

Sugar

Paper

BROOKLYN-PORT AUTHORITY
MARINE TERMINAL

Paper

Sugar   Paper

COLUMBIA STREET PIER

BROOKLYN

THE BRONX

Gypsum

HUDSON RIVER

MANHATTAN

EAST RIVER

Sugar

Paper

QUEENS

ATLANTIC   OCEAN

Traffic. – Every twenty-eight minutes, on the average, an ocean going vessel enters or leaves the port on a voyage with cargo, or passengers, or both. Each year, the port handles over 18,000 ship movements.

Cargo tonnages are increasing for foreign trade and total port tonnages. The principal export commodities are machinery, chemicals, steel products, textiles, vehicles and parts. The main imports are petroleum ; steel products ; vehicles ; newsprint and food products such as sugar, bananas, meat and coffee.

Passengers. – Some 382,000 passengers entered and left the port in 1976 using the **New York City Passenger Ship Terminal.**

Opened in 1974, it consolidates all passenger ship operations for the port of New York. The piers, providing six berths, are located on the Hudson River between 48th and 52nd Streets. This efficient, modern terminal has three levels : the street level is for supplies, the second or passenger level has comfortable traveler and visitor lounges, the upper level is a roof-top car park providing spaces for 1,000 vehicles. To facilitate arrivals and departures cars have direct access to the passenger level by means of a ramp. The terminal built at the request of the City of New York cost $40 million.

The world's largest and most luxurious cruise ships regularly call at the port. They include the *Quèen Elizabeth 2, Rotterdam, Statendam, Oceanic, Leonardo da Vinci, Mikhail Lermontov, Sagafjord, Royal Viking* and *Gripsholm.*

Port Services. – The Conrail system and five terminal railroads link the port with the rest of the country. The network of tracks leads into vast storage yards on the New Jersey side, and the freight is then moved to the piers either on barges or car floats, or is carried by truck on the last step of the shoreside journey.

Every day, some 10,000 long haul trucks move through the port area. Some 140 steamship lines regularly call at the port.

The Port Authority. – One of the agencies involved in the administration of the harbor is the Port Authority of New York and New Jersey, founded in 1921 by a compact between these two states. It was given responsibility to plan, build and operate a variety of transportation facilities, and to promote and protect the commerce of the great port. The agency's area of jurisdiction covers 1,500 square miles, equivalent to the area within a 25-mile radius of the Statue of Liberty.

The Port Authority built and operates seven waterfront terminal areas. In addition to the Passenger Ship Terminal, it runs three groups of general cargo piers in Brooklyn, a pier development in Hoboken, and the great container ship terminals in Newark and Elizabeth, New Jersey.

The Port Authority also is responsible for six tunnels and bridges connecting New York City with New Jersey, the world's busiest bus terminal, the Port Authority Trans-Hudson (PATH) rail rapid transit system, two heliports and three airports (for information, see p. 17).

In lower Manhattan, the Port Authority has undertaken the development of the **World Trade Center** on a sixteen-acre site bounded by West Street, Barclay and Vesey Streets, Church Street and Liberty Street. The World Trade Center features two tower buildings each 110 stories tall, or 1,350 feet (see p. 87).

Another organization operating within New York City, the **Triborough Bridge and Tunnel Authority,** has constructed bridges and tunnels to improve the flow of traffic within the city.

Commerce and industry. – New York is a powerful financial center. Whoever visits Manhattan is struck by the number and appearance of banks revealing the self-assurance of an old well-established banking system.

As early as the end of the 18th century, in fact, New York's economic life revolved around credit : the Bank of New York was founded in 1784, the Bank of the United States in 1791, and the Bank of the Manhattan Company in 1799. Today, New York banks finance about one-third of the foreign trade of the United States.

New York is the seat of the famous New York Stock Exchange *(see p. 91)*, the American Stock Exchange, and major stock and commodity exchanges which trade in such products as silver, rubber, cotton, cocoa and coffee.

The shipping industry, which handles 15 % of the country's overseas commerce, has attracted to the city the leading marine insurance companies and stimulated the development of warehousing and transportation.

With the attraction of its financial community, the city hosts more than 2,500 major American corporations, twice as many as second-ranking Chicago. Recognizing New York's leadership in international commerce, 60 % of all foreign corporations represented in the United States have chosen New York as their headquarters.

Highly specialized industries. – New York is not what one would envision as the typical industrial city. Traditionally skilled labor has played a significant role in New York's industrial development. From the 19th century's clothing workshops has emerged the modern fashion industry *(see garment center.p. 97)*, New York's first ; publishing, printing, food products and electrical equipment rank next. A number of medium and small-sized establishments are located in Brooklyn, Queens and the Bronx, but more than half the city's manufacturing is centered in Manhattan.

The "service industries". – New York is also the leader in communications and in the service industry. Over 4,000 companies specialize in business services : advertising, management and consulting, public relations, commercial research computer services and equipment rental.

Excellent educational facilities make New York an outstanding center for higher learning and scientific research : more than 60 two and four year colleges and universities.

With the location of all national television networks, many American and foreign newspapers and two of the major news wire services in the city, New York is the communication center of the nation.

Readily available contacts with major corporations, high-quality entertainment and first rate hotel accommodation have made New York an important convention center and attractive tourist spot.

ARCHITECTURE AND CITY PLANNING

From the wooden warehouse of the Dutch trader to the proud skyscraper of the great international corporation, New York's architecture has gone through many stages before achieving its current dominant position in the art of the industrial and atomic age. Through the work of the New York Landmarks Preservation Commission, landmarks and historic sites have been preserved.

Colonial architecture. – This style flourished when the "American provinces" were still British colonies. At its height in the 18th century, the colonial tradition persisted until well into the 19th century. Colonial architecture is also often called **Georgian,** because it was inspired by the style which prevailed in England under the Kings George (I-IV, 1714-1830). Frequently painted white, colonial buildings are usually constructed of wood or brick, and sometimes adorned with a portico or a colonnade. Steps lead up to the front door, sometimes crowned by a fan window, and the corners are often decorated with quoins (wooden blocks imitating stonework). Among examples of colonial or Georgian architecture to be found in New York are Fraunces Tavern, the Morris-Jumel and Gracie Mansions and St. Paul's Chapel *(see p. 85).* Over 100 pre-1800 houses still exist throughout the city.

The "Revivals". – The 19th century brought a multiplicity of styles reminiscent of the classic or medieval manner : "Greek Revival", or "Gothic Revival", for example.

Greek Revival architecture, inspired by the monuments of ancient Greece, was more widespread for churches and public buildings than for private homes, at least in the city. Examples of this style which have survived include : St. Mark's-in-the-Bouwerie, the Federal Hall National Memorial, which reproduces the proportions of a Doric temple, Colonnade Row and Grant's Tomb which reflects the style of the mausoleum of Halicarnassus.

With their Ionic porticoes, the houses of Washington Square attest the popularity of the neo-Grecian style which flourished in the mid-19th century.

Slightly rarer than Greek Revival, but fully as persistent, **"Gothic Revival"** was exemplified in the first St. Patrick's Cathedral *(see p. 82)* built early in the 19th century by the French architect Mangin, and is evident today in the present St. Patrick's Cathedral, Trinity Church and Grace Church.

At the end of the 19th and the beginning of the 20th centuries, New York architects cultivated the art of the Revival with enthusiastic eclecticism, recreating almost every imaginable European style for the magnates of industry and finance : feudal, Louis XII, Renaissance and Tudor competed in splendor. However, there was a distinct preference for the Italian Renaissance, the hands-down favorite of the most famous architects of the day, McKim, Mead and White, who designed the Morgan Library, the Villard Houses and the Vanderbilt Mansion.

The Brownstones. – These town houses were built primarily in the second half of the 19th century with brownstone from Connecticut and New Jersey. Usually three or four stories high, their steps are perpendicular to the façade, often forming geometrical patterns on streets where rows of brownstones have survived. Their cast and wrought iron banisters and railings are quite striking.

Originally family homes of the wealthy middle class, sometimes richly appointed brownstones slipped down the social ladder a bit, and most have been divided into apartments. A few years ago there were still large numbers of brownstones in the midtown area, but now not many are left except for those surviving in Harlem, the Murray Hill and Gramercy Park areas, Greenwich Village, Chelsea and Upper West Side and several areas of Brooklyn (Park Slope, Cobble Hill, Brooklyn Heights, Boerum Hill, Fort Greene and Clinton Hill). Many young couples reluctant to leave the city, artists and writers have discovered their charm giving impetus to the "Brownstone Renaissance".

THE SKYSCRAPERS

The famous New York skyline, a human challenge to the forces of nature, has given the city a gigantic Promethean character which is particularly impressive to a visitor.

Yesterday's Skyscrapers. – At the beginning of the 20th century, New York's population grew very rapidly *(see p. 24).* The price of real estate rose accordingly, a fact which caused the promoters to build higher and higher. The weight of building material first limited the architects, but they were soon freed by the use of steel, then reinforced concrete. Fireproof skeleton frame, projection for columns and beams, caisson foundation skeleton frame, cage and a skeleton construction also aided the architects in the conception of the "skyscraper". The invention and subsequent improvement of elevators removed the last barriers.

These techniques did not at first inspire a new architectural style. One of the first large skyscrapers, the Flatiron Building *(see p. 122)* erected in 1902 on a steel framework, was decorated in Florentine Renaissance style, with pilasters and a wide cornice. The Woolworth Building, on the other hand, which was finished in 1913, is a "Gothic cathedral of commerce", with its pinnacled tower and the rosettes of its gabled niches. Others were inspired by the French classical period, with Versailles as a constant model, and still others sometimes known as **wedding cakes,** were covered with ornate sculpture in the 1900 **"Gay style".**

However, shortly after the First World War, changes in design occurred. A new **zoning law** regulated the height of buildings in relation to the width of the streets, so that pedestrians would not find themselves in utter darkness. One result of these regulations was the type of building with successive setbacks, admittedly not always esthetically satisfying, one must admit, but still to be found on certain New York streets.

Gradually, there was an evolution in style : the new trend was toward the vertical, underscored by obvious structural requirements. The Chrysler Building, the Empire State Building and the RCA Building (in Rockefeller Center) are the finest examples of this period of architectural pioneering.

Today's Skyscrapers. – After an interruption due to the Second World War, skyscrapers once more sprouted in Manhattan, but built with different techniques and styles of construction.

In recent years, steel and reinforced concrete have given way to aluminum and glass, a weight and time-saving combination. The conventional skyscraper has normally a maze of interior columns but lately a new technique has been employed, in which the exterior walls consisting of closely spaced columns of steel, are used as load bearing walls leaving a maximum of open column free space. (The Towers of the World Trade Center and One Liberty Plaza).

Once completed the buildings often rise straight up, but are set far from the street, leaving free space for patios or gardens, often graced with fountains. The pure, straight lines of these buildings may sacrifice warmth for sophistication.

Architects of great renown have designed some of New York's skyscrapers finest buildings among them : Mies van der Rohe and Philip Johnson (Seagram Building) ; Gropius and Belluschi (Pan Am Building) ; and Saarinen (CBS Building).

Almost all the skyscrapers are office buildings, with batteries of elevators, express and local, which sometimes travel as fast as 20 miles an hour. The washing of all that glass is another problem : it's a fulltime job, calling for permanent, movable platforms, ofen manned by Indians, who are generally not susceptible to dizziness.

(From photo Éd. Sun, Paris.)

Park Avenue — View of the Pan Am Building

The main groups of skyscrapers are downtown and in the midtown area. The oldest are downtown, around Wall Street, but this area can also take pride in the Chase Manhattan Bank, completed in 1962, the twin towers of the World Trade Center, which surpass the record height of the Empire State Building and the buildings of Water Street. Newer buildings are clustered in mid-Manhattan, particularly on Park Avenue, Fifth Avenue (Rockefeller Center) and, most recently, the Avenue of the Americas (formerly Sixth Avenue), Third Avenue and Lexington Avenue (Citicorp).

City development. – City development and redevelopment are planned, guided and carried out by a number of local public agencies. The New York City Planning Commission is the major policymaking body concerned with the city's future. Its functions include zoning regulation and capital budget preparation. A number of operating agencies, including the Economic Development, Housing Development, Transportation and Parks, Recreation and Cultural Affairs Administrations plan and execute major programs and projects. Under the Office of the Mayor, development offices have also been created to concentrate on the future of particular regional centers. In addition several New York State agencies undertake their own development projects in the city, primarily in the areas of housing, transportation and parks.

The City is now implementing some of its major programs, including : innovations in zoning concepts through the creation of special districts such as the Times Square Theater District in which the City offers private developers incentives to build theaters in their new buildings ; the comprehensive redevelopment of major commercial business districts using a series of design controls to shape private development such as in Lower Manhattan ; and the creation of regional subcenters for example in downtown Brooklyn and Jamaica, Queens.

PAINTING (The New York School)

Prior to the 1930's it had been necessary for American artists to travel abroad to find out what was going on in experimental art. But as war fermented and the depression lingered in Europe, many foreign artists began to arrive in the United States. The best talents came, some to stay for a brief time, some to remain. This infusion of talent and ideas helped a great deal to make possible the establishment of an art that was truly American.

The establishment of the Museum of Modern Art, the Whitney Museum and the efforts of Peggy Guggenheim had extended ideas and a sympathetic audience was eager to embrace the new forms of artistic expression.

A precursor : Marcel Duchamp. – Early in this century most American painters were inspired by European masters. Some artists from the West Coast pioneered original forms but few others followed their example.

Brother of the sculptor Raymond Duchamp Villon and of the painter Jacques Villon, Marcel Duchamp, who was born in 1887 near Rouen, France, settled in New York in 1913. That same year he created a sensation by exhibiting at the Armory Show his *Nude Descending a Staircase* in which he expressed the results of his studies on the representation of movement.

Along with Picabia, he laid the basis for "Dada" *(see p. 40)* and created his provocative ready-mades", which consist of simple, even ordinary objects, which the artist exhibits as works of art (having intervened only to give them names) ; thus *The Bicycle Wheel* and *A Fountain,* was nothing more than a basin bought in a department store.

29

Action Painting. — The events of the 1940's brought many painters fleeing wartime Europe to New York : Frenchmen such as Chagall, Léger and Masson, along with the German Max Ernst and the Dutch Mondrian, contributed to a new artistic atmosphere in New York.

But it was only with Action Painting that the New York school found its own personality. Action Painting is a form of abstract art where instinct plays the greatest role : the artist, in a sort of reverie expresses himself with great brushstrokes, in an exalted hand-to-hand struggle with the canvas.

Jackson Pollock (1912-1956) was a master of Action Painting. He used to lay out the canvas unstretched, on the bare floor, and throw his pigments on it, sometimes mixing them with sand or crushed glass to form a sort of paste which he worked with sticks, trowels and knives.

Along with Pollock there were Kline (1910-1962), whose huge black and white compositions exude anxiety, and Rothko (1903-1970), of Russian origin, whose vast compositions in subtle colors are compelling. Other artists include Willem and Elaine de Kooning, Jack Tworkov, Adolph Gottlieb, Barnett Newman and William Baziotes.

Pop and Op Art. — Around 1960 a new trend appeared in New York art circles, which its adepts call Pop Art.

The artists swung the pictorial imagery of art from the purely abstract back to recognizable subjects. But it was an all new imagery — comic strip characters, street signs, light bulbs, movie stars — popular imagery transformed, demanding a new approach to looking. **Rauschenberg**, the "Pope of Pop Art", won the Grand Prix at the Venice Biennial in 1962. Among his contemporaries were Roy Lichtenstein, Ellsworth Kelly, Jasper Johns, Frank Stella, Claes Oldenburg and Andy Warhol.

By the mid 1960's two new movements appeared on the scene : "Op" and "Minimal" art. Op Art seeks to reveal movement to the beholder.

Inspired by the works of Delaunay and Duchamp, it is illustrated by the transformable paintings of Agam, the kinetic compositions of Vasarely, and the cybernetic constructions of Schöffer.

MODERN SCULPTURE IN MANHATTAN

Many visitors to New York have been welcomed by the town's most famous sculpture, Bartholdi's Statue of Liberty. Sculptures of various styles and periods are represented but the town is particularly rich in twentieth century works.

Very often sculptures decorated the early religious and civil constructions : Jean-Jacques Caffieri (Major General Montgomery's tomb at St. Paul's Chapel) ; Daniel Chester French and Augustus Saint-Gaudens (façade of the former U.S. Custom House). A. Stirling Calder (a statue of Washington in general's uniform on the north side of Washington Arch).

Parks, greens and squares were also decorated by commemorative statues, often to the town's and America's past leaders : Peter Stuyvesant, the Dutch Governor of New Amsterdam (Stuyvesant Square) ; equestrian statue of George Washington and a statue of Abraham Lincoln by Henry Kirke Brown (Union Square) ; Benjamin Franklin by Plassman (near Pace University), and statues of Washington and Lafayette by F.A. Bartholdi (Morningside Park).

The recent phase of construction in New York has seen the introduction of plazas and mini parks as integral parts of the urban landscape. The installation of modern art works, in many of these plazas gives every New Yorker the opportunity to appreciate and enjoy modern sculptural works. Among the most striking examples are the great architectural ensembles such as the United Nations, Rockefeller, Lincoln and World Trade Centers.

The Rockefeller Center is adorned on the lower plaza by the gilded bronze statue of Prometheus stealing the sacred fire for mankind and that well known landmark, the monumental bronze statue *(see p. 37)* of Atlas supporting the world in front of the International Building by the artist L. Lawrie.

The United Nations is a center of great international art works, among which are the Statue of Peace in the gardens presented by Yugoslavia and in the pool in front of the Secretariat Building a sculpture by Barbara Hepworth.

The Chase Manhattan Bank, famous for its art collection, has on its lower plaza a fountain by the Japanese sculptor Isamu Noguchi. A new and striking feature of the upper plaza is Jean Dubuffet's *Group of Four Trees*. This fiberglass construction painted black and white, rises to 42 feet and weighs 25 tons. The work was commissioned by D Rockefeller to celebrate the bank's 25 years on Wall Street.

Lincoln Center is famous for the outstanding art object displayed in the interior of the various buildings. Also worthy of note are Henry Moore's bronze *Reclining Figure* in the plaza pool and Alexander Calder's work *Le Guichet* on the plaza north.

The plaza of the World Trade Center has as a centerpiece a fountain and pool. At the center of the pool is the bronze sculpture by Fritz Koenig of Munich, representing a free form globe, which revolves almost imperceptibly.

The great centers are not alone to have architectural decoration, many individual buildings are enhanced by a sculptural work on the sidewalk or plaza : Yehiel Shemi's *Window Sculpture* (Jewish Museum) ; Ivan Chermayeff's No. 9 sign (9 W 57 th Street) ; Robert Cook's bronze and Luis Sanguino's *Amor* (345 Park Avenue) ; Noguchi's cube (140 Broadway) ; Beverly Pepper's *Contrappunto* (777 Third Avenue) ; Louise Nevelson's environmental sculpture *Night Presence IV* (center island on Park Avenue at 92nd Street) and Lipchitz's bronze *Bellerophon Taming Pegasus* in front of the Law Building at Columbia University.

The various sculpture gardens in the city also provide a collection of works by different artists : the New School for Social Research at 66 West 12th Street between Fifth Avenue and Avenue of the Americas ; 55 Water Street ; the Whitney Museum of American Art and the Museum of Modern Art where recent acquisitions include Picasso's *Monument* and works by Alexander Liberman, Barnett Newman and Tony Smith.

NEW YORK AND LITERATURE

From Knickerbocker to the "New Yorker". – In the rich literary life of contemporary America New York is doubtless the most vital force. Attracted by its intellectual climate and a receptive public, publishing and printing have been leading industries in New York for over a century.

A distinguished literary tradition goes back to Washington Irving *(see p. 139)*, a native New Yorker, author of *A History of New York* (written in 1809 under the pen name of Diedrich Knickerbocker), an irreverent account of the city's first Dutch families which shows that the satyrical strain embodied in today's *New Yorker* magazine has firm roots in New York soil.

Classics and bohemians. – A galaxy of outstanding figures in American literature were associated with New York throughout the 19th century, either because they lived there for some time *(see Greenwich Village p. 78 and Brooklyn p. 127)* or because they chose New York as the setting for their work.

These include the poet and short story writer Edgar Allan Poe *(see details p. 125)* ; the author of *Moby Dick* New York-born Herman Melville *(Bartleby, A Story of Wall Street)*, the poet and New York journalist Walt Whitman *(Mannahatta* and *Crossing Brooklyn Ferry)*, the New York-born novelists Edith Wharton *(The Age of Innocence)* and Henry James *(Washington Square)*, Stephen Crane the author of *The Red Badge of Courage (New York City Sketches)* and Mark Twain (a correspondent for Western newspapers in his early days in New York).

In the first decades of the 20th century, artistic and literary life in New York centered around Greenwich Village, so much so that it has been described as "the home of American arts and letters" during this period. The names of the poetess Edna St. Vincent Millay, the playwright Eugene O'Neill and the novelist Theodore Dreiser are remembered for their close associations with Greenwich Village.

"All around the Town". – Further uptown, and somewhat later, a group of wits, writers and wags made the Hotel Algonquin their headquarters. Among these poker-playing "knights" of what became known as the "Round Table" *(see p. 42)* were the raconteur and drama critic Alexander Woollcott, the humorist Robert Benchley and the editor of the *New Yorker,* Harold Ross, Dorothy Parker, short-story writer and master of the barbed witticism, and Franklin P. Adams ("F.P.A."), columnist and New York diarist, were also members of this group.

Carl van Vechten and Langston Hughes presided over the literary and artistic renaissance in the Harlem of the 1920's.

The "Age of Jazz", which was also the age of the flapper, bathtub gin, the New York speakeasy and the "Lost Generation", saw the emergence of its prophet in F. Scott Fitzgerald *(The Great Gatsby)* and of a then left-oriented critic in John Dos Passos *(Manhattan Transfer, U.S.A.).*

Broadway had its chronicler in Damon Runyon, who was in some ways the successor of an earlier historian of *Bagdad-on-the-Subway,* O'Henry author of many short stories. Ring Lardner cast a critical eye on the *Big League* that was New York. John O'Hara *(Butterfield 8)*, James Thurber, and more recently, John Updike were among the *New Yorker* writers who made that journal uniquely typical of New York. The essayist E.B. White *(Here is New York)* may be called a New Yorker's New Yorker. In our day, the novelist Norman Mailer has commanded wide attention, he grew up in Brooklyn and acquired fame with his novel *The Naked and the Dead* (1948).

'The Center of the Universe". – New York has always acted as a magnet, drawing into itself the best the country had to offer.

Long before the term "brain drain" was coined, the migration of the brightest young talents from farms, small towns and other "outlying precincts" to the big city was already an established phenomenon.

One of the most brilliant success stories of this type was that of Thomas Wolfe *(Look Homeward, Angel, You Can't Go Home Again)*, the ebullient North Carolina writer who used to dash out of his Brooklyn room after protracted sessions of work to celebrate by pouring pitchers of beer over his head in a nearby saloon.

But New York has attracted writers not only from the United States. Among those who have come from abroad and who have written, in praise or in blame, we may mention the Russian poet Vladimir Mayakovsky *(Brooklyn Bridge)*, the Spanish poet Federico Garcia-Lorca *(Poet in New York)*, the Irish playwright Brendan Behan *(Brendan Behan's New York)*, the French novelist Paul Morand *(New York)*, the English photographer and decorator Cecil Beaton *(Cecil Beaton's New York)* and the Russian poet, Andrei Voznesensky *(Airport in New York)*.

New York has stimulated the imagination of writers, foreign and American alike, because of the fascination exercised by this greatest and most exciting of all cities, "the center of the universe", as one of its mayors called it, constantly changing its skyline and even its population, full of contrasts and paradoxes : poverty amidst riches, cosmopolitan-ism befitting a world capital alongside strong neighborhood loyalties, local patriotism and ethnic pride, loneliness in spite of the crowds, toughness and cynicism mingling with sentimentality and soft-heartedness, essentially American but shaped by immigrants from a hundred lands.

These are some of the elements which make up the unique human adventure of New York, whose challenge to the creative imagination is as great as that of life itself.

> *"New York is a sort of anthology of urban civilization. The song that any city sings she sings. All that anybody can seek for that can be housed in steel and cement is here, and with it, never lost in all the city's drabness, respect for the striving, combative beauty-loving spirit of man."*
>
> R.L. Duffus.

BOOKS TO READ

Picture Books

Old New York in Early Photographs by Mary Black *(Dover Publications, New York, 1973)*.
New York : Sunshine and Shadow by Roger Whitehouse *(Harper & Row, New York 1974)*.

History and Architecture

Under the Guns, New York, 1775-1776 by Bruce Bliven Jr. *(Harper & Row, New York, 1972)*
History Preserved, a Guide to New York City Landmarks by Harmon Goldstone and Martha Dalrymple *(Simon & Schuster, 1974)*.
Beyond the Melting Pot by Nathan Glazer and Daniel Patrick Moynihan *(M.I.T. Press, Cambridge, Mass., 1970)*.
The Campaign of 1776 Around New York and Brooklyn by Henry P. Johnston *(Long Island Historical Society, Brooklyn, 1878 - Reprint : De Capo, New York, 1971)*.
The Story of New York by Susan E. Lyman *(Crown Publishers, New York, revised edition 1975)*
The AIA Guide to New York City by Norval White and Elliot Willensky *(Macmillan Company, New York, 1978)*.

Literature

See also p. 31 : New York and Literature.

A Walker in the City by Alfred Kazin *(Harcourt, Brace Jovanovich Publications, 1951)*.
Here is New York by Elvin Brooks White *(Harper & Row, New York, 1949)*.

SOME BOOKSTORES ON FIFTH AVENUE

Doubleday Book	673 724 *Fifth Avenue*
Rizzoli International	*712 Fifth Avenue*
Scribner Book	*597 Fifth Avenue*

A TOURIST CALENDAR OF EVENTS

DATE	LOCATION	EVENT
January-February	Chinatown	Chinese New Year
March 17	Fifth Avenue	St. Patrick's Parade
May	Washington Square 9th Avenue from 36th to 57th Street	Outdoor Art Exhibit International 9th Avenue Festival
June	Fifth Avenue	Puerto Rican Parade
	Between Second Avenue and 9th Avenue	52nd Street Festival
	Central Park and throughout the City	Summer Festival : (through August) free concerts on the Mall and Shakespeare at the Delacorte Amphitheater. Performances in many parks.
July	Throughout the City	Newport Jazz Festival
	Lower Manhattan	July 4th in Old New York
September	"Little Italy" (Mulberry Street)	Festival of San Gennaro : Patron Saint of the Neapolitans
	Fifth Avenue	Steuben Parade : German American celebration
	Atlantic Avenue, Brooklyn	West-Indian-American Day Carnival
	Washington Square	Outdoor Art Exhibit (see May also)
October	Fifth Avenue	Columbus Day Parade
	Fifth Avenue 29th to 52nd Streets	Pulaski Day Parade : Polish celebration
November	Madison Square Garden	Horse Show
	Broadway, Herald Square	Macy's Thanksgiving Day Parade
December	34th to 54th Streets	Fifth Avenue Holiday Festival
	Rockefeller Center	Giant Christmas Tree

A FEW FILMS EVOKING THE NEW YORK SCENE

A Tree Grows in Brooklyn	*1945*	*Elia Kazan*
On the Town	*1949*	*S. Donen and G. Kelly*
On the Waterfront	*1954*	*Elia Kazan*
West Side Story	*1961*	*R. Wise and J. Robbins*
Midnight Cowboy	*1969*	*J. Schlesinger*
Next Stop : Greenwich Village	*1975*	*Paul Mazursky*
Annie Hall	*1977*	*Woody Allen*

MANHATTAN

The island of Manhattan is by far the smallest of the five boroughs of New York City (see map p. 16) and the one which is the most popular with the tourists. It is 13,4 miles long, but only 2.3 miles across at the widest point. Between 1950 and 1960 the move to the suburbs and the more residential boroughs of Queens and Staten Island caused a decline in the total population of Manhattan, but it now seems to be fluctuating, due either to new arrivals, and perhaps a return from the outer fringes of suburbia.

Manhattan is the nerve center of the city.

Broadway, its longest and best known thoroughfare, winds from south to north, following an old Indian trail. The name "Manhattan" itself is an Algonquin word for "Island of the Hills". The city also grew from south to north, an explanation for the irregular pattern of streets in the oldest part of the town. Beyond Union Square, geometrical regularity takes over, and the neat pattern of numbered streets and avenues crossing at right angles covers most of the rest of the island.

Feverish activity and extraordinary feats in construction are typical of Manhattan. The tallest skyscrapers, the biggest banks, the largest and best stocked department stores, the greatest variety of cosmopolitan restaurants, and the densest crowds in the world tend to overwhelm the visitor. The Manhattan of today incorporates extensive flower and tree decked plazas, cascading fountains, vest pocket parks in the most unexpected places and brightly colored sculptures.

As the tourist comes to know New York better, he will discover the unusual variety of Manhattan : busy avenues lined with luxurious shops, quiet side streets lined with brownstones, residential areas with their striped canopies and doormen. Whole cities within the city, like Chinatown or Harlem, offer fascinating background for sociological studies.

At night, Manhattan is an unforgettable spectacle, seen from Brooklyn Heights or the top of the Empire State Building. The towers shining with myriads of lights, the flashing neon signs, the passing boats and planes, the processions of cars form an illuminated pattern of animation.

New York presents a diversity of attractions for the visitor : traveling there on business or pleasure, he is swept up in the exciting pace of the city. A sort of New Babylon, New York offers all types of amusements, heralded by the bright lights of Broadway or the tinsel of Greenwich Village. As a shopping center, New York City is a vast bazaar where you can buy absolutely anything you wish. There are the famous department stores such as Macy's, Gimbels, Bloomingdale's as well as the specialty shops for everything : boutiques, antique shops, gift shops, jewelry shops, camera stores, etc.

New York also offers the cosmopolitan distinction of a major center of the arts. Moreover excellent educational facilities make New York an outstanding center for higher learning and scientific research.

New York symbolizes for the foreign visitor the historical America and the fascination of the New World.

Lower Manhattan

RATING OF THE WALKS
AND SIGHTS

★★★   Very highly recommended

★★   Recommended

★   Interesting

Distance : about 1 mile — Time : 3 1/2 hours (not including guided tours, or museums).

Located in the heart of Manhattan, between Fifth and Seventh Avenues and 47th and 52nd Streets, Rockefeller Center is an imposing group of harmoniously designed skyscrapers, most of which were constructed before World War II. The various buildings are connected by the Concourse, a maze of underground passages lined with shops. A private street, Rockefeller Plaza, crosses the area from north to south. Once a year, it is closed for a day so that it does not become public property.

The 19 buildings cover about 22 acres and are used mostly for business purposes. The total of 557 stories house a working population of more than 60,000. If we add the number of tourists who visit each day we have a "population" nearly the size of Alaska's (250,000). Columbia University, which owns half of the land, receives a base rental of 9 million dollars a year.

RCA BUILDING	Ⓐ
RADIO CITY MUSIC HALL	Ⓑ
STEVENS TOWER	Ⓒ
CELANESE BUILDING	Ⓓ
McGRAW-HILL BUILDING	Ⓔ
EXXON BUILDING	Ⓕ
TIME & LIFE BUILDING	Ⓖ
SPERRY RAND BUILDING	Ⓗ
EQUITABLE LIFE BUILDING	Ⓙ
CBS BUILDING	Ⓚ
J.C. PENNEY BUILDING	Ⓛ
AMERICANA HOTEL	Ⓝ
NEW YORK HILTON	Ⓟ
BURLINGTON HOUSE	Ⓡ
MUSEUM OF AMERICAN FOLK ART	Ⓢ
AMERICAN CRAFTS COUNCIL	Ⓣ
MUSEUM OF CONTEMPORARY CRAFTS	Ⓤ
DONNELL LIBRARY CENTER	Ⓥ
INTERNATIONAL BUILDING	Ⓦ
THE MUSEUM OF MODERN ART	Ⓧ

ROCKEFELLER CENTER AREA

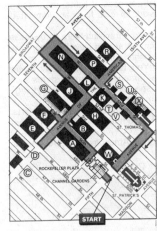

Fields and meadows. — At the beginning of the 19th century, the site now occupied by Rockefeller Center was part of the "Commons Lands" vacant or unpatented lands of Manhattan. **Dr. David Hosack**, a professor of botany, acquired 15 acres from the City for $5,000 to establish a public botanical garden which he called "Elgin Garden". Hosack soon found the upkeep of the gardens too expensive. So, in 1811, he decided to sell the land to the State of New York, which turned it over to Columbia University. The University then rented the land to farmers for $100 a year.

City blocks and brownstones. — By 1850, the present gridiron pattern of streets and avenues was laid out, and the first buildings appeared on the site. By the end of the 19th century it was part of a fashionable residential district. Splendid mansions rose side by side with more modest brownstones, a few of which survive today on 53rd Street.

In the early 1900's the neighborhood began to decline. It had become noisy especially after the construction of the Avenue of the Americas "El" (the elevated railway). The millionaires and the middle class moved away, leaving their fine houses to poorer tenants. The area later became famous as the "speakeasy belt" during the Prohibition era.

John D. Rockefeller, Jr. — Son of the oil multi-millionaire and father of the "Rockefeller Brothers", "John D., Jr" leased the land from Columbia in 1928. The initial lease ran 24 years and was made renewable until 2015, when the land and the buildings would revert to the University. In 1953, the renewal options were extended to 2069. With associates from the Metropolitan Opera, Rockefeller had first planned a gigantic opera house, but the crash of 1929 put an end to this project.

(From document, Museum of the City of New York.)

Rockefeller Center area early 19th century.

Taking another tack, he decided to construct a "city within a city". The central part of the project, including the RCA Building, was completed in 1940. One of the architects in charge was Wallace K. Harrison, later one of those mainly responsible for the design of the United Nations Headquarters *(see p. 65)*, and Lincoln Center *(see p. 102)*.

During the building of Rockefeller Center a practice was initiated which New Yorkers now take for granted. It is said that Rockefeller himself stopped by to watch progress one day, and was energetically asked to move on. That was the origin of the peephole, now routine procedure on every construction site.

VISIT

We suggest the following itinerary for a brief visit (see opposite) to the main buildings of Rockefeller Center and the Avenue of the Americas (formerly called Sixth Avenue). Guided tours of Rockefeller Center leave approximately every 30 minutes from 9:30 AM to 5:30 PM; the tour lasts about an hour, and costs $2.35. You may purchase tickets in the Guided Tour office, main floor of the RCA Building (see p. 35) and go downstairs to the Concourse Waiting Room.

Start on the sidewalk in front of Saks Fifth Avenue. From here you have a good view of the Channel Gardens, a promenade between the Maison Française on the left and the British Empire Building on the right, both topped by roof-gardens. Beyond, the silhouette of the RCA Building rises against the sky.

■ THE CHANNEL GARDENS★★★

A relaxing spot, the **"Channel Gardens"** (so named because they separate the French and British buildings) contain a series of pools, surrounded by flower beds which are changed regularly during the season, beginning with Easter Lilies on Good Friday. During World War II, a model "Victory Garden" was cultivated here. You may appreciate the benches along the flower beds after too much window-shopping. At Christmas time, spectacular lighting displays attract a crowd.

The Channel promenade leads down to the Lower Plaza, an open area below street level around which are flown the flags of the United Nations member countries. At the top of the steps leading to the Lower Plaza is a plaque citing "John D. Jr's" Credo. An outdoor restaurant in summer, the Plaza serves as a skating rink in winter.

(From photo Rockefeller Center, Inc.)

Channel Gardens.

On the other side of the Lower Plaza stands a bronze statue leafed in gold of Prometheus stealing the sacred fire for mankind. Every December, a huge Christmas tree towers from 65 to 90 feet above the statue. Visitors come to admire the colored lights or to hear occasional concerts of Christmas carols.

■ RCA (RCA Corporation) BUILDING★★★

Seventy stories tall, soaring 850 feet above street level, the loftiest of Rockefeller Center's towers is also the most harmonious architecturally. Slight indentations soften the severity of its lines.

The main entrance at 30 Rockefeller Plaza leads to the lobby, decorated with immense murals depicting man's progress by the Spanish artist José Maria Sert. Notice the particularly striking effects of perspective. These murals are actually the second series executed for the RCA Building. The first set, designed by the fiery revolutionary, Diego Rivera, were found to be too radical by "John D. Jr". Murals with a similar theme are now displayed in the Bellas Artes Place in Mexico City. *The Rockefeller Center Guided Tours office is located on the main floor of this building.*

On the first floor, the Control Center, introduces you to the running of the building and of the other buildings of Rockefeller Center.

Observation Roof★★★. – *Open from 10 AM to 9 PM from April 1 to October 1; from 11 AM to 7 PM the rest of the year.*

The ticket, booth is located on the 65th floor of this building. ($1.60). (The Observation Roof is included in the guided tour mentioned above). Take the express elevator which goes 16 miles an hour – 2 floors a second.

From the top the RCA Building you will discover a magnificent **panoramic view★★★** of New York, which is particularly spectacular towards lower Manhattan and the twin towers of the World Trade Center. Beyond the island in the left background, you can see the Verrazano-Narrows Bridge *(see p. 129)*. It is easy to spot such landmarks as the Empire State Building to the south and the Chrysler Building, partly hidden by the Pan Am Building, to the southeast. You will also notice the National Weather Service radar sphere on the upper level of the roof. On the 65th floor is the Rainbow Room, a well-known restaurant.

The Concourse★. – On the first level below the main floor, you will find the Concourse, which links all the buildings of Rockefeller Center. If you have time, you will enjoy a stroll in these underground passages, lined with attractive shops and exhibits.

Continuing along West 50th Street towards Avenue of Americas you will pass by **Radio City Music Hall**, the motion picture and musical theater where during the afternoon and evening shows the famous Rockettes danced. *(Future uncertain ; for shows telephone in advance)*.

A striking series of elegant tower buildings with spacious plazas, line the west side of the Avenue of the Americas.

Walk southwards to **Stevens Tower** at 1185 Avenue of the Americas, between 46th and 47th Streets. This 42-story office tower of glass and white marble incorporates a legitimate theater *(private : admission by membership only)* and a restaurant. Across 47th Street is the **Celanese Building**, a 45-story building similar in design to the other two new additions to Rockefeller Center to the north.

■ McGRAW-HILL BUILDING★

Setback from the street this 51-story building is surrounded by spacious plazas, which are paved with granite. Built of flame finished granite and solar bronze glass the building climbs to 670 feet.

A lower plaza in front of the building contains a unique pool demonstrating the planet Earth's relation to the Sun. This plaza leads to the lower concourse and the McGraw-Hill Bookstore. In addition, the new McGraw-Hill Park, along the western edge of the building, features New York City's only walk-through waterfall. It leads to a tree-shaded mall with an ornamental pool, hanging plants, umbrella-covered tables and chairs, curved teakwood benches, and refreshment facilities.

"The New York Experience" is a revolutionary new multiscreen and multi sensory show that unfolds the story of New York City, past and present *(11 AM to 7 PM Monday through Thursday ; 11 AM to 8 PM Friday and Saturday ; noon to 8 PM Sundays and holidays. $2.90)*. On your way to the New York Experience Theater pass through Little Old New York a colorful exhibit *(free)* of New York at the turn of the century.

■ EXXON BUILDING

This the corporate home for Exxon Corporation, with a height of 750 feet and 53-stories, is the second tallest skyscraper in Rockefeller Center after the RCA Building, which it faces across the Avenue of the Americas. Rising from a landscaped plaza, piers of limestone alternate with windows and beams enframed in bronze-tinted aluminum, situated behind the tower a peaceful mini-park with flowers, trees and cascading waterfall provides a welcome refuge.

Inside the 2 1/2 story high spacious lobby with its giallo beige marble walls and striking reddish floor, with gold filets making a geometric pattern, note the tapestry reproduction of a theater curtain painted by Picasso and the abstract hanging sculpture *Moon and Stars*.

■ TIME & LIFE BUILDING★★

Across from Radio City rises the smooth and shinning building where *Time, Money, People, Sports Illustrated* and *Fortune* are published. Erected in 1960, the building was the first modern skyscraper on the west side of the Avenue of Americas.

You may admire the pure vertical lines of this 48-story building, 587 feet in height, covered with limestone, aluminum and glass. On two sides of the building we see the America Plaza paved, with two-toned terrazzo pattern. The wavy design contrasts pleasantly with the rectangular pools and their fountains.

We find the same type of serpentine design on the floor of the spacious lobby. On the east side a large abstract mural by Fritz Glarner, a modern American painter, harmonizes with the stainless steel panels, alternately polished and dull, which cover the walls.

Our itinerary next takes us between the **Sperry Rand Building** and the **Equitable Life Building**. The latter, named for the insurance company, thrusts straight up, and is covered with alternating panels of black and clear glass. Every morning 7,000 employees come to work here.

Beyond 52nd Street is the **CBS Building** designed by the architect Eero Saarinen. The framework of reinforced concrete is covered with Canadian granite. On the other side of the Avenue of the Americas is the **J.C. Penney Building**, headquarters of the chain stores of the same name ; in front is a sunken sculpture garden.

Turn left on 52nd Street to have a good view of the south side of the Americana Hotel.

■ AMERICANA HOTEL★★

The sixth largest hotel in the world, its tapered silhouette is particularly elegant seen from the south, where the line is slightly broken. Built almost entirely of glass over a stone framework, it was erected in 1962, and contains 1800 rooms on 50 floors. Many conventions meet here. Off the lobby you will find a variety of shops.

■ NEW YORK HILTON★★

Covered with steel and glass panels, this 46-story hotel employs 1500 persons who speak a total of 27 languages. Finished in 1963, the building includes a four-story base, with service and reception facilities and a high tower given over to the 2131 rooms.

The interior is as modern as the architectural lines. Below street level are an art gallery and the "Taveerne", an informal Dutch coffee house. On the main floor, next to the lobby, you will find the charming International Promenade. Here are several attractive restaurants and bars.

On the upper floors are elegant suites for business meetings, some of which are decorated in French period styles.

Across 54th Street is **Burlington House** which although it does not belong to the Rockefeller Center, prolongs the row of impressive tower buildings on the west side of the Avenue of the Americas.

This brown tinted building, climbing to 50-stories, is surrounded by a spacious plaza with a vest pocket park behind and in front two pools with original fountains which when operating form attractive spheres of water.

The Mill at Burlington Exhibition Center *(open May through October Tuesday through Saturday 10 AM to 7 PM, 6 PM November through April ; admission free)* allows the visitor to make an intriguing 8 1/2 minute journey, via a moving walkway through the world of textiles. The exhibition displays the various fibers which are the raw materials of textiles, the operation of machines used in the manufacturing process such as the spinning frame, dye vats, warper, hosiery knitting machine and shuttleless loom. The journey ends with a fast-moving array of projected images showing the many ways Burlington fabrics serve man.

Take 53rd Street, the site of several museums including the Museum of Modern Art *(see p. 38)*.

Museum of American Folk Art. – *49 West 53rd Street. Open Tuesday through Sunday from 10:30 AM to 5:30 PM ; closed on Mondays and holidays. $1.00.*

This small museum, occupying one floor of a studio building, shows the American folk arts, historical and contemporary, in a series of four to five annual exhibitions ranging from textile crafts to early American portraiture.

Practical demonstrations sometimes accompany certain exhibits.

American Crafts Council. – *44 West 53rd Street. Open Monday through Friday 11 AM to 5 PM.*

The council maintains a crafts information center featuring a museum of contemporary crafts and a library *(open Tuesday, Wednesday and Friday noon to 5 PM)* specializing in 20th century crafts.

Museum of Contemporary Crafts. – *29 West 53rd Street. Open Tuesday through Saturday 11 AM to 6 PM ; Sundays 1 to 6 PM ; closed on Mondays ; $1.00.*

Maintained by the American Crafts Council the museum presents changing exhibits covering a wide range of American and foreign crafts in textiles, areas of design and environment.

To return to Fifth Avenue you will pass, across from the Museum of Modern Art, the **Donnell Library Center** at 20 West 53rd Street. This branch of the New York Public Library *(see p. 46)* houses such special features as the famed Central Children's Room one of the largest and most varied collections of childrens books ; the Nathan Straus Young Adult Library ; a special foreign language section with literature in more than 80 languages ; art, film, and record libraries.

Cross Fifth Avenue to the steps of St. Patrick's Cathedral *(see p. 47)* to admire Lee Lawrie's monumental statue of Atlas supporting the world. For taking part in the war against Zeus (Jupiter), Atlas was condemned to uphold the sky. The figure of the giant stands in front of the International Building.

■ INTERNATIONAL BUILDING

This 41-story building was originally intended to house consulates and other offices of foreign countries – whence its name. You should cross Fifth Avenue once more to enter the lobby inspired by ancient Greece, with its columns and walls of marble from the Greek island of Tinos. The ceiling is covered with very thin copper leaf. If all this copper were removed from the ceiling, it would weigh about a pound and, melted down, could

(From photo Samuel Chamberlain.)

Atlas.

be held in the palm of your hand. There are many services on the Concourse level of the building : bookshops, galleries of prints, a barbershop, passport office, restaurants...

You will find on pp. 16 to 19

two suggested programs for a short visit to New York City,

depending on the time you have available.

THE MUSEUM OF MODERN ART★★★

A pleasant place to relax or meet a friend any time of the year, the Museum of Modern Art is a particularly delightful haven of coolness in New York's oppressive summer heat, thanks to its airy garden and the air-conditioned interior. But above all it is the Museum's masterworks of the visual arts that attract, along with an intellectual elite, a colorful range of visitors of the most varied backgrounds.

The growth of the Museum. – Founded in 1929 by five collectors, the Museum of Modern Art was first housed in a few rooms of an office building. Its permanent home on 53rd Street was erected in 1939 after a number of donations, particularly the Lillie P. Bliss Bequest (235 works), had enriched the collections. Movable partitions separate the exhibition areas in this functional geometric building designed by Philip Goodwin and Edward Durell Stone.

In 1964 two new wings, the work of the architect Philip Johnson, were added. Within the next few years the museum will be undergoing extensive construction with a view to enlarging its exhibition space.

Development in the Museum's expansion project may necessitate changes in scheduled program and temporary closing of galleries.

Its organization. – A private institution, the Museum is directed by a board of trustees which includes such distinguished members as Nelson and David Rockefeller, among others. 38 thousand members who pay yearly dues of from $25 and up are the Museum's « stockholders ». Operating funds are provided in large part by membership dues, admission fees, the sale of publications and contributions.

But the Museum is more than a repository of masterpieces. It is also a cultural center, with such divisions as the **Lillie P. Bliss International Study Center,** which can be thought of as, a university of modern art. Among its resources are a library of 30,000 books, a film library, a department of architecture and design, an auditorium, and a collection of photographs.

An attractive cafeteria opening onto the garden caters to visitors, and the Members' Penthouse is a rendezvous for painters, critics and other members of the art world.

The collections. – Although the first exhibit sponsored by the Museum was intended to introduce the painters of the School of Paris with, artists such as Cézanne, van Gogh, Gauguin, the Museum now embraces the whole range of visual arts – not only painting and sculpture but also drawings and prints, architecture, industrial design, graphic design, photography and the cinema.

The many trends in modern art since 1880 are illustrated by more than 40,000 works of art. These include 3,000 paintings and sculptures, 3,000 examples of furniture, 10,000 prints, 4,000 architectural drawings and 2,000 posters.

Obviously, only a small fraction of this great collection can be shown at any one time (less than 10 %) so that the works on display are changed frequently : only the most representative are on permanent display. The Museum organizes significant temporary exhibits, drawing upon its own collections as well as outside loans. Many of these are then shown throughout the United States and abroad, contributing to the national and international appreciation of modern art.

VISIT *(about 2 1/2 hours)*

Open daily 11 AM to 6 PM (9 PM on Thursdays) ; closed Wednesdays and Christmas Day ; admission : $2.00. Admission also includes film showings on request. Pick up a folder at the entrance.

Main Floor. – Here glass and marble predominate. Various Museum services, one bookstore and the information desk and large temporary exhibits are to be found here.

Galleries to the right of the main hall display changing exhibitions in all the visual arts, as well as recent works from the collection.

The far side of the main lobby opens into the garden, one of the Museum's most popular attractions.

Sculpture Garden. – The architect Philip Johnson designed it in 1953 to serve as a setting for the Museum's sculptures, which are shown to best advantage outdoors ; they can be studied from different angles, and their appearance changes with the natural light. Marble paved walks, fountains, curtains of trees and terraces add to the charm.

Various schools are represented : romanticism by Rodin *(Monument to Balzac) ;* classicism with the buxom nudes by Renoir and Maillol ; expressionism and abstrac-

(From photo Museum of Modern Art.)

Museum of Modern Art. — The Garden.

tion by Germaine Richier, Miró *(Moonbird),* Lipchitz, Henry Moore *(Family Group),* Calder *(Whale)* and Picasso's *She Goat :* her belly is made of a basket.

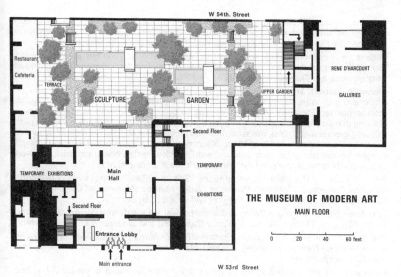

THE MUSEUM OF MODERN ART
MAIN FLOOR

0   20   40   60 feet

Upper Floors. – These floors house the Museum's permanent collection. Historical continuity is clearly apparent in the installation of the galleries. Outlined below are the different schools and trends of modern art and their main representatives.

Large scale reorganization sometimes changes the location of certain works of art, therefore the following descriptions are subject to verification.

Second Floor

Post Impressionism to Early Expressionism. – At the turn of the century, the fluidity of the Impressionists palette gave way to clearly defined shapes. Post-Impressionists include such artists as the Pointillist Seurat, who uses dots or rectangles instead of the fluid palette of the Impressionists, as seen in his luminous landscapes *(Evening at Honfleur)*. Also included are the visionary van Gogh *(The Starry Night, Hospital Corridor at St Rémy)*, and that lucid observer of contemporary mores Toulouse-Lautrec *(La Goulue at the Moulin Rouge)*. The « Douanier » Rousseau was hailed as the greatest of naive painters *(The Dream, The Sleeping Gypsy)*, pure in heart and dazzled by nature. Cézanne's firm, structural design and intense search for visual effects were to become a source of inspiration to the Cubists *(The Bather, Still Life with Apples)*. The "Nabis" or Prophets, proclaim that "a painting is essentially a surface covered with colors arranged in a certain order". This idea is developed in the works of Gauguin *(Still Life with Three Puppies, Moon and Earth)*, Vuillard *(Mother and Sister of the Artist)* and Bonnard *(The Breakfast Room)*. De Chirico's *Nostalgia of the Infinite* and Ensor's *Masks Confronting Death* are already expressionistic interpretations of these artists' tormented world.

Cubism. – Pioneers of this movement were Picasso and Braque, from 1907 to 1914, followed by Léger and Juan Gris from 1914 to 1921. Cubists try to interpret the sensation which the object creates rather than its physical image ; they dissociate the elements of the objects and rearrange the fragments in new, often geometrical order ; front and profile views may appear simultaneously, this conception opened a new era in art as seen in Picasso's *Les Demoiselles d'Avignon*. Picasso's colorful, clownish *Three Musicians* contrast with Léger's *Three Women*, a highly decorative but severe composition. Braque's *Man with a Guitar* is outstanding for the economy of means used. Léger's *The City* evokes the dynamics of the modern city - a maze of pillars, cubes, cones and pipes.

The Philip L. Goodwin Galleries for Architecture and Design. – Glassware and furniture designed by Tiffany, Guimard, Mies van der Rohe, Wright, Le Corbusier, Saarinen and others.

Expressionists. – Anxiety and despair, but also compassion and social commentary, mark these painters who ask the viewer to partake in their emotional experience. Rouault's haunting *Christ Mocked by Soldiers* is reminiscent of stained glass. The German School is represented by Nolde *(Christ Among the Children)* and by Kirchner in his boldly colored street scenes (Dresden, Berlin).

The style of the Austrian Kokoschka is shown in his powerful portraits and self-portraits.

Two masterworks by Lehmbruck are the sculptures *Standing Youth* and *Kneeling Woman*.

Fauvism and Late Cubism. – The Fauvists delight in pure color, using a striking juxtaposition of colors to intensify their compositions. Champions of this early 20th century movement were Matisse, Derain *(London Bridge)*, Vlaminck *(Autumn)* and van Dongen.

Cubist fantasy appears in collages, a method introducing fragments of paper and cloth into painting, as shown in *The Breakfast* by Gris.

I and the Village reveals Chagall's poetic imagination.

De Stijl, Purism. – The principles of De Stijl, advocating the purification of art were laid down in a journal of the same name founded by a group of artists in Holland in 1917. Adopting a non-representational style, van Doesburg and Mondrian moved toward complete abstraction which they achieved in their compositions reduced to horizontal and vertical lines in natural and neutral colors.

Monet : Water Lilies. – Forms tend to dissolve in an extraordinary interplay of colors, and although Monet attempted to capture every nuance of the flowers floating on the water – admire the delicate shading of the hues – here he appears as a forerunner of abstract art.

Futurism. – Italian futurism appeared on the art scene in 1909. The futurists stress movement in their visions of the dynamic forces of the machine age. Two followers of this movement are Boccioni *(The City Rises)* and Severini *(Dynamic Hieroglyphic of the Bal Tabarin)*.

Matisse. – An entire gallery is devoted to Matisse who, starting out as a Fauve, later moved toward subtler colors and simpler figures set against flat surfaces. Among his early masterpieces are *The Blue Window, The Red Studio* and *The Piano Lesson*.

Geometric Abstract Art - The Blue Rider. – At the beginning of the century Delaunay *(Sundisks)* and some painters linked with the "Der Blaue Reiter" (The Blue Rider) laid the foundations for Geometric Abstract Art. The followers of this movement reject realism, claiming that art should move by the effect of forms and color alone. Malevich, a member of the Russian Constructivist group, which also included Lissitzky and Rodchenko, created rigourously geometrical abstractions *(White on White)*. Kandinsky, more spontaneous, abandoned himself in imaginative abstract color compositions ; and Paul Klee created poetic fantasies in a world peopled by humans, animals and symbols *(Actor's Mask, Equals Infinity)*.

School of Paris. – This gallery, devoted to the "School of Paris", displays works by Soutine *(Chartres Cathedral)*, Modigliani *(Reclining Nude)*, Matisse *(Memoirs of Oceania)*, Braque *(The Table)* and other masters of the first half of the 20th century.

Latin Americans. – Human suffering and social protest are the themes powerfully expressed by the Mexicans Tamayo *(Animals)*, Orozco *(Zapatistas)* and Siqueiros *(Echo of a Scream)*.

Primitives. – The primitive painters Hirschfeld *(Girl in Mirror)*, Pickett *(Manchester Valley)* and Seraphine *(Three in Paradise)*, ignorant of any particular movement, startle by their colorful figurative style.

Americans. – Powerful interpreters of the contemporary American scene are John Marin *(Lower Manhattan)*, Joseph Stella *(Factories)*, Ben Shahn *(Pacific Landscape)* and Edward Hopper *(Gas)*. Note the popular *Christina's World* by Andrew Wyeth.

Third Floor

Picasso after 1930. – Surrealism, cubism and expressionism combine in the famous composition in black and white, *Guernica* (1937) (painting is on loan from the artist's estate), inspired by an episode in the Spanish Civil War. Accompanying this main work are a series of studies showing the evolution of this famous composition.

Dada. – Members of the 1914-1918 war generation, the Dadaists denied all esthetic and moral value in art. Their works present parodies of reality and essentially aim to shock the public. Jean Arp in Zurich, Duchamp *(The Passage from Virgin to Bride)* and Picabia *(M'Amenez'Y)* in New York were exponents of "Dada". Other artists include Max Ernst *(Two Children are Threatened by a Nightingale)* and Schwitters *(Revolving)*.

Surrealism and its Affinities. – Dedicated to the projection of the subconscious and dreams, Surrealists tend to create fantasy objects with little reference to nature (Arp, *Mountain, Anchors, Navel ;* Miró, *The Hunter),* or they tend to paint realistic scenes set in hallucinating surroundings, such as Magritte, Delvaux and Dali ; *(The Persistence of Memory)*.

Also drawn from the unconscious are the emotionally charged configurations by Gorky.

An artist of great originality, the French Dubuffet, uses childlike images as satyrical commentary in his textured compositions.

Abstract Expressionism. – This art form emerged in the 1940's as an American, largely non-representational movement. Jackson Pollock, known for his "Action Painting", dripped paint on his canvases to form rhythmically intertwined lines. The structural arrangements by Kline and Motherwell are striking in their boldly dramatic style while Rothko uses subtle color changes to define geometric shapes. Tobey reveals a lyrical element in his art. Reinhardt's "Abstract Painting" is a square composed of nine smaller black squares of varying intensity. Unlike his peers, Willem de Kooning uses the human figure *(Woman, I)* in his tense and turbulent paintings.

Pop Art. – *Apply at desk for location.* A descendent of "Dada", Pop Art advocates introducing into art the most ordinary objects of daily life : tin cans, cigarette butts, tires photographs to create easily recognizable and often witty images. You will notice the Rosenquist *(Marilyn Monroe)* and Lichtenstein *(Drowning Girl)*.

Sculpture. – You go from Bourdelle *(Beethoven)* to Rodin *(St. John the Baptist)* to Brancusi whose streamlined forms and smooth medium (marble or polished copper) convey an impression of harmony and lightness. Further on, the sculpture of Giacometti is full of expression and movement. Finally, you may see the abstract sculptures of Henry Moore, Duchamp-Villon and Calder.

Drawings, Prints and Photographs. – Rotating exhibits at the far end of the Third Floor : the prints and drawings collections include significant series by Seurat, Toulouse-Lautrec, Rouault, Dali and others ; the Steichen Photography Center illustrates the history of photography and has changing exhibitions.

Car trouble
If you have car trouble in New York City,
Call Police Emergency
Telephone : 911.
Arrangements will be made for authorized tow.
24-hour service 7 days a week.

Time : 2 hours, preferably after dark or, even better, after the theater.

"The longest street in the world", Broadway has given its name to this famous area of pleasure and entertainment. Times Square is its center, but it extends approximately from 40th to 53rd Streets. Disappointing and even shabby by day, Broadway lights up to become "The Great White Way" at night, when a colorful crowd throngs beneath its huge illuminated billboards.

■ TIMES SQUARE★★

Located at the intersection of Broadway and Seventh Avenue (called with some justification the "Crossroads of the World"), Times Square takes its name from the *New York Times,* which moved here in 1905.

Yesterday. – Previously known as Longacre Square, it was a center for livery stables and harness makers. The American Horse Exchange remained at 50th Street and Broadway, the present site of the Winter Garden Theater, until 1910.

On the southeast corner of Broadway and 42nd Street, now occupied by an office building, was the Knickerbocker Hotel. At the turn of the century, its "free lunch", offering such delicacies as lobster Newburg was very popular. It was not quite free, however, for the customer was expected to down two beers (at ten cents a glass instead of the then prevalent five) before enjoying the buffet, and one more after. Enrico Caruso liked to entertain his friends here.

(From photo John B. Bayley, New York.)

The old Times Building.

The Hotel Astor, one of the oldest in New York, was opened in 1904 on the west side of the Square between 44th and 45th Streets and replaced in 1968 by an office building. To the north, on Duffy Square, are to be found the statues of Father Duffy, an Army Chaplain during the First World War, and George M. Cohan, the famous song and dance man.

Times Square is often, for various reasons, the setting for huge gatherings : election returns, scenes of mass enthusiasm such as the record turnout on VE Day (May 8, 1945), or the annual vigil to celebrate the twelfth stroke of midnight on New Year's Eve.

Today. – Noisy and congested, lined with movie houses, discount and record shops which are interspersed with bars, "adult" bookstores, shooting galleries and other tawdry establishments, Times Square by day reveals little of its former grandeur. However, Times Square after dark still generates great excitement ; it is here that the quick pulse of the city can best be felt.

Times Square is host to all : the theatergoer in search of cultural rewards, the pleasure seeker and the visitors who come from far and wide for a few days' exploration and fun. The ambience is uninhibited and tolerant.

A good time to visit Times Square is the evening when the milling theater crowd merges with the thousands strolling under the flashing neon signs. The brilliant lights of Times Square have always dazzled visitors. As early as 1921, the writer G.K. Chesterton exclaimed : "What a marvelous wonderland this would be for someone lucky enough not to know how to read !" Such attractions as the huge billboard with the Winston smoker and the fabled waterfall have disappeared from the scene, but other advertising displays, no less boisterous, vie for the attention of the passer-by.

A cosmopolitan cuisine caters to every taste and purse ; you may dine in style in French gourmet, continental or Oriental restaurants, enjoy the friendly atmosphere of the pub or join the crowd at one of the many coffee shops some of which never close.

One Times Square. – The Times Tower's 25 stories seemed prodigiously high at the time it was erected (in 1904). Demolished except for its steel framework in 1964, it was replaced by the Allied Chemical Tower, covered with marble.

The Times itself has now consolidated all its operations in a building on 43rd Street, just west of Times Square *(permission to visit the plant may be obtained by advance request in writing).* However, the famous moving electric news sign and the lighted metal ball, which falls to mark the arrival of the New Year, have survived the transformations. On top is the restaurant "Act One".

■ BROADWAY★★ (Theater District)

One of the first "Broadway" theaters was opened by Oscar Hammerstein in 1892 at 42nd Street and Seventh Avenue. This far-sighted gentleman was the grandfather of Oscar Hammerstein II, well known for the musicals "Oklahoma" and "South Pacific", among others. Many of these early theaters in the Broadway area specialized in vaudeville or burlesque.

Today, Broadway offers a far wider range of diversions, with its world-renowed legitimate theaters, its movies, night spots and bars offering entertainment. Legitimate theater has recently spread to other areas, referred to as "Off-Broadway" *(see p. 15),* of which Greenwich Village *(see p. 78)* is probably the most prominent example and "Off-Off-Broadway" *(see p. 15)*, mainly between Second Avenue and Lafayette Street, and Houston and 8th Streets. A special theater district, bounded by 40th and 57th Streets, Avenue of Americas and Eighth Avenue, has been designated to protect the character of the area. Incentives are offered to future developers who provide a theater in new office buildings (e.g. the Uris, Minskoff and Circle in the Square Theaters).

Movie theaters. – Scores of movie theaters are concentrated in the Broadway area, including some "grinds" open 24 hours a day, showing second-run films. Along 42nd Street, between Seventh and Eighth Avenues, there is a whole series of converted legitimate theaters, virtually a solid row of marquees. The once magnificent, New Amsterdam, built in 1903, welcomed such stars as Maurice Chevalier and the Italian actress Eleonora Duse, and offered "Midnight Folies" on its roof during the summer.

BROADWAY-TIMES SQUARE

Further north on Seventh Avenue, or Broadway, larger movie houses such as the Embassy, the De Mille, Loew's State, were originally built to accommodate two to three thousand spectators at a sitting. Occasionally, popular singing stars and entertainers appear in person in these houses. On their screens have passed such famous figures as Shirley Temple, Deanna Durbin, Gary Cooper, Irene Dunne, Clark Gable, Doris Day, James Dean and Marilyn Monroe.

Legitimate theaters. – Some forty theaters remain in the theater district, many of them grouped around 45th Street. One of their glories is the musical, which often runs many years to sold-out houses (sometimes 5 years and longer).

Just next to Broadway, behind the former Hotel Astor site, is the heart of the theater district, **Shubert Alley**. This short private street, reserved for pedestrians, was laid down in 1913, between 44th and 45th Streets and widened during the construction of the Minskoff Building. The Shubert Brothers built the Booth and Shubert Theaters, and were required to leave this passage as a fire exit. At intermission or after the show, many theatergoers drop into Sardi's nearby. This restaurant becomes a show-business headquarters on opening nights, and is well-known for the caricatures of celebrated theatrical personalities lining the walls, and their more or less famous successors who gather in the bar or the restaurant.

On 44th Street, between Fifth Avenue and Avenue of the Americas, is a landmark of the theatrical and literary world – the Algonquin Hotel. Here, in the 1920's, Alexander Woollcott organized the famous "Round Table", which counted Robert Benchley, Dorothy Parker and Robert Sherwood among its regulars. Some of the old aura of the period, and virtually the entire original decoration remain. The Algonquin is now noted for its after-theater suppers and bar.

Night clubs and bars. – There is a variety of night clubs and bars in this area. The celebrated Roseland Dance City has become a haven for devotees of ballroom dancing, both married and singles. It features an American orchestra and a Latin band.

Half-Price Tickets

Tickets are sold on the day of performance to Broadway, Off-Broadway, Lincoln Center and other performing arts events at half-price plus a small service charge.

The Times Square Theatre Centre – Duffy Square, Broadway and 47th Street, 354-5800.

> *evening performance tickets are sold Monday through Saturday 3 to 8 PM.*
> *matinée tickets are sold Wednesday and Saturday noon to 2 PM.*
> *matinée and evening tickets are sold Sunday noon to 8 PM.*

The Lower Manhattan Theatre Centre – 100 William Street, between John Street and Maiden Lane, 344-3340.

> *evening performance tickets are sold Monday through Friday 11:30 AM to 5:30 PM.*

From the Empire State Building to Grand Army Plaza (59th Street).

Distance : 1 1/4 miles — Time : 3 hours.

One is never tired of strolling on Fifth Avenue, the scene of New York's triumphal processions. The striking views of the principal skyscrapers, the frequently changing shop-window displays and the elegance and beauty of chic New York women contribute to make it one of the most fascinating walks in the city. It is preferable to follow this itinerary on a weekday morning : on Saturdays and Sundays some of the buildings are closed.

A BIT OF HISTORY

Millionaires Galore. — Laid out gradually beginning in 1824, Fifth Avenue was becoming a more fashionable residential section than Broadway by 1850. About 350 town-houses had been built there by the end of the Civil War. Each cost at least $20,000, a small fortune at the time.

By 1880 the avenue was a busy and noisy thoroughfare, teeming with carriages and fine horse-drawn omnibuses. Scattered among the mansions were private clubs and brownstones, more modest but still extremely comfortable. On the corner of Fifth Avenue and 34th Street, A.T. Stewart, a partner in several department stores, built his fancy marble home. Across 34th Street was the huge brownstone of William Astor. His wife, "the beautiful Mrs. Astor" — the former Caroline Schermerhorn — a descendant of an old Dutch family, presided over New York society. In the 1890's her nephew, William Waldorf Astor, replaced his palace next door by the Waldorf Hotel, an act of vengeance upon his aunt, from whom his wife had been unable to wrest the leader-

(From engraving, Museum of the City of New York.)

Fifth Avenue in 1900.

ship of New York society. He then left to live in England. Within less than a year, Mrs. Astor had decided to move north to Fifth Avenue and 65th Street, and by 1897 her son John Jacob Astor had built the Astoria Hotel next to the Waldorf. They were operated together, despite the family tiff, to the benefit of both branches until 1929, when they made way for the Empire State Building. *(See p. 73 for the "new" Waldorf Astoria.)* Further north, the Vanderbilt dynasty was established around 50th Street — in pseudo-Gothic or simulated Renaissance splendor.

Fifth Avenue forms the "great divide" between the east and west sides of New York.

The Talk of the Town. — In the spring of 1883, the "upper crust" was in a dither. William K. Vanderbilt, the grand-son of the famed "Commodore" *(see p. 71)*, was planning a ball in his Renaissance palace. Eighteenth century French court costumes were prescribed, complete with the appropriate dances. The richest young belles of New York, including Miss Astor, rehearserd tirelessly to perfect graceful curtsies and complicated steps.

However, when the invitations went out she was not included. Her mother, descendant of an "old family", had snubbed the "nouveau riche" Mrs. Vanderbilt by not including her in her circle of friends.

There was nevertheless a happy ending to this sad tale. Mrs. Astor sacrificed her pride on the altar of mother-love, and invited Mrs. Vanderbilt at last to her home. The precious invitation arrived in time and Miss Astor could cavort in her period gown, dancing the minuet and the gavotte to music by Rameau.

The Marriage Mart. — Later, other balls caused nearly as much excitement. In 1892, Mrs. Astor launched the term "the 400" by sending exactly 400 invitations to a ball. Apparently she thought there were only 400 persons worth knowing in New York, but it was also true that her art gallery-ballroom could accommodate only that number in proper style ! We can imagine the anguish of those who were not invited.

Fashionable balls at the Waldorf Astoria were often graced by young European aristocrats whose titles were more brilliant than their fortunes. The results were sometimes spectacular : in one year, 1895, Consuelo Vanderbilt married the Duke of Marlborough, Pauline Whitney the grandson of the Marquess of Anglesey, and Anna Gould the greatest dandy of them all : Boni de Castellane.

You will find an **index** at the back of the guide listing all subjects referred to in the text or illustrations (monuments, sites, historical and geographical items, etc.).

■ EMPIRE STATE BUILDING★★★

However you arrive in New York the Empire State Building stands out as a landmark, its tower rising above Manhattan, shining at a height of 1472 feet (the building itself measures 1250 feet). Named for New York the Empire State, its 102 stories make it the third tallest building in the world after the Sears Roebuck building, Chicago and the twin towers of the World Trade Center (see p. 88).

The view from the top is so splendid that it deserves two visits : first by daylight, to understand the layout of New York ; and then again in the evening, to enjoy the spectacle of the city's lights.

The construction. – Less than two years after the first excavations in October 1929, the building was opened in May 1931. Work progressed at a dizzy pace ; at times, more than a floor rose each day. There are only two stories of foundations, but 60,000 tons of steel beams (enough for a double-track railroad from New York to Baltimore) also support the tower. These were in place within three days of their production in Pittsburgh. The whole building weighs 365,000 tons, less than the weight of the 55 feet of dirt and rock excavated to build it.

At first the public was very apprehensive about the stability of the building but it seems to have proved durable. Specialists intended to use the last floor as a platform for dirigibles but the project was abandonned after one trial which was nearly a catastrophe. Seventy-three elevators serve the 102 floors, and 5 acres of windows are washed once a month. It takes half an hour to walk down the 1860 steps.

Empire State and Eiffel Tower.

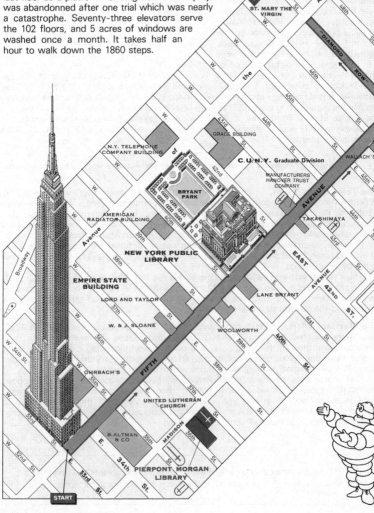

The 222-foot television antenna was added in 1951. It is a mere 22 stories high. In 1960 the beacon light was installed. The top 32 stories of the building are illuminated from dusk to midnight. They are turned off during foggy and cloudy nights and during the

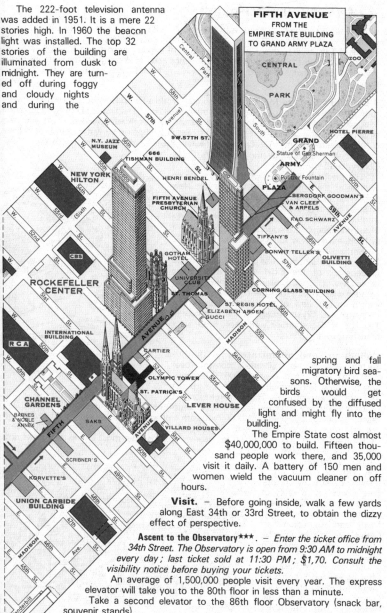

FIFTH AVENUE
FROM THE
EMPIRE STATE BUILDING
TO GRAND ARMY PLAZA

spring and fall migratory bird seasons. Otherwise, the birds would get confused by the diffused light and might fly into the building.

The Empire State cost almost $40,000,000 to build. Fifteen thousand people work there, and 35,000 visit it daily. A battery of 150 men and women wield the vacuum cleaner on off hours.

Visit. – Before going inside, walk a few yards along East 34th or 33rd Street, to obtain the dizzy effect of perspective.

Ascent to the Observatory★★★. – *Enter the ticket office from 34th Street. The Observatory is open from 9:30 AM to midnight every day ; last ticket sold at 11:30 PM ; $1,70. Consult the visibility notice before buying your tickets.*

An average of 1,500,000 people visit every year. The express elevator will take you to the 80th floor in less than a minute.

Take a second elevator to the 86th floor Observatory (snack bar, souvenir stands).

Here a rectangular open platform permits you to enjoy a magnificent **panoramic view★★★** for 50 miles in each direction when it is clear.

You may shudder to think that one July day in 1945, a bomber crashed into the building, at the level of the 78th and 79th floors.

For the full treatment, we advise you to take another elevator to the circular upper observatory *(102nd floor)* which is glass enclosed.

Window shopping along 57th street (see p. 121) is a must.
Some of the other large department stores are : Bloomingdale's, Macy's and Gimbels (see p. 120).

From 34th to 40th Streets (New York Public Library)

The section of Fifth Avenue between 34th and 40th Streets is bordered by many large department stores, such as B. Altman and Co, famous for its floors of fashions and fine foods and Lord and Taylor known for fine clothing and its attractive Christmas window decorations. Among the more unusual are Ohrbach's, just off the Avenue on 34th Street, a center for men's, women's and children's fashions, offering authentic line-for-line copies of French and Italian couture, and Lane Bryant (on the corner of East 40th Street) with its range of special size women's fashions.

This area also contains W & J Sloane (on the corner of 38th Street), noted for fine furnishings since 1843 and the "five and ten" store Woolworth which displays a dazzling variety of low-priced merchandise.

As you reach East 40th Street, the New York Public Library comes into view on your left.

■ NEW YORK PUBLIC LIBRARY★★

The New York Public Library was founded in 1895 to house the Astor Library, Lenox Library and Tilden Trust all under one roof. The library was opened in May 1911 with President Taft saying "this day crowns a work of national importance".

The famous marble lions, often called Patience and Fortitude, guard the entrance of the imposing Renaissance building designed by Carrère and Hastings. Behind the library is **Bryant Park**.

A popular Promenade. – In 1853 the first World's Fair in New York attracted crowds to the Murray Hill area, to gaze at three strange buildings. The first, on Fifth Avenue, dated back to 1842. Resembling a fort, it was topped by a walkway. Strollers could admire a large pool, for this pseudo-fort contained a reservoir, supplied by water from Croton Lake in Westchester County. **The Croton Distribution Reservoir** remained in service until 1899, when it was replaced by the New York Public Library, in 1911.

The **Crystal Palace**, with its main entrance on Avenue of the Americas, was built for the New York Fair in imitation of the London Crystal Palace, two years older. The iron and glass framework sheltered a large assortment of works of art and industrial products. A fire destroyed it in 1858, making way for Bryant Park.

Setback from 42nd Street, a pointed tower of timber braced with iron rose over 300 feet high, a predecessor of the Eiffel Tower. The **Latting Observatory**, as it was called, had three levels of wooden platforms. From the highest one, there was a superb view of New York, with Croton Reservoir and Crystal Palace in the foreground. The Latting Observatory was short lived as it burned down in 1856.

(From photo A. Devaney, New York.)

One of the Public Library lions.

Collections and organization. – The Research and Branch Libraries contain over 8,500,000 books and over 14,000,000 manuscripts, maps, phonograph records, tapes, prints and other library materials. The Research Libraries which are privately financed, house 5,000,000 volumes in four locations. Over 10,600,000 manuscripts, 136,000 prints, 317,000 maps are among the riches held by the Library. The second largest research library in the United States, after the Library of Congress, the New York Public Library has something for nearly everyone. The most interesting books and documents are displayed in temporary exhibits. Among the Library's rarities are a manuscript letter by Christopher Columbus, a draft of the Declaration of Independence in Jefferson's own hand, and an edition of Galileo's works which can be read only with a magnifying glass.

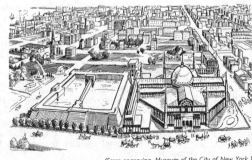

Included in the Research Libraries are the Schomburg Center for Research in Black Culture *(see p. 115)* and the Performing Arts Research Center *(111 Amsterdam Avenue, see p. 103)* which houses collections in the field of theater, music and dance.

(From engraving, Museum of the City of New York.)

Site of the Public Library in 1850.

The Branch Libraries through its network of 81 branches, serve Manhattan, the Bronx and Staten Island. The largest of these branches are located in the midtown area : the Mid-Manhattan Library *(8 East 40th Street)* ; the General Library and Museum of the Performing Arts at Lincoln Center *(111 Amsterdam Avenue, see p. 103)* ; the Donnell Library Center *(20 West 53rd Street, see p. 37)* and the well known Library for the Blind and Physically Handicapped *(166 Avenue of the Americas)* with thousands of braille and recorded materials, which provides a postage free service to residents of the five boroughs.

Visit. – *Open Mondays, Wednesdays, Fridays and Saturdays from 10 AM to 6 PM (Tuesdays to 9 PM). Closed on Thursdays, Sundays and holidays.*

The marble entrance hall on the first floor is impressive. On this floor are major temporary exhibits.

Take the elevator at the far end of the corridor to the right, up to the third floor. Along the walls are prints of American cities. An exhibition room displays interesting items from the Berg Collection of English and American literature ; on the walls are a number of portraits by noted American artists and printmakers. The large central hall is decorated with wood paneling and murals depicting the History of the Book.

To the right is the public card catalogue (10,000,000 entries) and the new Dictionary Book Catalog. Beyond are the main reading rooms which cover a half-acre. Beyond the central hall is the Print Gallery.

■ BRYANT PARK

In the summer, Bryant Park, between 40th and 42nd Streets on Avenue of the Americas, is an oasis of coolness in overheated Manhattan. At lunch time, employees of nearby offices come to relax and enjoy concerts of recorded music. In addition to the recorded concerts, Bryant Park offers live music during the day, flower displays and sometimes art exhibits.

Lawns and ivy filled flower beds border the promenades, shaded by sycamores. Bryant Park is named for William C. Bryant, author of the poem "Thanatopsis" and editor of the *New York Evening Post,* an influential paper during the Civil War.

At 40 West 40th Street is the American Radiator Building designed by Raymond Hood, New York City's first skyscraper to be named a landmark.

Two striking buildings can be seen from Bryant Park, to the west is the streamlined form of the New York Telephone Company Building with alternating columns of white marble and dark tinted glass. To the north is 1114 Avenue of the Americas (Grace Building), with its curvilinear base merging without break into a tower 50 stories tall, in travertine marble and tinted glass.

Continue north. The Graduate School and University Center, at 33 West 42nd Street is one of 20 individual educational units within the City University of New York. The Mall, a wide pedestrian arcade running from 42nd to 43rd Street between Fifth Avenue and Avenue of the Americas is the site of art exhibitions and concerts *(free of charge)*. At the corner of 43rd Street is a branch of Manufacturers Hanover Trust Company, one of the first banks constructed in glass designed by Skidmore, Owings and Merrill. For the public, used to thick-walled buildings, it was surprising to see the interior of a bank so visible to passerby, yet so ultramodern. One can even see the door of the vault through one of the windows. The bank is decorated in excellent taste ; with Macassar ebony furniture and Italian marble floors. The abstract sculpture may be more controversial - especially a spectacular composition by Harry Bertoia of metallic strips which hang from the ceiling.

Facing the Manufacturers Hanover Trust Company is a Japanese department store, Takashimaya, which evokes far away places. Further up the Avenue at the northeast corner of 46th Street is Wallach's specializing in quality men's clothing and ladies sports wear. Between 46th and 47th Streets is Korvette's, a discount house.

■ "DIAMOND ROW" ★

As you walk along 47th Street try to imagine that some 80 % of the diamond wholesale trade in America is transacted within this 750-foot block. A bewildering variety of languages - Spanish and Yiddish interspersed with Flemish - discuss carat, cut, color and clarity.

The street is lined with shops which display precious stones, but much of the trade is carried on in booths located on the upper floors and in the rear of the buildings. A sophisticated security system protects the dealers from unwelcome intruders. Policemen in and out of uniform maintain a constant vigil.

The merchants carry their precious bounty in suitcases, unobtrusive packages or in their coat pockets. The exchanges take place either right on the sidewalk or in one of the two clubs ; certain transactions are sealed by a mere handshake. Offenders transgressing this honor code are reportedly blacklisted throughout the diamond world.

Back to Fifth Avenue Between 48th and 49th Streets at 600 Fifth Avenue is the Barnes and Noble Annex selling bestsellers at discount prices. Scribner's bookshop, across the Avenue, has retained its handsome glass façade.

Across 49th Street is Saks Fifth Avenue, a specialty shop for the "chic woman".

■ ST. PATRICK'S CATHEDRAL ★

The Roman Catholic Cathedral of New York, St. Patrick's is dedicated to the patron saint of the Irish, heavily represented in the city. The festivities of St. Patrick's Day *(see p. 32)* amply demonstrate their veneration for the apostle of Ireland and even more for the " ould sod ". Until 1964, just before March 17th, you could see an army of workers painting a green line down Fifth Avenue to mark the occasion.

The cathedral was started in 1858 and opened in 1879 but its completion did not take place until 1906. At that time, churchgoers complained that it was too far out of town, but it is now in the heart of midtown, thanks to the northward growth of the city.

The cathedral was built of white marble and stone. Its Gothic architecture is patterned on the cathedral of Cologne, in particular the towers which rise over 330 feet. However the slender balanced proportions are dwarfed by the skyscrapers of Rockefeller Center. Three portals with fine bronze sculpted doors open into the nave. Bordered by side-aisles and apse, the nave is lighted by stained glass windows of the Gothic type, with particularly intense blues. Many of these windows were made in France. Thirty-foot pillars support the cross-ribbed Gothic arches which rise 110 feet above the nave. We should also mention the elegantly designed baldachin, over the main altar, and the monumental organ. On the way out, you will notice, on your right, the bronze figure of Pope Paul VI.

Beyond 51st Street rise the 51 stories of **Olympic Tower.** This elegant tinted glass building houses shops, offices and luxury apartments in its upper stories. Inside, Olympic Place, is a richly landscaped indoor park with fine trees and a waterfall.

On the same block is the French jeweller, Cartier, established in New York since 1847.

Across the street, at 666, the 39-story **Tishman Building (666)★**, was one of the more original architectural efforts of its time, with is façade of embossed aluminum panels. The inside is equally imaginative, with its unusual ceiling composed of thin wavy hanging strips, and a luminous cascade fountain on one wall. On the top floor, a restaurant and bar, "Top of the Sixes" richly decorated with tapestries and paintings offers, a magnificent view over most of Manhattan. Between 54th and 55th Streets next to Gucci is the well-known beauty and fashion salon of Elizabeth Arden.

■ ST. THOMAS CHURCH★

St. Thomas Episcopal Church was built at the beginning of this century in Gothic Revival style.

Amidst the wealth of statues and delicate tracery on the façade are carved the words "Thou art the King of Glory, O Christ". In the middle of the portal, St. Thomas welcomes the worshippers. Six of the apostles flank him, three on each side of the doors. The other apostles are arrayed centrally overhead in the tympanum. Below them are bas-reliefs of the legend of St. Thomas. To the left of the main portal is the narrow "Brides' Entrance", decorated with symbolically joined hands.

On entering the nave you will be struck by the huge **reredos★** of Dunville stone which rises above the altar. Spotlighted, it forms a lighter contrast to the darker vault. Numerous recesses shelter statues of Christ, the Virgin Mary, the Apostles, Saints of all denominations.

After this highlight, the rest of the decoration and furnishings recede into the background but you should also notice the stained glass windows, in deep reds and blues, the pulpit and the sculptured organ case. On entering you will see a particularly fine tapestry representing a Moses destroying the Tables of the Law when he found the Israelites worshipping the golden calf (Aubusson, 17th century).

In winter, October through May, there are organ recitals on Sunday afternoons at 5:15PM and the full choir and music every Wednesday at 12:10PM and Sunday at 11AM and 4PM.

Located between 53rd and 54th Streets, are the University Club (1899) and the Gotham Hotel (1905) both of the Italian Renaissance style.

Further on between 54th and 56th Streets are several Italian shops : one Gucci store (fashion and shoe boutique) and Buccellati which are both located on the main floor of the ornate Beaux Arts St. Regis Hotel.

■ FIFTH AVENUE PRESBYTERIAN CHURCH

One of the last churches built in brownstone *(for this term see p. 28)*, the "Fifth Avenue Presbyterian" was built in 1875. The Sanctuary, which has a seating capacity of 1800, is noted for its magnificent organ casing as well as intricately carved ash-wood pulpit.

In the sanctuary : organ recitals at 12:30PM every Tuesday, October through May.

Next to the church is Rizzoli's the international bookstore and gallery which has one of the largest selection of foreign language books. The southwest corner of 56th Street is occupied by the small Renaissance palace of the jeweler Harry Winston, whose specialty is diamonds and precious stones from $5,000 up. This is just the first of a series of luxurious shop windows.

Across the Avenue is the **Corning Glass Building★**, New York City headquarters of one of the world's leading producers of specialty glass, including Steuben crystal. Built in 1959, the 28-story building was the first on the Avenue to be sheathed in glass. It is mirrored in a corner pool.

The Steuben shop is on the ground floor. Here you will find examples of the American crystal often chosen as state gifts. There are occasional exhibitions of new or historic designs.

Between 56th Street and Grand Army Plaza, you will notice Bonwit Teller's (the exclusive specialty shop for men and women) and Tiffany, the jewelry store with its exquisite window displays. Inside, you may admire the Tiffany Diamond, a mere 128 carats. The Hallmark Gallery, a retail store and show place for the latest Hallmark products : greeting cards, party and gift items, is located on the northwest corner of 56th Street.

On the same side of the Avenue are I. Miller with its fashionable shoes, and at 10 West 57th Street, Henri Bendel, the fashion store for the sophisticated shopper. Across the street rises the striking and controversial form of **9 West 57th Street★** an elegant 50-story office building with tinted glass curtain walls and travertine marble edges. Unique in design and construction techniques, the building is fronted by plazas on 57th and 58th Streets, in travertine marble, the use of which is continued on the floors and walls of the lobby. The slightly distorted reflections of other buildings resulting from the slope produce extraordinary visual effects. Included in the project are a tri-level shopping mall, garage and a mini-park on 58th Street. The award-winning sculptured number nine sign on 57th Street was the work of Ivan Chermayeff.

Across the avenue, Bergdorf Goodman's is a bastion of haute couture and custom furs. The jeweler's store Van Cleef and Arpels, close to Bergdorf Goodman, has a sparkling array of treasures, including the diamond tiara of the Empress Josephine.

To the right, on your way uptown, stop to admire the 10,000 toys and games for young and old at F.A.O. Schwarz. They include teddy bears and other life size animals, antique toys, electrical and mechanical games, nearly live dolls, disguise kits, play houses and tree houses. (It is said that teddy bears were named after President "Teddy" Roosevelt, once depicted in a cartoon sparing the life of a bear cub.)

You have now reached Grand Army Plaza, the end of this walk.

If you want to plan your own visit to New York, please consult the **map of the walks and main sights.**

To reach the sight or district you wish to visit, please use **the subway and bus maps** folded into this guide.

Distance : 2 miles — Time : 4 1/2 hours (not including visits to museums).

Along Central Park, Fifth Avenue has long been New York's most prestigious residential section. Today, luxury apartment houses with spectacular views on Central Park, rise side by side with former mansions, most of which have now become museums, consulates, clubs, or cultural institutions. The sidewalk is dotted with awnings. Uniformed doormen greet the residents of the skytop palaces as they step out of their chauffeur-driven limousines.

A BIT OF HISTORY

The rush to the North. — During the last decade of the 19th century, Fifth Avenue millionaires began to migrate from the 34th Street area toward the open space of Central Park. Here, massive stone mansions and palaces replaced the old-fashioned brownstones. The interiors were often decorated with tapestries and antique furniture acquired sometimes for a fortune in Europe, but sometimes for a song.

(From photo John B. Bayley, New York.)

Fifth Avenue. — A former millionaire's mansion.

The boldest of these wealthy "migrants", Andrew Carnegie, moved all the way to 90th Street, while the haughty Mrs. Astor *(see p. 43)* stopped at 65th Street. Nearby lived the families of the financier Gould (67th Street) and the Whitneys (at 68th and 72nd Streets). W.A. Clark, the cooper king, built an edifice 150 feet high at the corner of 77th Street. These magnates of finance flourished in their palatial mansions until the crash of 1929 forced a number of them to sell, making way for apartment houses.

■ GRAND ARMY PLAZA★★

This square, a large and flowered breathing space, sometimes referred to, in short, as "Plaza Square", or "the Plaza" by New Yorkers, marks the division between the Fifth Avenue of luxury shopping, and the fashionable residential section. It is one of the few cool spots in town in the summer.

You may be tempted to take a ride in a hansom cab in Central Park. The horses are shod with rubber *(a 1/2 hour's ride costs $14 ; $10 for every additional 1/2 hour).*

Grand Army Plaza is surrounded by luxurious and distinguished hotels, like the Pierre and the Plaza of the continental type. The **Plaza,** built in 1907 in French Renaissance style, is a New York institution, where coming-out parties and charity balls draw the cream of New York society.

In front of the hotel, on the Fifth Avenue side, stands the figure of Abundance atop the Pulitzer Fountain with its gracefully cascading waters.

(From photo William Hubbell.)

Central Park South. — Horse-drawn cabs.

The fountain was built in 1915, and named for Joseph Pulitzer, the newspaper publisher who founded the literary prizes bearing his name. Just to the north, notice General Tecumseh Sherman on horseback, a statue by Augustus Saint-Gaudens.

Nearly as celebrated as the Plaza, the Hotel Savoy stood in front of it, across the square until 1966 when it was replaced by the **General Motors Building★**, a 50-story tower, clad in white Georgia marble, which was designed by Edward Stone.

In front of the building, the sunken General Motors Plaza adorned with flower beds and fountains, contains an outdoor restaurant and is lined by shops, a gallery, and an autopub. The main and first floor showrooms display General Motors automobiles and engineering advancements. *(Open Monday through Friday 9 AM to 9 PM ; Saturday 10 AM to 6 PM. Closed holidays.)*

On the northern corner of 60th Street, the **Metropolitan Club,** an Italian Renaissance palace, stands next to the **Hotel Pierre,** one of the most elegant in New York ; some of the rooms are occupied by permanent guests, but the hotel retains its continental style. Built in 1930, it is a sort of "40-story Versailles", with 600 rooms, topped by a tower in the form of the royal chapel designed by Mansart and Robert de Cotte. Behind, rises the glass-paneled **Getty Building,** a complete contrast in style.

Turn into **62nd Street,** passing the Knickerbocker Club, on the northern corner. This is one example of the residential streets which link Fifth Avenue to Madison and Park, with their old-world 18th-century style town houses. The modern façade of the Fifth Avenue Synagogue is a reminder of New York's large Jewish community.

Continuing up Fifth Avenue, on the corner of 64th Street you see a Tuscan Renaissance mansion built in 1896 by a coal baron, Edward J. Berwind. At 3 East 64th Street, the New India House, headquarters of the Consulate of India and the Indian delegation to the United Nations, illustrates what the Museum of the City of New York calls the "Gigi" style. It was built in 1903 by Warren and Wetmore. Further down the street, crossing Madison Avenue, at 112 East 64th Street is Asia House.

Asia House. – *Open 10 AM (1 PM Sundays and holidays) to 5 PM (8:30 PM Thursdays). Closed about 4 weeks between each exhibition. $1.00.*

The Asia Society was founded in 1956 under the guidance of John D. Rockefeller 3rd to promote better understanding and appreciation of Asia. Housed in this glass fronted structure, designed by Philip Johnson, is the Asia House Gallery, which displays four major exhibitions of Asian art a year.

Return to Fifth Avenue, and the former New York State **Arsenal**, built in the 1840's in pseudo-feudal style, houses the New York City Parks Administration. Behind it is the Central Park Zoo *(see p. 101)*.

Sixty-fifth Street is a typical residential street of the East Side. At No 49, Franklin and Eleanor Roosevelt lived next door to his mother, Mrs. James Roosevelt. Relations between the mother and her famous son were so close that she had several walls demolished between the two houses.

Temple Emanu-El. – *Open from 10 AM to 5 PM, guide available. Worship services Fridays 5:15 PM (organ recital at 5 PM) and Saturdays at 10:30 AM.*

The leading Reform synagogue in New York, and the largest in the United States, Temple Emanu-El (God with us) was built in 1929, in Byzantine Romanesque style.

The majestic nave can welcome 2500 worshippers. The ceiling, the marble columns in low relief and the great arch covered with mosaics are reminiscent of the basilicas of the Near East. Traditional Jewish symbols decorate the stained glass windows.

At the end of the nave, the Sanctuary harbors the tabernacle, or Holy Ark, which contains the Torah scrolls. On either side of the Sanctuary are placed the menorahs (seven-branched candlesticks).

Continue on Fifth Avenue to 70th Street where Henry C. Frick's former mansion, surrounded by terraced flower-beds, now houses his collection of fine art.

Frick Collection★★★. – One of the most beautiful private museums in the world. *Description p. 52.*

The French Consulate is located at 934 Fifth Avenue, in an Italian Renaissance mansion.

Just north of 75th Street, an attractive wrought iron fence protects **Harkness House**, a "Roman" palace with ornate sculptured cornices. It was built in 1907 for Edward S. Harkness, a partner of John D. Rockefeller in the then Standard Oil Company of New Jersey.

At the corner of Madison Avenue and 7th Street is the Whitney Museum.

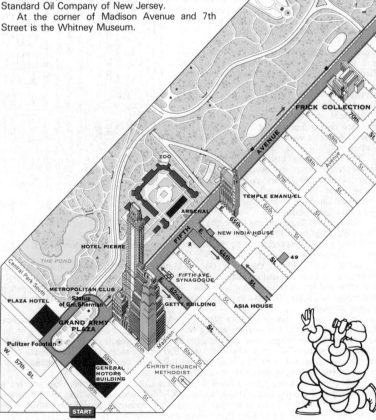

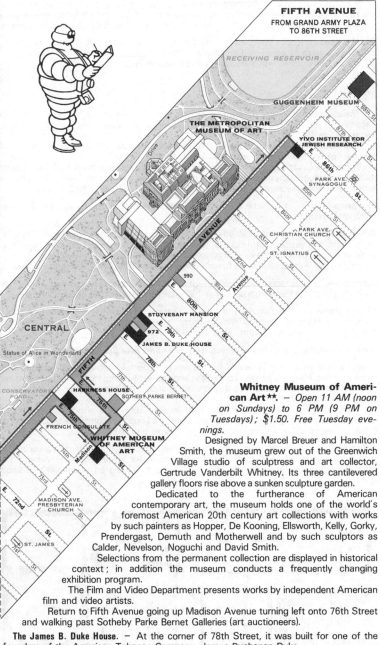

FIFTH AVENUE
FROM GRAND ARMY PLAZA
TO 86TH STREET

RECEIVING RESERVOIR

GUGGENHEIM MUSEUM

THE METROPOLITAN
MUSEUM OF ART

YIVO INSTITUTE FOR
JEWISH RESEARCH

PARK AVE.
SYNAGOGUE

PARK AVE.
CHRISTIAN CHURCH

ST. IGNATIUS

990

STUYVESANT MANSION

CENTRAL

972

JAMES B. DUKE HOUSE

Statue of Alice in Wonderland

HARKNESS HOUSE

CONSERVATORY POND

SOTHEBY PARKE BERNET

FRENCH CONSULATE

WHITNEY MUSEUM
OF AMERICAN
ART

MADISON AVE.
PRESBYTERIAN
CHURCH

ST. JAMES

Whitney Museum of American Art★★. – *Open 11 AM (noon on Sundays) to 6 PM (9 PM on Tuesdays); $1.50. Free Tuesday evenings.*

Designed by Marcel Breuer and Hamilton Smith, the museum grew out of the Greenwich Village studio of sculptress and art collector, Gertrude Vanderbilt Whitney. Its three cantilevered gallery floors rise above a sunken sculpture garden.

Dedicated to the furtherance of American contemporary art, the museum holds one of the world's foremost American 20th century art collections with works by such painters as Hopper, De Kooning, Ellsworth, Kelly, Gorky, Prendergast, Demuth and Motherwell and by such sculptors as Calder, Nevelson, Noguchi and David Smith.

Selections from the permanent collection are displayed in historical context; in addition the museum conducts a frequently changing exhibition program.

The Film and Video Department presents works by independent American film and video artists.

Return to Fifth Avenue going up Madison Avenue turning left onto 76th Street and walking past Sotheby Parke Bernet Galleries (art auctioneers).

The James B. Duke House. – At the corner of 78th Street, it was built for one of the founders of the American Tobacco Company, James Buchanan Duke.

The vestibule is decorated with a statue by Nicolas Coustou (1658-1733), representing Euterpe, the muse of Music.

At 972 Fifth Avenue, the cultural and press services of the French Embassy are housed in the former Payne Whitney home, designed by McKim, Mead and White.

The turreted mansion on the southeast corner of 79th Street is the **Stuyvesant Mansion**, built in Louis XII style by a descendant of the last Dutch governor of New Amsterdam *(see p. 81)*.

On the northeast corner of 80th Street is one of the most luxurious apartment houses on the avenue. It was built in 1910 by McKim, Mead and White in Italian style. Many of the apartments have two living rooms, dining room, four bedrooms, kitchen, pantry, and six servant's rooms. Others are duplexes.

The Metropolitan Museum of Art★★★. – *(Main entrance at 82nd Street).* Some of the richest collections of fine art in the world. *Description p. 54.*

On the southeast corner of 80th Street is the "Louis XIII" Miller Mansion. First occupied by William S. Miller, it later belonged to Mrs. Cornelius Vanderbilt III, one of the last to leave the "50's." After her death in 1953, it became the headquarters of the **Yivo Institute for Jewish Research.**

From the east side of Fifth Avenue, you will notice, two blocks to the north, the novel outlines of the **Guggenheim Museum** *(description p. 64).*

5 FRICK COLLECTION ***

For those who love Old Masters, as well as for those who simply like beautiful things, the Frick Collection is one of the high points of a visit to New York. The visitor may enjoy a glimpse of life in a luxurious private home as well as the varied collection of masterpieces.

The House. – It was designed in 1913 for Henry Clay Frick (1849-1919), a Pittsburgh industrialist. Here he assembled a collection acquired over a period of forty years.

It was transformed into a museum and opened in 1935.

VISIT

The museum is open : September through May, 10 AM to 6 PM Tuesday through Saturday ; 1 to 6 PM Sundays, Feb. 12, Election Day ; closed on Mondays, Jan. 1, Thanksgiving, Dec. 24, 25.

June, July and August, 10 AM to 6 PM Wednesday through Saturday ; 1 to 6 PM Sunday ; closed Monday, Tuesday and July 4. $1,00.

The entrance is at 1 East 70th Street ; children under ten are not admitted ; those under 16 must be accompanied by an adult. There are chamber music concerts on Sunday afternoons in winter, for which tickets are necessary *(they are free but must be applied for by mail).*

Entrance Hall. – In a niche on the right is displayed a bust of *Henry Clay Frick* by Malvina Hoffman.

Boucher Room. – You are carried back in time to an 18th century French boudoir, with its intimate and precious atmosphere. The woodwork frames eight Boucher paintings, commissionned by Madame de Pompadour. They represent the *Arts and Sciences.*

Among the 18th century French furniture are pieces by Martin Carlin, Riesener and Malle.

Anteroom. – This room is reserved for rotating exhibitions of drawings and prints from the collection. Note the marble bust of an Italian lady by Francesco Laurana (15th century).

Dining Room. – Decorated with English 18th century paintings in delicate colors : portraits by Hogarth, Romney and Reynolds, and *The Mall in St. James's Park* by Gainsborough. The silver is 18th century English.

West Vestibule. – Here are displayed the series of the *Four Seasons* (Boucher, 1755).

Fragonard Room. – It is named for the eleven decorative paintings by Fragonard, a hymn of inimitable grace to love. Four of the large panels were commissioned by Madame du Barry. They recount the various stages of a romantic encounter : *Pursuit, Meeting, Love Crowned* and *Love Letters.*

Outstanding furniture adds to the total effect : sofas and armchairs covered in Beauvais tapestry designed by Boucher and Oudry ; a Louis XVI commode by La Croix ; a delightful sewing table with lyre-shaped legs ; Sèvres porcelains, etc.

South Hall. – Foremost, among the beautiful furniture, we should mention a Louis XVI secretary-desk signed by Riesener, with bronzes made for Marie-Antoinette. Among the paintings, notice the *Portrait of His Wife* by Boucher (1743, signed twice) and two small

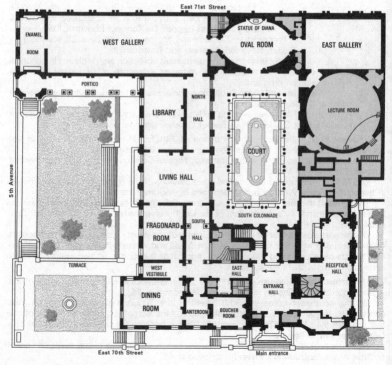

Vermeers, one of which, the *Officer and Laughing Girl,* is remarkable for its radiant luminosity. At the foot of the stairs is a thirty day Louis XV calendar clock, which also contains a barometer.

Living Hall. — Furnished with a desk by André Boulle and two cabinets in the style of this famous 17th century French cabinet-maker, this room displays 16th century masterpieces. The Venetian school is represented by a *Saint Francis in Ecstasy,* by Giovanni Bellini, against an outstanding landscape, and by two Titian portraits, one depicting the sensual features of the author of racy tales and comedies, *Pietro Aretino.* The fascinating figure of *St. Jerome* as Cardinal, by El Greco, represents the Spanish school. Typical of the best of the German school are two celebrated portraits by Hans Holbein the Younger : with great psychological perception he has depicted *Sir Thomas More* and *Thomas Cromwell.*

(From photo Frick Collection.)

Henry Clay Frick's Living Hall.

Library. — Henry Clay Frick himself looks down from a portrait in this room decorated with lovely examples of Chinese porcelain on black backgrounds and with small Italian and French bronzes of the 16th and 17th centuries.

You will also notice the charming terra-cotta bust of the Swedish miniature painter Peter Adolf Hall, done by the French sculptor Boizot in 1787, and a whole series of English paintings of the 18th and 19th centuries.

North Hall. — Above the blue marble Louis XVI table hangs Ingres' portrait of the *Comtesse d'Haussonville.* The marble bust by Houdon represents the *Marquis de Miromesnil,* Keeper of the Seals under Louis XVI. There is a spirited Baroque sketch by Tiepolo of *Perseus and Andromeda* (Venetian, 18th century) and a charming Chardin *The Lady with a Bird Organ.*

West Gallery. — In this room, decorated with 16th century Italian furniture and Persian carpets, are portraits and landscapes of the Dutch, French, Spanish and British schools.

Among the portraits notice Lodovico Capponi, a page in the court of Duke Cosimo I de'Medici, by Bronzino (Florence, 16th century) ; an El Greco of the Italian period *(Vincenzo Anastagi, a Knight of Malta)* ; works by Frans Hals ; three splendid Rembrandts of a great intensity of expression *(Self-Portrait, Nicolaes Ruts,* and *The Polish Rider) ;* two famous works by Van Dyck ; *Frans Snyders,* an Antwerp painter of still life, and his wife ; *Philip IV of Spain,* by Velazquez. There is also the well-known *The Forge* by Goya.

You may particularly admire, among the landscapes, the Ruisdael, the Hobbema (Dutch, 17th century), and *The Harbor of Dieppe* by Turner. A work by Georges de la Tour (French, 17th century) ; *The Education of the Virgin,* a typical example of this painter from Lorraine also deserves special attention.

Enamel Room. — A beautiful collection of Limoges painted enamels of the 16th and 17th centuries in intense blues and greens accompanies a *St. Simon* the Apostle (?) by Piero della Francesca and a Madonna and Child with St. Lawrence and St. Julian by Gentile da Fabriano.

There are also a few Italian Primitives and examples of Renaissance sculpture.

Here you may admire a great work by van Eyck (Flemish, 15th century) ; *Virgin and Child, with Saints and Donor.* The Virgin stands between St. Elizabeth of Hungary, to the right, and St. Barbara, to the left, with her hand resting on the shoulder of the donor, a Carthusian monk. The details and the extensive landscape reveal the fine brushwork of the painter.

Oval Room. — A life-size terra-cotta figure of *Diana the Huntress* by Houdon (French, 18th century) graces this gallery. It is a version of a statue executed for the Duke of Saxe-Gotha and acquired by the Russian Empress, Catherine the Great.

Four large portraits by Whistler flank this sculpture, including one of the poet, *Robert de Montesquiou.*

East Gallery. — An assortment of paintings from different schools and periods, all of fine quality. Claude Lorrain's dramatic *Sermon on the Mount* dominates the gallery. The other works on display are : Greuze's genre painting *The Wool Winder ;* the *Quay at Amsterdam,* by Jacob van Ruisdael (Dutch, 17th century),where the sail of the boat on the left seems to capture all the light ; and a portrait, by Jacques Louis David, of *Countess Daru,* the wife of Napoleon's Quartermaster General.

Court. — One of the most delightful parts of the Museum. It is a cool haven in summertime thanks to its marble floor, fountain and pool, tropical plants and flowers. From the south Colonnade you can admire the entire court and the statue of *Diana,* by Houdon, in the Oval Room beyond. Among other sculptures, there is a 15th century bronze *Angel* by Jean Barbet.

Richly endowed and supported, the Metropolitan presents magnificent collections from prehistory to the twentieth century, a veritable encyclopedia of the arts over 5000 years.

The growth of the Museum. – Founded in 1870 by a group of New Yorkers, members of the Union League Club, the Museum first opened in temporary quarters in 1872. The core of the collections was a gift of antiquities from General di Cesnola, a former consul in Cyprus, and a group of 174 paintings most of which were Dutch or Flemish.

The first permanent building, a modest red brick structure built around four small courtyards, rose between 1879 and 1898 on land belonging to the City of New York. It still forms part of the present building.

The monumental Renaissance façade (designed by Richard Morris Hunt), in grey Indiana limestone, was completed in 1902, although the sculptural decoration has never been finished. On the occasion of the Museum's Centennial Celebrations in 1970 a comprehensive architectural plan was devised which will eventually bring the entire Museum to physical completion. This master plan will include four new wings and necessitate the reorganization of the Museum.

During these decades, the collection also grew considerably, either from gifts of millionaires (Morgan, Rockefeller, Marquand, Hearn, Altman, Bache, Lehman...) or from purchases.

With the space limitations imposed by the master plan massive collecting will necessarily give way to a period of disposal and refinement. In this context the Museum plans to organize exchange exhibitions with other cultural institutions, notably the Louvre.

A few statistics : over three million visitors in 1977 ; 236 galleries ; over 2000 European paintings and 3000 European drawings ; over 1,000,000 prints ; 4000 objects of medieval art ; 3000 American paintings and statues ; 4000 musical instruments. About a fourth of the collection is on display at any one time.

The Departments. – The museum is organized into eighteen sections. *See the plan opposite.*

European Sculpture and Decorative Art★★★ *(see p.58)*
European Ceramics, Glass and Metalwork★★ *(see below)*
Costume Institute★ *(see p. 56)*
Junior Museum★ *(see p. 56)*
Egyptian Wing★★★ *(see p. 56)*
Greek and Roman Art★ *(see p. 56)*
Medieval Art★★★ *(see p. 57)*
Lehman Pavilion★★ *(see p. 57)*
Arms and Armor★★ *(see p. 59)*

Musical Instruments★★ *(see p. 59)*
American Wing *(see p. 60)*
The Michael C. Rockefeller Collection of Primitive Art *(see p. 60)*
Far Eastern Art★ *(see p. 60)*
Ancient Near Eastern Art *(see p. 60)*
Islamic Art★★ *(see p. 60)*
Drawings, Prints★ and Photographs *(see p. 60)*
European Paintings★★★ *(see p. 61)*
Twentieth Century Art *(see p. 63)*

General Information. – The main entrance of the "Met" is on Fifth Avenue, across from 82nd Street. You will enter the Great Hall around which are grouped various services ; checkroom, information desk, art and book shop. (Metropolitan Museum Christmas cards are very popular ; the Museum also sells reproductions of ancient jewelry and ceramics.)

Beyond the Greek and Roman galleries, at the far left of the building, in the south wing, is a cafeteria : the tables are grouped around a pool with sculpture by Carl Milles. The snack bar, Educational Services and Junior Museum are downstairs.

Special exhibitions, lectures, films, gallery talks and concerts are among the cultural activities of the Museum.

VISIT

Open Tuesday through Saturday from 10 AM to 4:45 PM (8:45 PM Tuesday) ; Sundays and holidays from 11 AM to 4:45 PM. Voluntary admission fee. Closed Mondays. Audio guides are available for certain departments and temporary exhibitions.

Ground Floor

EUROPEAN CERAMICS, GLASS AND METALWORK★★

Ceramics. – This term includes all objects of baked clay, glazed or not. Among the former a distinction is made between faience and hard and soft-paste porcelain. Some "rustic basins", with an aquatic decor, represent the work of Bernard Palissy (1510-1590). There are also samples of faience from such major French workshops as Nevers, Rouen, Moustiers, Sceaux, Marseilles and Strasbourg, as well as porcelains from St-Cloud, Chantilly, Mennecy, Vincennes and Sèvres, including two curious "pot-pourri" vases in the form of castles of soft-paste porcelain from Sèvres. Other galleries display Italian majolica ware from Urbino and Gubbio, with its metallic luster ; Dutch Delft and English wares (soft-paste porcelains, Wedgwood and Staffordshire), and German stoneware, faience and porcelain (Meissen, Nymphenburg and Hochst).

Metalwork, Collectors' Items. – Two galleries (38 and 39) display French Provincial and Parisian silver of the 17th and 18th centuries, including objects by N. Besnier, F.-T. Germain, E.P. Balzac and J.-N. Roettiers. In addition, there are galleries devoted to English silver and to Continental European metalwork and glass. You may want to pause in gallery 40 where Renaissance goldsmith's work and enamels from Limoges and Venice are displayed together with snuffboxes, toilet sets and dance cards of the 18th and 19th centuries.

You will also be interested in the watches, clocks and miniature portraits. Renaissance clockmaking is represented by the richly decorated clock of gilded bronze (1568), work of the Viennese Cospar Behaim.

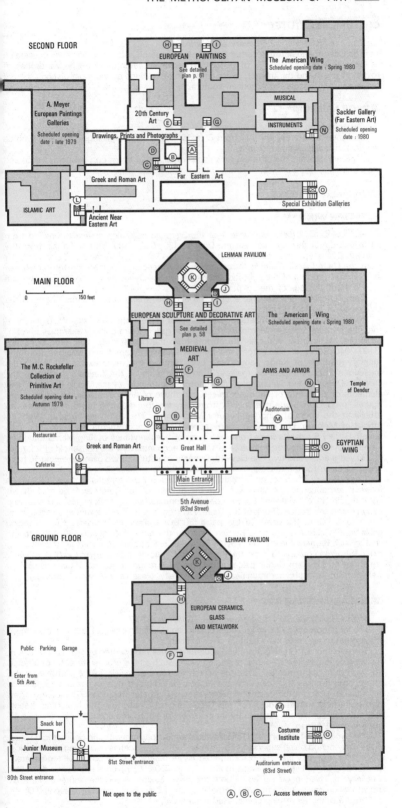

In view of the vast program of expansion and renovation undertaken by the museum, certain departments may be closed to the public for several months at a time and specific works of art may be exhibited in locations other than those indicated. Information regarding new installations and revised floor plans may be obtained at the information desk at the museum's entrance.

COSTUME INSTITUTE ★

The exhibits are changed every six months.

The Costume Institute, a center for costume research and study, has a vast collection – almost 30,000 articles – of period and regional costumes from the wardrobes of royalty, society and the theater, and a collection of fashions by the most distinguished of contemporary French and American couturiers.

JUNIOR MUSEUM ★

Entrance from within the main building.

Designed to interest children from 6 to 15 in art, using ingenious methods, such as illuminated tableaux and dioramas.

A gallery explains the different techniques of oil, water color, egg tempera, fresco and cave painting. There are also a library, studio, and auditorium.

Main Floor

EGYPTIAN WING ★★★

Displayed in 13 galleries, Phase 1 of the Egyptian collection covers the period from Paleolithic Egypt through the Eleventh Dynasty (300,000 - 1991 BC) and again from the Thirtieth Dynasty to the Coptic period (380 BC to 641 AD). The Temple of Dendur is a gift from the United Arab Republic in recognition of American help in saving the temples of Abu Simbel. Phase II of the collection ranging from the Dynasties Twelve to Twenty-nine will be the final stage of the Egyptian installation.

Comprehensive descriptions, a time line and wall maps introduce the visitor to the civilization of ancient Egypt.

Enter (gallery 1 a) the "mastaba" and chapel of Pernebi, the burial site of a dignitary of the Fifth Dynasty court at Memphis. Presented in gallery 2 are primary examples of relief, sculpture, architecture and daily life objects from the First through the Tenth Dynasties (3100-2040 BC) and reliefs from the famous Cheops Pyramid and columns from the funerary temples of Kings Sahura and Unis. Among the relics excavated during the museum's Thebes expedition (gallery 3) are fragments of the funerary temple of the Eleventh Dynasty king, Nebhepetra Mentuhotpe, the founder of the Middle Kingdom, and elements of the tomb of his major queen and those of his concubines. In gallery 4 are figures, models of boats and scenes from daily life found at the tomb of Mekutra, an official at the court of King Nebhepetra Mentuhotpe. The complete burial of Wah, an official of Mekutra, shows his mummy as well as the adornments with which he was buried. Gallery 5 exhibits finds from the tombs of five dignitaries of King Mentuhotpe ; an Eleventh Dynasty papyrus archive – letters and accounts from the household of a farmer (4,000 years ago) ; and two fine Eleventh Dynasty sculptures. Two galleries, 6 and 10 have been set aside for the museum's rich collection of color facsimilies of tomb and temple paintings. Gallery 7 focuses on Thirtieth Dynasty (380-342 BC) material : Prince Wennefer's massive sarcophagus ; granite relief from the temples of the Delta ; and the magnificent "Metternich Stela". Galleries 8 and 9 display stone sarcophagi, mummies and two long papyri (excerpts from a "Book of the Dead") all from the time of Alexander's conquest of Egypt (332 BC) to the death of Cleopatra (30 BC). Gallery 11 is reserved for changing exhibitions. Gallery 12 contains Roman art from the time of Augustus (30-1 BC) to 4th century AD. Remarkable are the "Fayum Portraits" eight portrait-panels (painted in wax in AD 2). Shown in gallery 13, from the Roman and Coptic periods in Egypt (30 BC - AD 641) are about 40 excellent Coptic pieces showing a wide range of objects of everyday life as well as from monastic communities (textiles, jewelry, glass vessels, wood carvings).

GREEK AND ROMAN ART ★

Main Floor (Galleries 1-9). Second Floor (Galleries 10-17).

The large collection of Cypriot Antiquities (6) and Cycladic objects (1a) show the variety of art created by these early centers of civilization.

The evolution of Greek pottery and sculpture is well represented by the rich collection. In sculpture the geometric period produced works such as the bronze statuette of a horse (16) with pure and simplified lines, the search for form especially in the portrayal of the human body (Kouros 1) dominates in the Archaic period grave monuments and reliefs while the Classic period produced sculptures showing greater freedom. These are often represented by Roman copies of the Greek original (2 and 3). The Hellenistic period becomes realistic as can be seen by the portrayal of youth and age (*Sleeping Eros* – 16 and *Peasant Woman* – 4).

The evolution of pottery (10-15) followed a similar pattern with the geometric designs of the early period being superseded by human forms with scenes portraying mythological subjects or everyday life. The black and red figure techniques are both well represented. Outstanding is the **Euphronios Krater** (bought for $1,000,000) which is excellently displayed in gallery 10. This work is signed by both the potter Euxitheos and the painter Euphronios and shows on one side the Body of Sarpedon, son of Zeus being lifted by Sleep and Death and on the other, an arming scene. (Red figured Calyx.)

In the first gallery next to the Great Hall is an interesting collection of sarcophagi, and a series of portrait busts typical of the realism of expression of the later Roman period.

In the southeast corner of the Great Hall, do not fail to visit the bedroom (cubiculum) from a villa at Boscoreale near Pompeii, which was buried by the eruption of Vesuvius in AD 79. The paintings, which depict architecture of the Roman period, may have been derived from traditional theatrical scenery. Notice the satyr masks and the characteristic Pompeian red.

MEDIEVAL ART★★★

On the left side of the main staircase is the **Early Medieval Gallery.** Early Medieval art is represented by the Treasure of Cyprus (7th century) discovered in 1902 and Byzantine ivories and enamels ; pass through an Italian Romanesque marble portal from San Gemini, in Umbria, to the Medieval Tapestry Hall.

Under the staircase is a **Romanesque chapel** containing a collection of Virgins Enthroned (French, 12th and 13th centuries) and a stained-glass window from Paris.

Tapestries. – Woven principally in the workshops of Flanders (Arras, Brussels and Tournai), these tapestries date from the 14th century to the early 16th century. At that time, they were as practical as ornamental, since they served to temper drafts and dampness.

The earliest, depicting the Crucifixion (Germany, 14th century), lacks any sense of perspective. A later Annunciation, begun early in the 15th century, is related to a painting by Melchior Broederlam, a court painter in Burgundy. A particularly arresting series is the rare group of the Sacraments, with Baptism, Marriage and Extreme Unction. Another series, commissioned by Charles the Bold, Duke of Burgundy, shows the arming of Hector during the Trojan War. In the same gallery is an unusual German saddle of bone. The decoration, in very low relief, shows scenes of courtly love.

Medieval Sculpture Hall. – Built to suggest a church, with nave and side aisles. A splendid baroque wrought iron choir screen is installed here. Begun in 1668 for the Cathedral of Valladolid, in Spain, the main part is 17th century, and the upper part more recent. At Christmas the Museum exhibits a magnificent tree and 18th century Neapolitan creche in front of the choir screen.

A large collection of sculpture and bas-reliefs traces the development of Gothic sculpture from the 13th to the 16th centuries. The most precious examples are displayed under glass, or spotlighted. Among these are an exquisite Virgin and Child (France, 13th century) in painted wood, on the right near the entrance of the gallery, and, on the wall nearby, an Italian crucifix of the early 13th century.

(From photo Metropolitan Museum.)

The Medieval Hall and the Spanish Grille.

The Mona Lisa was placed there, during her visit in 1963. This masterpiece from the Louvre drew a million and a half visitors to the Metropolitan.

Medieval Treasury. – In addition to the portable shrines, reliquary caskets and sacramental objects, the Treasury (to the right of the Medieval Sculpture Hall) also contains two fine sculptural groups (French, early 16th century) from the private chapel of the Château of Biron in southwestern France. On one side is the Entombment of Christ, and on the other the sorrowing Virgin holding the body of her son.

In the wall and central cases are precious religious objects : a 13th century Limoges enamel shrine, with scenes from the life of Christ in copper-gilt, the silver reliquary head of St. Yrieix (Limousin, 13th century) which once held fragments of his skull, and a small German Virgin and Child of the 15th century.

The richness of the collection of Romanesque and Gothic Limoges enamels rivals that of the Parisian ivories of the 14th and 15th centuries, including a rosary with beads in the form of skulls. We should also mention a curious carved bone reredos by Baldassare degl'Embriacchi (Italy, 15th century) : scenes from the life of Christ (in the center), St. John the Baptist (to the left) and St. John the Evangelist (to the right).

LEHMAN PAVILION★★

The Robert Lehman Collection can be seen in this pavilion where a series of period rooms and galleries built around a garden court have been especially designed to house the encyclopedic collection of some 3,000 works of art. The seven period rooms have been duplicated from the old Lehman home on West 54th Street.

The collection is famous for its Italian paintings of the 14th and 15th centuries. The Siennese School is represented by Sassetta *(St. Anthony in the Wilderness)* and others. The Florentine School is exemplified by Botticelli *(Annunciation)* and the Venetian School by Bellini *(Madonna and Child).* Among a distinguished group of works by painters of the Renaissance – Flemish, French and German – is the famous *St. Eligius* by Petrus Christus ; also shown are canvases by Gérard David, Memling and Cranach the Elder. Later period painting is exemplified by Rembrandt, El Greco and Goya. Also featured in the collection are French paintings of the 19th (Ingres' *Portrait of the Princesse de Broglie)* and 20th century. The Impressionist and Post-Impressionist style is personified by such artists as Renoir and van Gogh. Fauve canvases by Matisse and Vlaminck are also exhibited. Housed on the lower level the important collection of drawings ranges widely in the history of European art. Included are drawings by the masters of the Italian Renaissance : Leonardo da Vinci and Pisanello, a fine group of Rembrandt's, Dürer's and the great modern draughtsmen - Degas and Cézanne. 19th century American art is represented by a sketchbook by Prendergast.

The collection includes magnificent examples of the decorative arts : Gothic tapestries and embroideries, Persian faïence, Italian majolica of the 15th and 16th centuries, medieval bronze aquamanilia, Renaissance bronzes and medals, Venetian glass, Limoges enamels, superb goldsmith's work and jewelry and furniture of the Renaissance.

EUROPEAN SCULPTURE AND DECORATIVE ART★★★

The Blumenthal Patio (Velez Blanco). – To the left of the main staircase is the Renaissance patio from the castle of Velez Blanco in Andalusia. It was reconstructed here in 1964. The white marble galleries and the fine low relief decoration by Lombard sculptors transport you to the shores of the Mediterranean. The capitals reflect a refined Italian mode, and the tile ceiling adds a harmonious note of color. The Latin inscription beneath the cornice gives the name of the owner : Pedro Fajardo and the dates of construction : 1506-1515.

Northern Renaissance Galleries (1-5). – These include a wooden door, carved for the Château of Gaillon in Normandy and representing Louis XII and the builder of the château, the Cardinal of Amboise, wearing a square doctor's bonnet ; the chapel from the Château de la Bastie d'Urfé (French, 1550) ; the "Nelson Room" from the Star Hotel, Great Yarmouth (Norfolk) ; and the wooden paneled room from the village of Flims in Switzerland.

Italian Galleries (8-11). – Further on a vestibule provides an entrance to the bedroom from the Sagredo Palace (Venice early 18th century). In another gallery there are examples of Italian sculpture by Antonio Rossellino and Pietro Torrigiano, and small bronzes of the 16th and 17th centuries by Andrea Riccio, Giovanni da Bologna and others.

English Galleries (13-20). – To follow the development of English decorative art from 1660 to 1800, start with the gallery beyond Medieval Sculpture.

A staircase from Cassiobury Park, Hertfordshire, by Gibbons, represents the decorative art of the 17th century. The Rococo style of mid-18th century is reflected in the stucco decoration of a dining room from Kirtlington Park, Oxfordshire, now arranged as a drawing room.

The architect Robert Adam (1728-1792) gave his name to a style reminiscent of ancient motifs and exemplified by the stately dining room from Lansdowne House, London. Pastel colors, pilasters, niches for ancient statues, "Pompeian" stucco decoration all contribute to the refinement of the setting, in delicate contrast to the deep tones of the mahogany table and chairs. The Lamerie silver and an elaborate chandelier complete the arrangement.

The next gallery, formerly at Croome Court, Warwickshire, was also designed by Adam. The owner, Lord Coventry, ordered Gobelins tapestries designed by François Boucher.

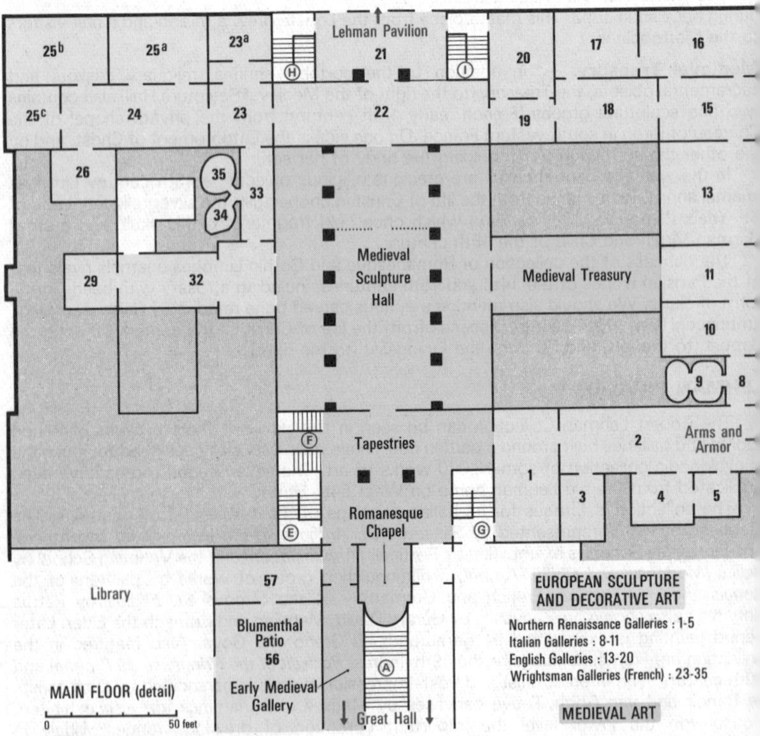

				Lehman Pavilion				
25ᵇ	25ᵃ	23ᵃ		21		20	17	16
			H		I			
25ᶜ	24	23		22		19	18	15
26			35					13
		33	34					
29	32			Medieval Sculpture Hall		Medieval Treasury		11
								10
							9	8
		F		Tapestries			2	Arms and Armor
						1		
		E		Romanesque Chapel	G	3	4	5
Library		57						
		Blumenthal Patio 56			A			
MAIN FLOOR (detail)		Early Medieval Gallery		↓ Great Hall ↓				

0   50 feet

EUROPEAN SCULPTURE AND DECORATIVE ART
Northern Renaissance Galleries : 1-5
Italian Galleries : 8-11
English Galleries : 13-20
Wrightsman Galleries (French) : 23-35

MEDIEVAL ART

*Manhattan Sightseeing

7th Ave.

150 W.49th St.

Ave. of America's

5th Ave.

Madison Ave.

49th St. & Park Ave.

WALDORF ASTORIA

Wrightsman Galleries. (23-35) – These galleries of 18th century period rooms and settings present a full and rich panorama in the French decorative arts.

The introductory gallery contains the Paris shopfront of 1775. Embellished with pilasters and fancifully carved garlands, this charming boutique façade is typical of the Louis XVI style. In its windows are displayed outstanding examples of Paris silver. Opposite, side by side are two elegant small rooms. The rococo boudoir from the Hôtel de Crillon is graced with pieces of furniture from the Château of St. Cloud including a daybed made for Marie-Antoinette. The Bordeaux Room is a delicately paneled circular salon decorated and furnished in the neoclassical style. Hung in the Louis XV room is the famous *Portrait of Louis XV as a Young Boy* painted by Rigaud ; included also are the richly carved four corner panels which represent the pleasures of the seasons. Among the porcelain in the Sèvres Alcove Gallery is the unique vase in the form of a ship and pieces from the Rohan service in the delicate turquoise-blue for which Sèvres was famous. Beyond the alcove is the graceful room from the Hôtel Lauzun, the setting for an exquisite collection of French furniture inlaid with Sèvres porcelain plaques. Masterpieces by the cabinetmakers Carlin, Weisweiler and Bernard II van Risenburgh (B.V.R.B.) are also displayed. The bronze and marble clock in the form of a Black woman is by André Furet, watchmaker to Louis XVI ; when one of the figure's earrings is pulled, the hours and minutes appear as numbers in her eyes. The focal point of the Louis XVI gallery is the splendid double portrait by Jacques-Louis David of *Antoine-Laurent Lavoisier and His Wife* of particular interest too are a pair of upright secretaries in black and gold Japanese lacquer signed by Weisweiler. Four 18th century rooms open into the gallery. The white and gold paneled salon from the Hôtel de Varengeville serves as an effective setting for magnificent Louis XV furniture, particularly the King's own desk from his study at Versailles. The carpet was woven at Savonnerie for the *Grande Gallerie* of the Louvre. In the room from the Palais Paar in Vienna, a late rococo room, in blue and gold tones are exquisite pieces of furniture among them a writing table and *commode en console* both by van Risenburgh and a rock-crystal chandelier. The neoclassical, oak-paneled salon from the Hôtel de Cabris in Grasse still retains the original gilding on the paneling. Among the treasures in the room is a *nécessaire de voyage* constructed to serve both as a small table for dining and as a bed table. The Hôtel de Tessé room with its white and gold neoclassical paneling was the grand salon of the Comtesse de Tesse's residence. The room displays a rare 17th century Savonnerie carpet and furniture made for Marie-Antoinette by Jean-Henry Riesener including a secretary and matching commode in black and gold Japanese lacquer encrusted with gilt bronze.

ARMS AND ARMOR ★★

From the great workshops of Milan and Brescia, Augsburg and Nuremberg, Greenwich, Solingen and Toledo during the 15th, 16th and 17th centuries came these masterpieces of "sculpture in steel". A large number of them once belonged to famous men.

The Equestrian Court. – A spectacular group of models of armored horsemen on their caparisoned mounts. A full suit of armor often weighed sixty pounds.

Most of the armor displayed here was intended for jousting. This is shown by the reinforced left side, protection against the shock of the lance. There is a fine example of German 16th century jousting armor : the horseman, wears a helmet topped with horns.

Some English pieces of the late 16th century, from Greenwich, accompany them : notice particularly the armor of George Clifford, of steel, "blued", etched and gilded.

Side Galleries. – Do not miss the examples of parade armor, and finely chiselled and embossed arms. The most arresting armor pieces are the parade helmet of Francis the first, by the great Milanese armorer Filippo Negroli, the shield and helmet of Claude Gouffier, Master of the Horse of Henry II, and the three quarter armor of Anne de Montmorency, High Constable under the same king.

Arms of tempered steel, often made in Toledo, Spain, include daggers, swords and rapiers, halberds, lances and pikes : especially handsome is the sword with the chiselled cup hilt which belonged to the Marquis of Spinola (16th century). Among the firearms are matchlock and wheel-lock pistols, as well as flintlock muskets and pistols, often accompanied by their powderhorn (note the double-barrelled pistol which belonged to Charles V).

Finally, you will also see a half suit of the Duke of Alba, a richly embossed suit and a shield designed for Henri II of France, by Etienne Delaune (1555), a gilded helmet of Cosimo II de Medici and a flintlock garniture made at Versailles for Napoleon Bonaparte by Nicolas Noël Boutet.

Second Floor

MUSICAL INSTRUMENTS ★★

Audio equipement (75 cents) enables the visitor to hear the instruments play period music.

This section presents an original and rare collection of more than 4,000 musical instruments from all periods and all parts of the world. You should not miss the three Stradivarius violins, made by the famous lutemaker of Cremona, and an outstanding series of keyboard instruments decorated with marquetry, sculpture and paintings, the first pianoforte, built in Florence by Bartolommeo Cristofori in 1720, and the spinettina made in 1540 in Venice for the Duchess of Urbino, all displayed here. Other interesting instruments include two Flemish double virginals of the 16th century decorated with musical scenes, lutes, zithers and guitars from the 17th century, and chamber organs of the 18th century. In addition there are Near-and Far-Eastern and African instruments.

Many of the instruments are in working order and are used for occasional concerts.

THE AMERICAN WING

Under reorganization – scheduled opening date : Spring 1980.
The American Wing will house the departments of American Paintings and Sculpture and American Decorative Arts. There will be permanent galleries for paintings, sculpture, prints and drawings from the 17th century to the early 20th century. Decorative arts installations will include 25 period rooms as well as galleries.

THE MICHAEL C. ROCKEFELLER COLLECTION OF PRIMITIVE ART

Scheduled opening date : Autumn 1979. This new department continues to show attractively displayed selections from its holdings while awaiting the construction of galleries in the new wing, which will include the collections of the former Museum of Primitive Art. The collection will include some 3,000 objects from Oceania, Africa and pre-Columbian America.

FAR EASTERN ART★

Around the main stairway and the balcony above the Great Hall, you can trace the development of Chinese porcelain. There are also a number of Chinese bronzes.
To the north of the Great Hall are several galleries. The first features Chinese Buddhist sculpture of the 5th and 6th centuries ; a huge mural from Shansi in northern China (14th century) forms a magnificent background ; it depicts Buddha and his assembly. The museum has greatly enlarged its holdings of Far Eastern Art, especially Chinese and Japanese paintings and sculptures, thus new galleries will be opening *(in 1980).*

ANCIENT NEAR EASTERN ART

On view are sculptures, pottery and metal work dating from the sixth millenium before Christ to the beginning of Islam with emphasis on Sumerian, Iranian and Assyrian civilizations. Notice a beautiful series of objects from Hasanlu and Dinkha Tepe in Iran and many finely carved ivories (8th century BC) from Nimrud, Iraq. The best of the Iranian objects are a number of drinking horns (rhytons) in the form of animal beads and some beautiful gold jewelry.

ISLAMIC ART★★

A wall-sized map and descriptions introduce the visitor to the culture of Islam which flourished during 12 centuries in a huge region ranging from Central Asia to Spain.
The opulence of a 18th century Syrian house appears in the richly panelled reception room decorated with an ornamented ceiling, stained glass windows and a magnificent marble floor ; a mosaic fountain graces the inner court.
The gallery devoted to the museum's excavations in Nishapur, a thriving Persian city from the early 9th to the 12th century, contains rare wall paintings and a collection of objects in metal, stone, ceramics and glass. Inscriptions and the famous arabesque appear already on some of the pottery.
As the centuries unfold, the treasures exhibited gain in refinement. On display in successive galleries are tile panels, intricate wood and metal work from the Mamluk period, ivory carving, artfully painted ceramic bowls, decorated glass lamps, bottles and jugs from Iran, jade vessels and jewelry from 17th century India. Pages from the Koran reflect the artistry of the calligraphers. Because of their sacred character prayer niches were decorated with meticulous care. The exquisite 14th century "mihrab" from Isfahan is an 11 foot high mosaic composed of glazed ceramic tiles in geometric and floral patterns and inscription from the Koran.
An array of sumptuous carpets attests to the importance of carpet weaving brought to perfection in the workshops of Egypt, Persia, Turkey and India.
An early 16th century painted wood ceiling comes from Moorish Spain. The beauty of the room is enhanced by the Egyptian "Simonetti" carpet thought to be the most precious carpet preserved from the 15th century.
Painting, which found a lively expression in the illustration of manuscripts, is represented by the delicate art of miniatures as practised in Persia, India and Ottoman Turkey. The rich collection is highlighted by the exquisite miniatures depicting episodes from the great Persian literary work known as the "Shah Nameh" or "Book of Kings".

DRAWINGS, PRINTS★ AND PHOTOGRAPHS

At the top of the main staircase, to the left. Presented in the form of temporary exhibits.

Drawings. – Of the 3000 drawings, one of the finest is by Raphaël : on one side is the Madonna and Child with the infant John the Baptist, and on the other a study of a nude male figure. Others, of interest, are the *Redemption of the World* by Veronese, and the *Garden of Love* by Rubens.
The collection includes important works by masters from Italy (Michelangelo with study for the Lybian Sibyl, Parmigianino, Pietro da Cortona, Pordenone, Romanino of Brescia) ; France (Poussin, Claude Lorrain, Vouet, David, Ingres, Delacroix) ; or Holland and Flanders (Rubens, Rembrandt, Lievens, Breembergh) and Spain (Goya).

Prints. – All techniques are included : woodcuts, lithographs and all forms of engraving.
Among the most memorable we should mention : for the Renaissance, a *Battle of the Ten Naked Men,* by Antonio Pollaiuolo ; *Battle of the Sea Gods,* by Andrea Mantegna ; *The Four Horsemen of the Apocalypse,* by Albrecht Dürer ; *Summer,* after Pieter Bruegel.
For the 17th century : *Time, Apollo and the Seasons,* by Claude Lorrain ; *Rembrandt Faust in His Study,* and *Christ Preaching ;* and a landscape by Seghers, also a Dutch painter.
The 18th century artists represented include the Englishman Hogarth, the Roman Piranese, the French Moreau le Jeune and the Spaniard Goya. Particularly noteworthy among 19th century artists are Daumier *(Rue Transnonain)* and Toulouse-Lautrec *(Aristide Bruant).*

EUROPEAN PAINTINGS★★★

Recorded tours are available for the galleries. This department occupies 40 galleries, partially furnished with chairs, chests of drawers, hangings and sculpture that create a felicitious atmosphere for the admiration of the works of art. Arranged by national schools in chronological order, all paintings of a particular school appear against walls of the same color.

If you set out to see a particular school of art call ahead to see if the gallery is open.

Italian Galleries (1-8).

Primitives and 15th Century : Galleries 3, 4 and 5. – Usually religious scenes with golden backgrounds, painted on wood. However with the Florentine Giotto or the Sienese Sassetta, there is a beginning of modelling and landscape.

The Epiphany (3), from Giotto or his workshop, brings together the Angel appearing to the Shepherds, the Nativity and the Adoration of the Magi. Taddeo Gaddi, a follower of Giotto, painted the 5 panel altarpiece, *The Madonna and Child Enthroned with Saints* (3). Works by Giovanni de Paolo and Segna di Buonaventura illustrate the Sienese School. The Venetian Carlo Crivelli is represented by a *Pietà,* originally part of an altarpiece.

Pintoricchio Gallery : Gallery 4a. – The ceiling of an Italian palace, painted by Pintoricchio (1454-1513), has been remounted here. Notice the allegorical and mythological scenes *(Triumphs after Petrarch,* the *Three Graces* and the *Judgment of Paris).* Also on display are frescoes of mythological figures and signs of the Zodiac from a villa in Rome by Guilio Romano.

The Florentine School is represented by Botticelli and his masterpiece *The Last Communion of St. Jerome* (4b) and Domenico Ghirlandajo's double portrait, *Francesco Sassetti and His Son Teodoro* (6). Notice the contrast between the firm features of the man and the soft features of his son. Note also the *Man and Woman at Casement* (5) by Fra Filippo Lippi.

Renaissance 16th Century : Galleries 1, 2 and 6. – High Renaissance paintings are represented by the Venetian School which is characterized by vivid colors, large foreground figures and backgrounds often depicting real landscapes. In gallery (2) a number of "Cassoni" (marriage chests) are placed against the walls. In the center stands a monumental table inlaid with alabaster and semi precious stones. It was designed by the architect Jacopo Barozzi da Vignola for the Farnese Palace in Rome, and bears the arms of Cardinal Alessandro Farnese.

Decorative canvases by Titian *(Venus and the Lute Player)* and Tintoretto *(Finding of Moses)* (2) are hung here. Andrea del Sarto's *(Holy Family)* (6) is worth noticing. However, works by comparatively minor artists are as interesting : for example the various portraits soberly executed by Moretto da Brescia *(Entombment)* (1) and Moroni.

17th Century : Gallery 8. – Among the works exhibited in this gallery are Caravaggio's. *The Musicians* with their sensuous and effeminate features and the *Coronation of the Virgin* by Annibale Caracci and his pupil Reni's *Immaculate Conception.*

18th Century : Gallery 7. – Three great Venetians at the height of 18th century Baroque style stand out : Francesco Guardi with his views of Venice ; Pietro Longhi, whose intimate scenes, drawn with minute care, depict the daily life of the Venetian nobility ; and Giovanni Battista Tiepolo, with his huge canvases depicting scenes executed in luminous colors.

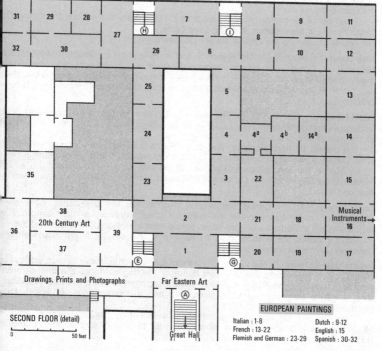

SECOND FLOOR (detail)
0   50 feet

Drawings, Prints and Photographs

Far Eastern Art

Great Hall

20th Century Art

Musical Instruments→

EUROPEAN PAINTINGS

Italian : 1-8   Dutch : 9-12
French : 13-22   English : 15
Flemish and German : 23-29   Spanish : 30-32

Dutch Galleries (9-12).

The collection concentrates on works of the 17th century artists : the "golden age" of Dutch painting.

The "Met" owns 33 of **Rembrandt's** works covering all phases of his career. Using light with great ingenuity the painter gave careful attention to the hands, jewels, collars and cuffs. Among his earlier portraits are *Man and Woman* (9) and *Man in Oriental Costume (The Noble Slav)* (9), dating from the 1630's. *The Crucifixion with the Virgin and St. John* (9) is by Terbrugghen, who was greatly influenced by Caravaggio.

The high point of this collection is the celebrated *Aristotle With a Bust of Homer* (10), a symbol of philosophic reflection. This imaginary portrait was signed and dated 1653. The lively activity in Jan Steen's *Merry Company on a Terrace* (10) contrasts with these introspective portraits.

In Gallery 11 the later Dutch paintings show serene interior scenes, seascapes and landscapes with vast skies. A masterpiece by Vermeer, *Young Woman with a Water Jug*, bathed in a soft light, immediately attracts the eye. Note also *Curiosity* by Ter Borch and landscapes by Molyn and Goyen.

Rembrandt's later works comprising self-portraits and portraits of his fellow citizens reveal the painter's deep psychological insight. The vivacious and colorful group portraits by Frans Hals record a different aspect of the life of the burghers. *(Revellers or Merrymakers) of Shrovetide.* The poetic landscape, *Wheatfields,* by Jacob van Ruisdael demonstates his profound observation of nature.

In gallery 12, as part of the Altman Collection, you should not overlook Rembrandt's *Toilet of Bathsheba,* notable for its uncompromising realism ; a portrait by Frans Hals *(Young Man and Woman in an Inn)* and several Van Dyck portraits (gallery 28).

French Galleries (13-22).

17th Century : Gallery 13. – An impressive *Fortune Teller,* by Georges de la Tour, illustrates the restraint and strength of expression of the French school.

Of the two "Roman" French painters, Claude Lorrain and Nicolas Poussin, Poussin is represented by *The Blind Orion Searching for the Rising Sun,* guided by the oracle Cydalion Lorrain in *Sunrise* and *Roman Campagna* created a classical type of landscape combined with subtle luminosity.

18th Century : Galleries 14 and 14a. – Portraits are displayed, showing the French interest in outward appearance, and in psychological analysis. You can follow the development of the art of the portraitist, from the amiable and polished figures by Largillière *(The Baron and Baroness de Prangins)* to the sober and austere works of Duplessis *(Benjamin Franklin)*.

Along the way, one encounters Nattier, Drouais *(Madame Favart),* Fragonard, Vestier and Madame Vigée-Lebrun, whose portrait of *Madame Grand,* the future wife of Talleyrand, symbolizes the charm of the "gracious century". Two works by Chardin move by their frank simplicity *(Still Life with Hare,* and *Boy Blowing Bubbles).* Along the walls is arranged a succession of "fêtes galantes", which were popular during the reign of Louis XV. Among them are the tender and sad *Mezzetin,* a character from the *Commedia dell'Arte,* a small but celebrated work by Watteau ; the *Dispatch of the Messenger, a* pastoral scene by Boucher painted with a refined technique ; and the *Broken Eggs, an* ambiguous subject by Greuze. Interspersed among them are a few portraits, such as that of Madame Vigée-Lebrun, by her student Mademoiselle Lemoine and Greuze's portrait of the Comte d'Angiviller.

A number of handsome genre paintings by Fragonard are also exhibited, including *The Italian Family,* a lively sketch, and *The Love Letter.*

For details concerning the English Gallery (15) see p. 63.

19th Century : Gallery 16. – The French School is represented by Delacroix *(Abduction of Rebecca),* J.L. David – severe and solemn in the *Death of Socrates* but lucidly observant in the *Portrait of Maréchal Gérard* – and by Ingres whose psychological insight is evident in his *Portrait of Joseph Antoine Moltedo,* and in portraits of *Monsieur Leblanc* and *Madame Leblanc.*

Late 19th century : Gallery 18. – The unabashed-realism of Courbet is expressed in his landscapes and portraits : *Young Ladies from the Village,* which depicts the native region of the painter and *The Sea.*

The canvas by Rosa Bonheur, *The Horse Fair* was considered a masterpiece, in its time, Cornelius Vanderbilt bought it for $58,000 and presented it to the museum in 1887.

By Manet, the Met possesses the *Dead Christ with Angels, The Spanish Singer* and *Mademoiselle Victorine in the Costume of an Espada.* More Impressionist is his river scene *Boating* (19).

Corot Gallery (17). – During the artist's lifetime, his airy landscapes were most appreciated ; today many prefer his human figures, attractive in their simplicity of expression and attitude. Among the latter, notice *Woman Reading, The Letter,* and *Sybille.*

Corot's works are accompanied by sombre landscapes by Millet, Rousseau and Daubigny, of the Barbizon school.

Impressionist Galleries (19 and 22). – This school took its name from a canvas, painted by Monet, called *Impression, Soleil Levant* (Sunrise). Painting outdoors, the Impressionists innovated painting by rendering transitory visual images gathered from nature. In addition they aimed to transmit their visual sensations and to capture light on canvas, by juxtaposition of pure tones of color.

There are a large number of landscapes by Monet. Some are luminous such as *La Grenouillère à Chatou* (22) ; and others are veiled by mist or smoke *Rouen Cathedral* (19).

At about the same time Toulouse-Lautrec was viewing his models and objects without sentimental indulgence ; the movement he attains in his paintings – *Englishman at the Moulin Rouge*, (19) – is suggested by the tension and animation of his lines.

Renoir is represented by several portraits, above all *Madame Charpentier and Her Children* (Gallery 22) a warm expression of intimacy radiates from this imposing group portrait. An exceptional series of paintings by Degas (Gallery 22) : portraits, nudes, and dancers show a restrained but acute sense of observation : note the powerful *Woman with Chrysanthemums* and *Dancers Practising*.

Post-Impressionist Galleries : Galleries 20 and 21. – All facets of Cézanne's highly structured art encompassing both classic and modern concepts can be admired here (21) : landscapes *The Gulf of Marseilles seen from Estaque, The Cistern of Jas de Bouffan, Mont Sainte Victoire) :* almost geometrical paintings of still life, the first hints of cubism, and figures, such as *The Wife of the Artist in Red Dress* and *Cardplayers*. In Gallery 20 are hung works by Seurat, Utrillo, Gauguin and van Gogh (*Irises* and *Cypresses*).

English Gallery (15)

18th Century (The Age of Reason). – Here are hung a number of portraits, brilliantly executed in fresh colors, but somewhat superficial in their charm. The artists are Thomas Gainsborough, Sir Henry Raeburn, Sir Joshua Reynolds *(Colonel Coussmaker),* Sir Thomas Lawrence : notice his spirited portrait of *Elizabeth Farren,* later Countess of Derby, and an early work of William Hogarth : *The Wedding of Stephen Beckingham and Mary Cox.*

19th Century. – Turner's *Venice, Grand Canal,* and *The Whale Ship* show concern with the problem of dissociation of colors and of light, in order to create a luminous atmosphere. He was a forerunner of Impressionism. Among the landscapes, John Constable's *Salisbury Cathedral* is outstanding.

Flemish and German Galleries (23-29).

15th Century : Gallery 23. – This room displays paintings of the 15th century in Flanders, centered around the van Eyck brothers. Depicting sacred subjects almost exclusively, these works are characterized by a taste for picturesque and familiar details.

Jan van Eyck is represented by *The Last Judgment* and *The Crucifixion.* These dramatic scenes were designed as side panels of a triptych, whose central panel has disappeared. By his contemporary, Petrus Christus, we have *The Annunciation* with a luminous landscape which was formerly attributed to van Eyck.

The works by Rogier van der Weyden *(Christ Appearing to His Mother* and *Francesco d'Este)* and his follower Hugo van der Goes (portraits) show a different style in Flemish art.

15th-16th Centuries. – This gallery (24) contains religious works by Gerard David and Memling. Among them is the *Annunciation* by Memling, formerly attributed to van der Weyden, which is set in the room of the Virgin, and the figures occupy most of the foreground : the tunic of the angel Gabriel, with its fine gold embroidery, is especially striking.

The Flemish and German schools are represented in the Altman Collection (Gallery 25) by the *Marriage of St. Catherine* by Memling. Dürer's *Virgin and Child with St. Anne,* and fine portraits by Holbein. In the display cases are beautiful enamel portraits by Leonard Limosin (French, 16th century) representing *Francis I, Henry d'Albret* and others.

Gallery 26 is the more interesting with two works by Lucas Cranach the Elder *Judgment of Paris, Martyrdom of St. Barbara),* portraits by Hans Holbein, who was court painter to Henri VIII, and especially *The Harvesters* by Bruegel the Elder.

17th Century : Gallery 27. – This gallery presents Rubens and his circle. Notice Rubens' flamboyant *Venus and Adonis* (27). In Gallery 28, you will see *The Triumph of Henry IV,* a preparatory oil sketch for one of the paintings commissioned by Marie de Medici, and portraits by van Dyck.

Spanish Galleries (30-32).

The Spanish character, grave, mystic and passionate, is expressed by such great painters as El Greco, Velázquez, Murillo and Ribera.

Gallery 30 contains the works of El Greco : *View of Toledo, The Vision of St. John,* where the Evangelist appears elongated in the foreground, and a portrait of the *Cardinal Guevara, Grand Inquisitor.* Note Ribera's *Holy Family with St. Catherine* and the richly colored *Virgin and Child* by Murillo.

Among the four works by Velázquez in Gallery 31 are two early works : *Supper at Emmaus* and the *Portrait of Philip IV, King of Spain.* Outstanding, however, is the portrait of *Juan de Pareja,* Velázquez's assistant and traveling companion. This masterpiece, an example of the artist's mature style, is astounding for its vitality and lifelike appearance. In the Goya Gallery (32) among the portraits of children and personal friends, note the *Majas in a Balcony.*

TWENTIETH CENTURY ART (35-39)

Created in 1970 this department presents the best of recent art in all its manifestations, by means of changing exhibitions.

Included amongst the early 20th century paintings are works by Pierre Bonnard still in the Impressionist tradition and Picasso's *Portrait of Gertrude Stein,* with the first cubic forms. In the post war (1946) period New York was the center of the art world and witnessed the development of Abstract Expressionism with such artists as Jackson Pollock *(Autumn Rhythm),* F. Kline and the leader of the school de Kooning *(Easter Monday).* Color field painting followed with Ellsworth Kelly and Morris Louis *(Alpha-Pi).* There is also a large gallery for decorative arts made since 1900, highlighted by a large wall of glass panels designed by Jean Dupas in 1933, which formed part of the decoration of the Grand Salon of the luxury liner *Normandie.*

Time : about 1 hour.

Located on Fifth Avenue, between 88th and 89th Streets, The Solomon R
Guggenheim Museum is particularly interesting, both for its original architecture and the
works of contemporary art it displays.

Two Innovators. – **Solomon R. Guggenheim,** a copper magnate, was fascinated by
modern painting. An enthusiastic collector, he established the Solomon R. Guggenheim
Foundation to promote non-objective art and art education. In 1943 he commissioned
Frank Lloyd Wright to design a museum and set aside the sum of two million dollars for
this purpose. He died in 1949, seven years before construction started (completed in 1959).

Frank Lloyd Wright (1867-1959) was the son of a minister. He first married at 21 and had six
children. However, he moved alone to Chicago to participate in the "Chicago school" which
pioneered, at the beginning of the century contemporary architecture. In all, he designed more
than 600 buildings (such as Johnson Wax Company Research Laboratory Towers in Wisconsin
or Kaufmann House "Falling Water" in Pennsylvania) and left many more plans and projects.

The Museum is one of Wright's most controversial works. To those who criticized his
"corkscrew", or "monstrous mushroom", he replied that "one should no more judge a
building from the outside than a car by its color". This seer dreamed of building a
skyscraper in Chicago 510 stories high, with atomic elevators, but condemned the
skyscrapers of New York.

Exterior. – From the Central
Park side of Fifth Avenue
you can see the entire building, constructed in cream-
colored concrete. The administration building is on the
left. The form is almost reminiscent of a carrousel. A
sweeping concrete overhang,
which contains the Thann-
hauser Collection, joins the
administration building solidly
to the museum proper. This
latter building is a cone composed of a four-layer spiral,
which becomes larger as it
rises. In addition, each section is inclined outward toward the top. There are no
windows on this side of the
building.

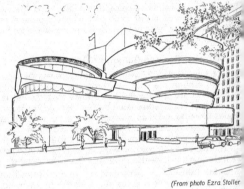

(From photo Ezra Stoller

Guggenheim Museum. — Exterior.

Interior. – *Open from 11 AM to 5 PM Wednesday through Sunday and holidays, 11 AM
to 8 PM Tuesday. Closed Monday (except holidays) and Christmas Day. $1.50.*

Enter the main lobby. The continuous spiral ramp, over a quarter of a mile long, rises
gradually to the glass dome, ninety-two feet high. Frank Lloyd Wright has designed a
dome completely covered with glass, but planning authorities' required the addition of
concrete arches and the reduction of the dimensions.

Although the diameter of the museum increases as it rises, this is not evident from
here, since the ramp becomes wider as it ascends. The oval basin, compared to a seed
pod by the architect, has a central symbolic value : the form is followed in the decoration
pedestals for sculpture, tables, flower pots, etc.

Take the elevator to the top floor and make your way down easily, passing in front of
sculpture and paintings. These are attached to the circular outside wall and to the side
panels, which form separate compartments, a sort of vast chambered nautilus. Wright had
wanted the paintings to be displayed as if on an artist's easel and lighted by natural light
from windows in the ceilings immediately above, changing with the movement of the sun
and the seasons. Although the lighting in the museum now comes from spot lights and
fluorescent tubes in the ceiling above the paintings, the present director, Thomas M
Messer, follows Wright's concept by hanging the paintings unframed directly on the walls
A few feet in front of the paintings, a slight step reminds visitors to remain at a suitable
distance.

Collections. – The core is composed of works left to the Museum by Solomon
Guggenheim. Among the 4000 works are the largest Kandinsky collection in the world
over 70 Klees and important groups by Chagall, Delaunay, Léger and others. However, the
Museum usually presents a temporary exhibition of one artist or school through its own
permanent collection and loan exhibitions.

Thannhauser Collection. – Presented on the second floor just off the central ramp, this
collection is the bequest of Justin K. Thannhauser who died in 1976. It includes some of
the most significant works of the past 100 years, from the Impressionists to Picasso
Among the Impressionists, the best represented are Pissarro *(Les Coteaux de l'Hermitage a
Pontoise)*, Renoir *(Woman with a Parrot)*, and Manet *(Before the Mirror)*. Other highlights
are works by Cézanne (still lifes), van Gogh *(The Viaduct, Mountains at Saint-Rémy)*,
Gauguin, Toulouse-Lautrec *(au Salon)*, Degas, Modigliani and Vuillard, whose *Place
Vintimille* sparkles with the light of Paris.

Picasso is most bountifully represented : notice his early works, *The End of the Road*
Le Moulin de la Galette and *The Fourteenth of July. Minerva, Woman Ironing, The
Harlequins*, the still lifes, the doves and the portraits of Dora Mar and Françoise Gilo
illustrate the classic and restrained side of his artistic temperament.

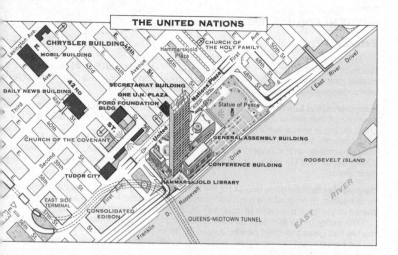

On the banks of the East River, the headquarters of the United Nations is dominated by the Secretariat building, which rises toward the sky, simple and smooth as a mirror.

A Philanthropist. – The Charter of the United Nations was drafted at San Francisco in 1945. The following year, the General Assembly met first in London, then at Hunter College in the Bronx, and finally at Flushing Meadow, Long Island *(see p. 133)*. The decision was made to locate the permanent headquarters in the United States.

In December 1946, John D. Rockefeller, Jr *(details p. 34)*, financier and philanthropist, offered the sum of $8,500,000 in order to acquire the present site on the East River, between 42nd and 48th Streets. This « Turtle Bay » area was then covered with slums, slaughter houses and breweries. The city of New York has since participated in a joint program of improvements, resulting in the complete renovation of the area. The U.N. buildings were designed under the direction of the American architect Wallace K. Harrison.

Building the U.N. – The construction program cost about $67,000,000. The government of the United States made available an interest-free loan of $65,000,000, which is being reimbursed by annual payments. The balance was met from the regular United Nations budget. Among the numerous architects consulted on the project were such famous figures as Le Corbusier (France) and Oscar Niemeyer (Brazil).

The Secretariat building was occupied in 1950, and two years later the first meetings of the Security Council and the General Assembly could be held at the permanent site. In 1961, the new Dag Hammarskjöld Memorial Library was constructed. The entire group of buildings and gardens occupies 18 acres of land, which enjoy a degree of extraterritoriality.

The organs of the United Nations. – Governed by a charter of 70 articles, the United Nations is composed of six principal organs, and working closely with the U.N. are a number of specialized agencies. The Secretary General, at present Kurt Waldheim, is the chief administrative officer of the Organization. He performs such functions as are necessary to carry out decisions or recommendations adopted by the General Assembly and the Councils.

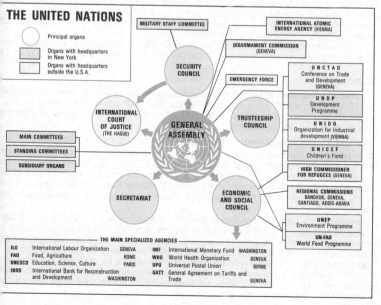

■ **THE HEADQUARTERS★★★** *(Time : about 3 hours.)*

Exterior

From the corner of 45th Street and First Avenue, you have an excellent view of the buildings, with the flags of member states (as of January, 1978 : 149 ; there were 5' original members). These flags are arranged in English alphabetical order, the same order in which delegations are seated in the General Assembly.

Hammarskjöld Library. – The library, a gift of the Ford Foundation, is dedicated to the memory of the former Secretary General, Dag Hammarskjöld, killed in 1961 in a plane crash during is peace-keeping mission to the Congo.

Its marble walls enclose 400,000 volumes for the use of UN delegates, Secretaria' staff members and scholars. In addition, there are newspapers, reading rooms, a collection of 60,000 maps, a microfilm laboratory, tape recording services and ar auditorium.

Secretariat Building. – Except for the parts seen during the guided tours, it is not oper to the public. In front of it is a circular marble pool, donated by American schoolchildren placed in the pool is a piece of sculpture by Barbara Hepworth of Great Britain.

The purity of its architectural lines is striking. Entirely constructed of white Vermon' marble and glass and steel panels, it rises 39 floors without a break.

Air conditioning, 18 elevators, escalators, a cafeteria and a complete medical cente contribute to the efficiency and comfort of the 5,000 international civil servants and other employees who work here. Drawn from many of the member nations, these include, among others : interpreters and translators, experts in international law and economics, press officers, printers, librarians, statisticians, 200 United Nations guards and other supporting staff. Some 50 charming young people in uniform or their native dress are responsible for guiding approximately one million visitors who come each year.

The Buildings.

Conference Building. – Thus named because of its council and commitee meeting rooms, this building forms a link between the Secretariat and the Assembly buildings. The meetings of the Security Council, the Economic and Social Council, and the Trusteeship Council are held here. The main façade faces the Eas River.

General Assembly Building. – Long and low in form with an elegantly curved roof, the Assembly Hall is covered by a central dome.

Diagonally across from the U.N. Secretariat and the General Assembly Building at the northwest corner of 44th Street and First Avenue, rises the 39-story **One United Nation Plaza Building**, one of New York's newest and most beautiful skyscrapers. Designed b' Kevin Roche, John Dinkerloo and Assoc., as a combined office and hotel building, I U! Plaza is entirely sheathed in a green reflecting glass.

Continue to the north of the buildings on the esplanade in front of the visitors entrance. From here you have an attractive view of the gardens (statue of Peace, a gift from Yugoslavia

Interior

Guided tours including visits to the main meeting rooms leave at frequent intervals from 9 : 15 AM to 4 : 45 PM ; buy tickets ($2) at the Tour Desk at the south end of the mar lobby. Children under 5 are not admitted. The Information Desk in the center of the lobby distributes free tickets to meetings.

General Assembly Building. – The building is the heart of the United Nations.

Main Lobby. – Enter through one of the seven doors donated by Canada and turn around Notice that the exterior wall of concrete and glass, which seemed opaque from th outside, now appears translucent. Beyond the **Information Desk** is the curved wall of th Assembly Hall. On the right is the entrance to the **Meditation Room**, a small V-shaped room in the center of which stands a single block of iron ore symbolizing timelessness. At th narrow end is an abstract fresco.

Assembly Hall. – Lighted from above, the oval Assembly Hall measures 165 by 115 fee and is 75 feet high. The speaker's rostrum is surmounted by a dais with the President the General Assembly seated in the center, assisted by the Secretary General and th Under Secretary General for the General Assembly. The emblem of the United Nations represented above. On either side are glass-enclosed booths for radio and television, an for the interpreters who work in the five official languages : English, French, Spanish Russian and Chinese. The side walls are decorated with abstract paintings designed b Fernand Léger and executed by Bruce Gregory.

The General Assembly meets in regular annual session for about three months, starting on the third Tuesday in September and lasting until mid-December. Special sessions may be called at the request of the Security Council or of a majority of the Member States. The Assembly may discuss any matters within the scope of the Charter, unless they are under consideration by the Security Council. It also receives and discusses annual reports from the other organs and votes the budget. Decisions on important questions are made by a two-thirds majority of members present and voting ; a simple majority suffices for other matters. The Assembly may pass resolutions, initiate studies and make recommendations for the maintenance of peace and security and to promote international cooperation. It also elects its own President and Vice Presidents, admits new Members on the recommendation of the Security Council and chooses the non-permanent members of the Security Council.

Conference Building. – The five stories of the Conference Building house, from the basement up, technical installations (air conditioning, printing presses, television and recording studios, photographic dark rooms), Conference Rooms, Council Chambers and Delegates' Lounges, the Delegates' Dining Room and the cafeteria for the members of the Secretariat.

A number of works of art are shown during the visit, which goes on to the Secretariat Building : a Persian carpet and a carpet from Ghana, a mosaic from Morocco, a huge Belgian tapestry, two Brazilian murals depicting Peace and War and a stained glass window by Chagall, unveiled in 1964 as a memorial to Dag Hammarskjöld and contributed by the members of the staff of the United Nations and the artist. In the garden, in front of the Conference Building and the Secretariat is a Japanese peace bell, made of coppetr coins from 60 countries.

Security Council. – The chamber, donated by Norway, is decorated with gold and blue hangings, and a mural symbolizing Peace and Liberty, Equality and Fraternity. There are 200 seats for the public.

The Security Council has primary responsibility for the maintenance of international peace and security. Amendments which were adopted by the General Assembly and which came into force in 1965 have increased the number of members of the Security Council from 11 to 15 ; 10 are elected every two years, and the other 5 (United States, France, United Kingdom, USSR, China) are permanent. Votes on procedural matters require an affirmative vote of 9 members, and for important questions, these 9 must include the 5 permanent members. This rule of unanimity for the « great powers » is better known as the veto, but an abstention by a permanent member does not in practice prevent a decision from being adopted. The members of the Security Council preside in rotation ; the President changes every month.

Trusteeship Council. – This room was contributed by Denmark. The walls, covered with precious woods, are decorated with a large teak statue of a woman carrying a bluebird, which symbolizes Hope and Independence.

The Trusteeship Council supervises the Trust Territories administered by Member States. Only one territory remains which has not become independent : the U.S. Strategic Trust Territory of the Pacific Islands, which includes the Marshalls, the Carolines and the Mariana Islands, except Guam.

Economic and Social Council. – This functional room was donated by Sweden. The plain walls and exposed heating apparatus contrast with the vivid colors of the large « window wall ».

Eighty per cent of the UN staff works in the domain of economic and social problems. This Council considers a wide variety of subjects ranging from the environment and population to women's rights and including health, transportation, human rights, crime prevention and freedom of information, etc.

(From photo United Nations.)

General View of the UN from the East River in 1973.

Distance : about 1/2 mile — Time : about 2 hours.

From the East River to Fifth Avenue, 42nd Street which extends just a little over three miles across Manhattan Island is one of the liveliest and busiest thoroughfares in New York. Some of the City's most important buildings and useful facilities (railway, bus and airline terminals) are near or flanking it.

Thousands of workers swarm in and out of the office buildings which are beehives of activity. Constructed at different times, these buildings illustrate changing architectural styles since 1900.

(From documents, Library of the Boston Athenaeum.)

The site of 42nd Street in 1850.

A BIT OF

HISTORY

From the shanties to the skyscrapers. — It was here at Kips Bay that the British landed in September, 1776. Forty-second Street was officially opened in 1836 by the mayor, who encouraged the inhabitants to move uptown to enjoy the pure, clean air. However, as late as 1860, it became an area of shanties where squatters eked out an existence amid their pigs and goats. As the city moved northward, the municipal government had great difficulty in dislodging these occupants.

The development of the area really began early in this century, when the land, which had been rocky and sloping, was levelled. This growth has continued, with the construction of the present Grand Central Terminal and, much more recently, the Pan Am Building.

■ TUDOR CITY

Located between First and Second Avenues, this group of apartment houses was built during the 1920's on the site of "Corcoran's Roost". This was the hideout of Paddy Corcoran, a notorious bandit.

The 12 buildings, from 10 to 32 floors in height, contain 3,000 apartments and accommodating 12,000 people. The brick architecture with Flamboyant or Tudor Gothic touches was intended to be reminiscent of an English period style.

Here 42nd Street burrows between two halves of a small hill, and is crossed by a bridge. You can reach Tudor City by taking 41st Street. These comfortable buildings enjoy a relative isolation and calm which are rare in the center of New York. You will be refreshed by the sight of the green lawns and neat footpaths, but this private park is restricted to residents of the neighborhood.

From the bridge over 42nd Street there is an interesting **view** of the United Nations *(see p. 65)* to the east and the Chrysler Building *(see opposite)* to the west.

■ FORD FOUNDATION BUILDING★

Between 42nd and 43rd Streets stands the headquarters of the Ford Foundation, completed in 1967.

Its eleven glass and steel stories, supported by granite pillars, surround a pleasant inner garden decorated with flowers, plants and shrubs around a pool.

The three underground floors include a garage with space for fifty cars, a 175-seat auditorium and conference room and a library containing more than 20,000 books.

The Ford Foundation, a private, non-profit institution, finances philanthropic organizations which specialize in research, education and community improvement. It has assisted some 7,200 organizations in all 50 states and 83 foreign countries.

■ DAILY NEWS BUILDING★

Opened February 1930 as the new home of the *Daily News* (The News was founded in June 1919 as the Illustrated Daily News and was published at 25 Park Place). The *Daily News* is a tabloid with the largest circulation in America : 1,914,819 daily and 2,788,731 on Sunday. It puts out an average of 100 pages every day and about 600 on Sundays.

The News owns WPIX-TV and two radio stations WPIX-FM and WICC in Bridgeport, Connecticut. The lobby of the News Building *(220 East 42nd Street)* is famed for its giant globe of the world and clocks showing the correct time around the world. The floor of the lobby indicates both distances and flying times to major cities throughout the world.

The 37-story News Building was one of the first in New York to be built on a steel framework, which is marked on the outside of the building by white brick pilasters. The vertical geometric effect thus achieved is far from old-fashioned. On the other hand, the carved figures above the main entrance are typical of the stylized design of the 1930's. The newest wing of the building, in architectural harmony with the original building, is at Second Avenue and 42nd Street.

■ MOBIL BUILDING★

This 45-story skyscraper is composed of a central section and two wings and it is sheathed in a self-cleaning stainless steel skin. When it was finished in the fall of 1956, it contained 1 600,000 square feet of air-conditioned office space becoming the largest skyscraper in the world to be completely air-conditioned.

The lobby is faced with luxurious grey and black marble. The 32 completely automatic elevators were considered a model of efficiency when the building was opened. There are entrances to the subway and Grand Central Terminal here, carefully disguised to preserve the harmony of the decoration. The floor is slightly sloped.

■ CHRYSLER BUILDING★★

At the northeast corner of Lexington Avenue is the main entrance to the Chrysler Building designed by William Van Alen. Despite its venerable age, it is still one of the most famous New York landmarks. Its top reminiscent of the 1929 Chrysler radiator cap, can be seen from afar. When it was completed in May 1930 there was stiff competition for the record in height from the building at 40 Wall Street, but the addition of the spire to bring the Chrysler Building to 1046 feet tipped the balance in its favor. With its 77 story, rising 1048 feet, it was briefly the highest building in the world, taking second place after the completion of the Empire State Building. It takes the sixth place as the World Trade Center is now completed *(see p. 87)*.

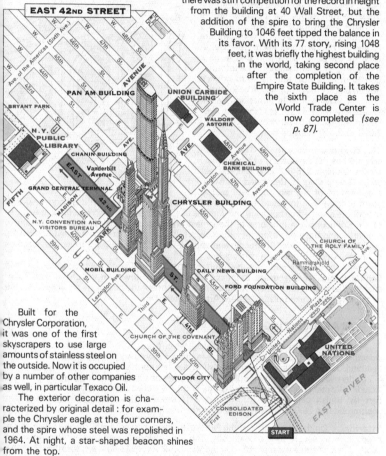

Built for the Chrysler Corporation, it was one of the first skyscrapers to use large amounts of stainless steel on the outside. Now it is occupied by a number of other companies as well, in particular Texaco Oil.

The exterior decoration is characterized by original detail : for example the Chrysler eagle at the four corners, and the spire whose steel was repolished in 1964. At night, a star-shaped beacon shines from the top.

Arcades link the building with Grand Central Terminal and the 42nd Street subway station.

■ CHANIN BUILDING

Lower in profile than its neighbors, but rising 56 stories nevertheless, the Chanin Building, designed by Sloan and Robertson, is also decorated in the style of the 1930's, with friezes of bas-reliefs on the exterior and, in the lobby, copper doors ornamented with plant motifs. It is considered one of New York City's great art deco buildings.

■ GRAND CENTRAL TERMINAL★

One of the two main New York stations, Grand Central has the distinction of showing virtually no evidence of the hundreds of trains which arrive and depart every day. They are hidden away in underground galleries on two levels. They include more than 400 weekday suburban trains as well as long distance trains.

The Terminal is operated by Conrail under service agreements with the New York State Metropolitan Transportation Authority and the Connecticut Department of Transportation.

From Grand Central take the train to the Hudson River Valley described on p. 138.

From Depot to Terminal. — In the 1840's the former New York, New Haven and Hartford Railroad used a depot on Fourth Avenue at 23rd Street. Horse-drawn trolleys converged there to be converted into locomotive-drawn trains for the outgoing trip. Railroads were not yet taken very seriously ; it was said that if a locomotive collided with a cow, it would have to be repaired (hence the « cow-catchers » in the front of early models).

Founded in 1853, the New York Central was bought in 1862 by Commodore **Cornelius Vanderbilt**, whose earlier interest had been in shipping. First limited to Harlem and the east bank of the Hudson, the line (New York Central System, now a part of Conrail) was extended to Buffalo in 1872, and to Chicago one year later. The depot, on the site of the present Terminal, had seven platforms protected by a huge glass cage.

The present Terminal was completed in 1913. Of its 123 underground tracks, 29 on the upper level and 17 on the lower level are platform tracks where passengers are loaded and unloaded. There are 11 tracks which feed into loop tracks permitting the trains to turn within the confines of the Terminal. An average of close to 150,000 commuters and suburban passengers are served at the Terminal each weekday. A total of up to a half-million people pass through Grand Central daily. The Information Booth surmounted by a four-faced golden clock provides all kinds of information. A Telephone Information Center exclusively for Harlem, Hudson and New Haven line suburban services handles from 2,000 to 3,000 inquiries daily.

(From photo John B. Bayley, New York.)

Grand Central Terminal.

The Grand Concourse. — This impressive hall has the dimensions of a cathedral : ten stories high, 275 feet long and 120 feet wide. The ceiling is decorated with the constellation of the sky, but few people seem to have time to notice it. Grand Central is a city within the city, it is connected with major hotels and office buildings and with the city's subways. Among outstanding features of the Concourse are a colorama, the largest photo transparency in the world (changed regularly), and the world's largest indoor clock (12 feet in diameter). The Grand Concourse, together with the Lower Concourse and upper levels of the terminal building, have scores of shops, stores and service concessions.

Controversy has raged over the future of Grand Central since the proposition by Penn Central, Conrail's predecessor, to erect a 59-story office tower on top of the Terminal or even to demolish it altogether. Designated as a landmark the building is considered as one of the city's best examples of Beaux-Arts architecture.

■ PAN AM BUILDING★★★

The octagonal mass of the Pan Am Building, which rises above Grand Central, caused considerable controversy at the time of its construction. Many now agree that the building itself is beautiful. Judge for yourself by walking a short distance north or south on Park Avenue.

Undertaken in 1960 and completed in 1963, it was designed by a group of architects including Walter Gropius. It was one of the first New York buildings to be financed in large part by British capital. One of the largest (civilian) office buildings in the world, it accommodates 25,000 employees in 50 acres of offices.

Interior. — On the street floor of the Pan Am Building, powerful grey granite pillars give a majestic, even severe tone to the lobby. The ivory-colored areas used by Pan American World Airways add a warmer note. On the Vanderbilt Avenue side is a **composition**★★ by the sculptor Richard Lippold, a spectacular arrangement of brass wire representing a globe and a network of rays.

On the Lobby Floor there is a control room for the technical equipment : an impressive panel with flashing lights, a closed circuit television network, etc. The street floor also has shops and restaurants.

In EUROPE

use the **MICHELIN "Green Guides"** in English for :

AUSTRIA	**and for France :**
GERMANY	
(West Germany and Berlin)	
ITALY	BRITTANY
LONDON	CHATEAUX OF THE LOIRE
PORTUGAL	DORDOGNE
SPAIN	FRENCH RIVIERA
SWITZERLAND	NORMANDY
	PARIS

Distance : 3/4 mile — Time : 1 1/2 hours.

Graced by a series of traffic islands, often decorated with flowers or greenery, this Avenue was essentially residential until recently. Every Christmas,

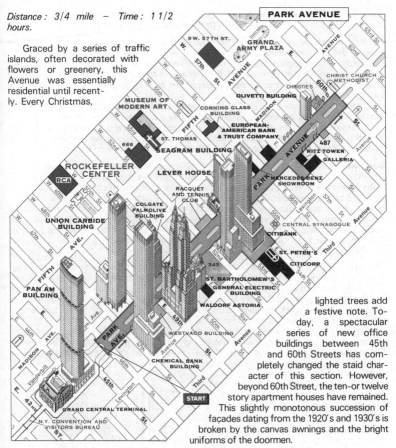

PARK AVENUE

lighted trees add a festive note. To-day, a spectacular series of new office buildings between 45th and 60th Streets has completely changed the staid character of this section. However, beyond 60th Street, the ten-or twelve story apartment houses have remained. This slightly monotonous succession of façades dating from the 1920's and 1930's is broken by the canvas awnings and the bright uniforms of the doormen.

The imprint of the Railroad. – At the beginning of this century this part of Fourth Avenue, which was later renamed Park Avenue, was hardly fashionable. The open railroad tracks of the New York Central were crossed by bridges carrying the crosstown streets. The smoke and noise were almost unbearable.

The Avenue changed in name and appearance after the trains were electrified and covered over in 1907. By the 1920's the problem of building over two levels of railroad tracks had been solved by the use of concrete piles, and the boom began. Park Avenue rapidly became a particularly sought-after address.

From Grand Central Terminal to 60th Street

Union Carbide Building★★. – Located between 47th and 48th Streets on the west side of Park Avenue, this building is slightly set back. Built between 1957 and 1960 for the Union Carbide chemical company, the various construction materials present a striking contrast : shining glass windows and unpolished black and white steel.

Another interesting feature is the asymmetrical design. On the right is a 52-story tower, on the left a low wing set still futher back with an entrance on Madison Avenue. Like Lever House *(see p. 72)* the building is set back from the building line providing an open pedestrian space ; this plaza (on the Park Avenue side) is paved in pink marble-chip terrazzo. Another innovation is the location of the main lobby and the elevators on the second floor, which can be reached by escalator. (There are two exhibit galleries : the Lower Gallery, at street level, and the Main Gallery, 2nd floor facing Park Avenue ; *monthly exhibits are open Monday through Friday 9:30 AM to 4:30 PM)*.

On the opposite side of Park Avenue the **Chemical Bank Building**★, with its 50 glass-covered stories, balances the Union Carbide Building. Across 48th Street rises the dark slender tower of the 42-story Westvaco Building.

Waldorf Astoria★. – This hotel, known the world over, contains 1,800 rooms served by 1,700 employees. The massive 42-story building was built in 1931 *(see p. 43 for the earlier history of the hotel)*. The luxury apartments and suites have witnessed such a succession of celebrities that a protocol service has been organized to decide delicate questions of precedence and etiquette ; thus, certain dignitaries who stay at the Waldorf are entitled to see their national flags floating in front of the hotel. Among the suites in the Towers, some were occupied for years by such notables as President Hoover, General MacArthur, Adlai Stevenson and the Duke of Windsor. Another is reserved for presidents and heads of state (the Presidential Suite). There are also many small suites and single and double rooms in the hotel proper occupied by guests from every part of the United States and from abroad.

Stop at the corner of 49th Street to admire the succession of modern buildings on the west side of Park Avenue : from left to right, Union Carbide, Bankers Trust, Colgate Palmolive, ITT, Manufacturers Hanover Trust and Lever House.

Colgate Palmolive Building. – Directly across from the Waldorf, this 25-story building, finished in 1955, is covered with glass over an aluminum frame.

St. Bartholomew's Church. – The ornate Romanesque Byzantine style and compact form of this Episcopal church, which opened in 1918, provide a curious contrast with the surrounding skyscrapers. Located between 50th and 51st Streets, on the east side of Park Avenue, it stands apart from the ITT Building across the street and the high Flamboyant Gothic tower of the **General Electric Building** at the back of the church (on the corner of Lexington Avenue).

Choral concerts are given on Sunday afternoons from last Sunday in October through Easter at 4 PM. The Vanderbilts donated the richly sculptured bronze doors.

The semi-dome of the apse is lighted by alabaster windows and decorated with mosaics depicting the Creation and the Transfiguration. Pass the skyscraper at 345 Park Avenue with its plaza, pool, fountains and sculpture. The Cadillac motor showroom is on the left.

Seagram Building★★. – The headquarters of Joseph E. Seagram & Sons Inc., located at 375 Park Avenue between 52nd and 53rd Streets was designed by **Mies van der Rohe** and **Philip Johnson**. The first bronze-sheathed skyscraper ever constructed is set back half an acre on a twin fountained granite and marble plaza. The subtle color scheme of the exterior bronze panels and topaz-grey windows and the refinement of the interior lobby with its travertine walls and continuation of the granite plaza floor, give an air of classic distinction to the building. A large Picasso painting done in 1919 as a stage curtain for the ballet *Le Tricorne*, can be seen. *Guided tours available Tuesdays at 3 PM.*

Take a right on 53rd Street to Citicorp on Lexington Avenue.

Citicorp. – A spectacular aluminum and glass tower is the focal point of Citicorp Center (Citibank's multipurpose development) which occupies the block between Lexington and Third Avenues, 53rd and 54th Streets. Four gigantic square columns support the 59-story building which is topped by a 160-foot sloping crown. The natural colored aluminum and reflecting glass facing of the tower and an innovative energy system help reduce energy requirements and adapt energy consumption to demand.

Also part of the complex are a seven story building, surrounding a sky lit atrium, an arcade, a sunken pedestrian plaza and (at the corner of Lexington Avenue and 54th Street) the modern **St. Peter's Church.** ''**The Market**'' spread over three levels of the lowrise structure, accomodates a diversity of inter-national shops and restaurants.

Walk around the **Citibank Building** which covers the entire block between 53rd and 54th Streets and Park and Lexington Avenues.

Lever House★★. – Lever House, across from the Citibank building, raises its slender silhouette against the City's sky. Designed by Skidmore, Owings and Merrill, this first ''glass house'' after the United Nations Secretariat Building *(p. 66)*, was opened in 1952. The 21-story tower, which is raised on supporting pillars according to the concept of Le Corbusier, enjoys a justified reputation of esthetic and technical quality. Art exhibits are displayed in the Lever Lobby *(open Monday through Friday 10 AM (1 PM Sundays and holidays) to 5 PM. Closed Saturdays).*

The building is flanked to the south by a survivor of early Park Avenue, the 1918 Italian Renaissance palace of the exclusive Racquet and Tennis Club. To the north are two adaptations of the ''wedding cake'' principle whose upper stories are set back in layers to conform with zoning regulations.

Continuing up Park Avenue, after 55th Street you will pass the **Mercedes-Benz showroom** designed by Frank Lloyd Wright in 1955. At 450 Park Avenue rises the dark

(From photo Lever House.)

Lever House.

silhouette of the **European-American Bank & Trust Company** with its distinctive façade.

At the northeast corner of 57th Street is the **Ritz Tower**. On the ground floor is the First Women's Bank, organized primarily by women to provide a full range od banking services to men and women. Turning right onto 57th Street, **Galleria** at No. 117 with its unique architectural design is an interesting example of a ''multi-purpose'' building, a 57-story residential tower with offices and a through block arcade lined with shops, picture galleries and café. Farther up Park Avenue, at the southeast corner of 59th Street, an Italian Renaissance building harbors the Chapel of Faith, Hope, and Charity and Cardinal Spellman's Servicemen's Club. Cross the avenue, stopping on the central island to admire the outstanding **view★★★** of Park Avenue south to the Pan Am Building.

Olivetti Building. – Designed by Skidmore, Owings and Merrill, and built between 1958 and 1960, this building has 11 floors. Located on the southwest corner of 59th Street, it seems dwarfed by the skyscrapers farther downtown. Nevertheless, the geometric rigor of its lines, with glass panels resting on supporting pillars, is impressive. Across the street at the corner of 59th Street is Christie's, fine Art Auctioneers since 1766.

Beyond 60th Street is the residential section of Park Avenue, one of the most fashionable addresses in town, as you will gather from a short stroll uptown.

Distance : 1 1/2 miles - Time : 1 hour (not including visit to the Pierpont Morgan Library).

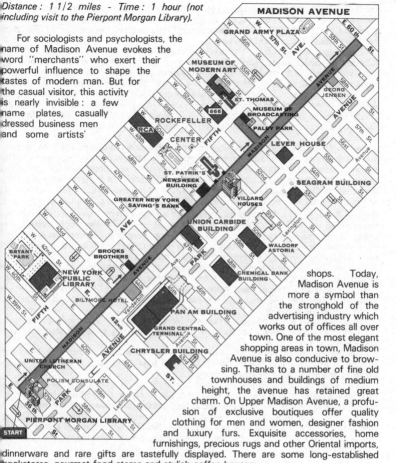

For sociologists and psychologists, the name of Madison Avenue evokes the word "merchants" who exert their powerful influence to shape the tastes of modern man. But for the casual visitor, this activity is nearly invisible : a few name plates, casually dressed business men and some artists' shops. Today, Madison Avenue is more a symbol than the stronghold of the advertising industry which works out of offices all over town. One of the most elegant shopping areas in town, Madison Avenue is also conducive to browsing. Thanks to a number of fine old townhouses and buildings of medium height, the avenue has retained great charm. On Upper Madison Avenue, a profusion of exclusive boutiques offer quality clothing for men and women, designer fashion and luxury furs. Exquisite accessories, home furnishings, precious rugs and other Oriental imports, dinnerware and rare gifts are tastefully displayed. There are some long-established bookstores, gourmet food stores and stylish coffee houses.

The proximity of the great museums has attracted art and antique dealers ; galleries, among them the most prestigious, abound between 57th and 90th Streets, some just off the avenue and some installed on the second floor.

From 36th to 60th Streets

The first three blocks still bear reminders of the era when Madison Avenue rivalled Fifth Avenue as a fashionable residential area. The area, known as Murray Hill, was named for the family whose mansion was located at about what is now the intersection of Park Avenue and 38th Street. It is said that in 1776, the mistress of the house served tea to the British General Howe while Washington's troops escaped to the north.

■ PIERPONT MORGAN LIBRARY★★

A cultural treasure trove, the walls of the Morgan Library enclose rich collections of rare books, manuscripts, drawings, engravings and works of art assembled by **J. Pierpont Morgan** (1837-1913) and preserved here since his death. The accumulation of objects, the magnificent furnishings and decoration, the shadowy silence of his study and library recreate the atmosphere which must have existed during the lifetime of this great collector. In 1924 the Library was transferred from the Morgan family to a Board of Trustees.

The Buildings. – At the southeast corner of 37th Street, the **United Lutheran Church** occupies the former home of J.P. Morgan, son of J. Pierpont. It possesses the only surviving garden on Madison Avenue.

The Library itself is on the corner of 36th Street. An excellent example of 16th century Italian Renaissance style, in pink Tennessee marble, it was finished by McKim in 1906. The annex on the corner was added in 1928 on the site of the elder Morgan's home. On 36th Street you will see the steps leading to the entrance, guarded by two lions.

The Library and the Museum★★. – *Open Tuesday through Saturday 10:30 AM to 5 PM ; Sundays 1 to 5 PM. Closed Sundays in July and in August, only the reading room is open. Admission free.*

The vestibule is resplendent in marble polychrome. On the left is the main Exhibition Hall for rotating exhibitions and on the right a reading room open *(except Saturdays and Sundays)* to accredited scholars.

From the vestibule, you can continue along a corridor which houses a rotating exhibit of material selected from the Library's collections or on loan.

The West Room. – From the entrance to Mr. Morgan's study, the visitor is struck by the atmosphere of studious meditation in this room. Although rather dark in tone, it is opulent, thanks to the painted and carved Italian ceiling (16th century), the red damask hangings, and the massive black wood furniture.

Paintings and statuettes, enamels and metalwork of the Middle Ages and the Renaissance, Swiss stained glass of the 16th and 17th centuries, and rock crystal Italian cups (16th and 17th centuries) blend harmoniously with the decoration. Above the Florentine marble chimney (15th century) is a portrait of Morgan himself.

Among the paintings, notice two small Bohemian panels of the 14th century : *The Adoration of the Magi* and *The Death of the Virgin*, the portraits by Hans Memling, the *Mystic Marriage of St. Catherine* by Cima da Conegliano (Venice, early 16th century) and the wedding portraits of Martin Luther and his wife by Lucas Cranach the Elder (Germany 16th century).

Among the sculpture are a number of small Florentine marbles of the 15th century such as the bust of *Marietta Strozzi* by Desiderio da Settignano and the *Virgin and Child* by Antonio Rossellino. Among the enamels and gold-work we should mention two Saint Porchaire salt cellars (16th century), the Stavelot Triptych, a portable altar made by Godefroid de Claire about 1150, a Viennese ciborium of the early 14th century and two salt cellars decorated with scenes from the life of Jacob (Nuremberg, 16th century).

The East Room. – This library is decorated with a large Flemish tapestry (16th century representing the Triumph of Avarice. Three tiers of rare books are visible through iron grilles. Changing exhibitions of books, autograph manuscripts and letters, and illuminated manuscripts are shown in display cases. A copy of the Gutenberg Bible and an illuminated manuscript of an Antiphonary are permanently displayed.

Beyond the Pierpont Morgan Library, notice on the northeast corner of 37th Street the granite palace built for the Dutch sea captain, De Lamar, for a million dollars. (The land cost a mere quarter of a million). His fortune came from African gold mines and Wall Street speculation. Between 1925 and 1973, the National Democratic Club occupied the building which is now the home of the Polish Consulate.

Further uptown is one of the last hotels in Manhattan to have a Victorian atmosphere, the Biltmore, whose lounge serves as a convenient meeting place for students, New Yorkers and out-of-towners.

On the northwest corner of 44th Street is **Brooks Brothers,** which has been the stronghold of men's and boy's clothing for more than 150 years ; it now also carries exclusive selected clothing items for women.

A little further, at the northwest corner of 48th Street, is a branch of the **Greater New York Savings Bank**. This rustic brick Colonial house is rather a surprise in the midst of Manhattan, and contrasts with the steel and glass **Union Carbide Building** opposite *(see p. 71).*

From the corner of 50th Street, you will have a good view of Rockefeller Center. On the west side of Madison Avenue itself is the **Newsweek Building,** where the well-known weekly news magazine is published. At the top of the building, the time and the local temperature are shown in lights.

Villard Houses. – The Florentine Renaissance palace, a group of 6 mansions, built in 1885 by McKim, Mead and White for Henry Villard, founder of the Northern Pacific Railroad, was later the home of several notables, among whom Whitelaw Reid, editor-in-chief of the *New York Herald Tribune* and ambassador to England. This was for some 25 years after World War II, the Archdiocese of New York.

On the west side of the Avenue, on either side of the apse of St. Patrick's, are two small town houses, the rectory of the cathedral and the residence of the Archbishop of New York, Cardinal Cooke, who administers the richest diocese in the world.

Paley Park on East 53rd Street, accessible through the shopping arcade, is one of the new vest pocket parks where office workers and visitors alike can rest beside cascading water which mutes the city noises.

Museum of Broadcasting. – *1 East 53rd Street. Open Tuesdays through Saturdays noon to 5 PM. Closed holidays. $1.50.*

The first of its kind, the museum contains a collection of tapes of significant radio and T.V. programs of the first 50 years of broadcasting, which are available for public viewing. Included in the collection are drama and sports events ; speeches by each of the 10 presidents of the United States, since broadcasting began ; the Graham McNamee coverage of Charles Lindbergh's triumphant return to the U.S. in 1927 ; the earliest version of Amos n' Andy and the comedy routines of Bert Lahr and Beatrice Lillie to name only a few.

Returning to Madison Avenue pass several new office buildings before reaching, 601 Madison Avenue, Georg Jensen, an outpost of Scandinavian design : silver, gifts and ceramics.

OTHER GREAT COLLECTORS AND THEIR TREASURE TROVES

Distance : about 3/4 mile –
Time : 1 1/2 hours.

Gramercy Park*. – Gramercy Park, Irving Place and the immediate surroundings form an elegant residential enclave in an area which is otherwise undistinguished. The neoclassic town houses dating from the nineteenth century and the calm streets with few shops attract artists and intellectuals. It is one of the spots in New York which most recall the past.

A fashionable area. – In the 18th century, this site was a "crooked little swamp" ("Krom Moeraije" in Dutch, which was later transformed into Gramercy). When the swamp had been drained, Samuel Ruggles bought a farm here, part of which he divided in 1830 to form the present park.

In the middle of the last century, a number of New York notables settled in Gramercy Park.

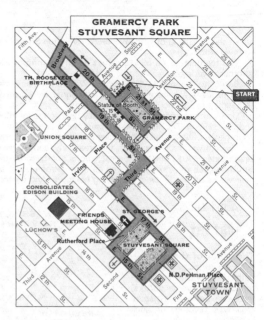

GRAMERCY PARK
STUYVESANT SQUARE

The Park. – The park is pleasantly shady, but its use is reserved for the nearby residents. In the center is a statue of Edwin Booth in his favorite role of Hamlet.

Around the park are charming neoclassic town houses, with their outside staircases. Notice the fine cast iron bannisters, balconies and street lamps. The richly decorated interiors give an impression of warmth and intimacy.

Numbers 1, 2, 3 and 4 Gramercy Park West, in red brick, date from about 1840. Number 4 was the home of James Harper, Mayor of New York in 1844 ; it is still graced with the traditional cast iron "Mayor's Lamps".

The present site of the National Arts Club at number 15 (south) was the home of Samuel J. Tilden, a Democratic adversary of Tammany Hall, Governor of New York State in 1874-1876, and unsuccessful candidate for the presidency in 1876. At number 16 lived Edwin Booth, who founded the Players Club in 1888. Notice the ornate street lamps and the second floor balcony decorated with actors' masques. Number 18 was the domain of Mrs. Stuyvesant Fish, whose innovations included reducing the time for a formal dinner to one hour.

Theodore Roosevelt Birthplace. – *Open Memorial Day through Labor Day, Monday through Saturday 9 AM to 4:30 PM (4 PM the rest of the year). 50 cents.*

Between Broadway and Park Avenue, at 28 East 20th Street, a flag flies from the house where **Theodore Roosevelt** (1858-1919) was born and lived until he was 15.

A typical wealthy New Yorker's home of the mid-nineteenth century, with its austere exterior and elegantly overstuffed interior, the birthplace has been restored with appropriate period furniture and numerous memorabilia. It is now a National Historic Site.

Theodore Roosevelt was a colorful personality. The first New York Police Commissioner to have attended Harvard, the organizer of "Roosevelt's Rough Riders", the Vice President who succeeded to the presidency when McKinley was assassinated in 1901, later to be elected president in his own right, big game hunter, explorer and litigant, he was often in the public eye. Teddy was the uncle of Eleanor Roosevelt.

Weekly chamber concerts are given on Thursday evenings at 7:30 PM. Fall, winter and spring only. Admission free.

Stuyvesant Square*. – Occupying part of the farm of **Peter Stuyvesant** *(see p. 81)*, Dutch Governor of New Amsterdam, Stuyvesant Square was a focal point of fashionable New York in the middle of the 19th century. Located between 15th and 17th Streets, and First and Third Avenues, it is now surrounded by hospitals, churches, and schools. It seems part of a country town lost in the immensity of New York. **Rutherford Place,** to the west, is most typical.

From Stuyvesant Square you can see, along the East River from 14th to 23rd Streets, Stuyvesant Town and Peter Cooper Village. These middle-income housing projects were built after the Second World War by the Metropolitan Life Insurance Company.

Friends Meeting House. – One of the latest examples of the Federal style with strong neoclassic elements, in New York, it was built in 1860 as the meeting place of the "Religious Society of Friends", otherwise known as Quakers. The white marble base of the building identifies it as having been designed to be a station in the Underground Railroad - a place where escaped black slaves could stay on their way from slave states to Canada. *You may ask to visit the meeting room during the week.*

St. George's Church. – Near the Friends Meeting House is St. George's Episcopal Church, founded in 1749. The present building was erected in 1848 in red sandstone. The façade with its twin towers is in the early Romanesque tradition, although the rose window is Gothic ; the elder J.P. Morgan *(see pp. 73 and 91)* was a parishioner here ; occasionally it was called "Morgan's Church". In front of the Church, in Stuyvesant Square, is the bronze statue of Peter Stuyvesant, easily identified because of his peg-leg.

Time : about 1 hour.

At the beginning of Fifth Avenue, Washington Square forms a large rectangle planted with venerable trees.

The fountain in the middle serves as an impromptu wading pool for children during summer dog days.

Bordering Greenwich Village *(see p. 78)* and used as a campus by the students of New York University, Washington Square, although usually quiet and even a little melancholy, is sometimes the scene of picturesque events.

On warm summer evenings you may hear formal or informal concerts of guitar, banjo and folk singing. During spring and summer it is a training ground for lasso throwers or pogo players, while chess or checkers experts battle silently under the trees.

Twice a year, spring and fall, the area is invaded for two full weeks by the **Washington Square Outdoor Art Exhibit** (any artist who is approved by the jury can pay the small enrollment fee may exhibit as long as there is room available). Minor poets used to tack their works on the fence in the spring hoping to find customers.

A BIT OF HISTORY

The ashes of the past. – Who would suspect that the paths and lawns of Washington Square cover a potters' field. Even earlier, this marshy area was favored for duck hunting.

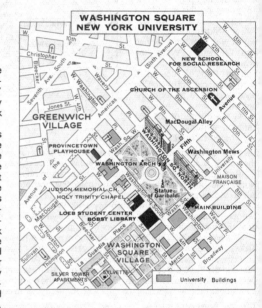

Later the cemetery was closed, and the field became a parade ground where troops marched by on the Fourth of July. In 1828 it became a public park. The first elegant town houses were built in 1836, and Washington Square became a fashionable address ; red brick neoclassic houses rose in the area. **Henry James's** novel *Washington Square,* later adapted to become the play and film *The Heiress,* depicted the life of the local aristocracy. Mark Twain, O'Henry, Walt Whitman and later Edward Hopper, also frequented Washington Square and evoked it in their works.

New York University : foundation and development. – An independent institution, N.Y.U. was founded in 1831 by **Albert Gallatin**, Secretary of the Treasury under Jefferson and Madison.

The first hundred students and their fifteen professors occupied rented quarters until 1836, when the University moved into a Gothic Revival building of its own on Washington Square.

In 1894 the present classical building on the east of the Square with is triangular pediments replaced the original one. To the south of the square are the Silver Tower Apartments designed by I.M. Pei, where there is an impressive sculpture, the *Sylvette* by Pablo Picasso, executed by Carl Nesjar in 1968.

Today, New York University numbers thirteen colleges and schools and about 41,000 students, including 2,350 foreign students, divided among six centers. The principal campuses are : Washington Square (Sciences, Arts and Letters, Business, Law, Education), and N.Y.U. Medical Center *(see p. 118)* on First Avenue (Medicine and Dentistry). The Graduate Business School is located on Trinity Place in the Wall Street area, and the Institute of Fine Arts in the Duke House on Fifth Avenue and 78th Street. The seven libraries of N.Y.U. have more than 2,500,000 books.

University alumni have included Walter Reed, conqueror of yellow fever ; William Gorgas, whose sanitation work made possible construction of the Panama Canal ; the political notables Elihu Root, Samuel Tilden, Mayors Fiorello La Guardia and Edward Koch and Senator Jacob Javits ; composers Deems Taylor and George Kleinsinger ; authors Countee Cullen, Joseph Heller and Lillian Hellman ; motion picture producers Kermit Bloomgarden, Martin Scorsese and Stanley Kramer ; and Drs. Jonas Salk and Albert B. Sabin, developers of the polio vaccines.

Famous University professors have included Samuel F.B. Morse, inventor of the telegraph ; the composer Percy Grainger ; among authors, Joyce Kilmer, Thomas Wolfe, and Leon Edel, the biographer of Henry James ; the mathematician Richard Courant ; the philosopher Sidney Hook ; and economist Wassily Leontief, 1973 Nobel Prize Winner.

VISIT

We recommend a visit to Washington Square late in the afternoon or in the evening, especially during warm weather, to enjoy the atmosphere and local color to the fullest.

Washington Arch. – It was erected to commemorate the centennial of Washington's inauguration in 1789 *(details p. 91)*. A triumphal arch placed at the beginning of a triumphal way (Fifth Avenue), the permanent white marble Washington Arch was finished in 1892.

One can identify on the north side, toward Fifth Avenue, two statues of Washington, one in his general's uniform and the other in mufti. The first is the work of A. Stirling Calder, the father of Alexander Calder, well-known creator of "mobiles" : what a contrast in styles !

On the south side, notice the frieze with the American eagle and Washington's initials in the center. Trumpet-blowing statues of Fame embellish the corners.

Statue of Garibaldi. – Erected in 1888, it forms a rallying point for inhabitants of nearby "Little Italy" *(see p. 79)*. A hero of the Italian struggle for independence, Garibaldi visited New York in 1850. N.Y.U. students claim that Garibaldi turns his head when a virtuous girl goes by : no one has yet seen him do it, but perhaps he has been looking in the wrong direction.

New York University. – N.Y.U. buildings rim the Square. The newest, the **Bobst Library** on Washington Square South, is a red stone-faced building. Among the largest are the classical **Main Building**, built in 1894, on the east side, and on the south side, the **Loeb**

Student Center and the Holy Trinity (Catholic) Chapel, all in glass. It contrasts strangely with the Lombard Romanesque Baptist Church nearby, with its arcades and separate bell tower. On Washington Square East, is the Grey Art Gallery *(open Tuesday through Friday 10 AM (1 PM Saturdays) to 5 PM (8:30 PM Wednesdays)*.

Washington Square North★. – This is the most attractive side of the Square, thanks to the graceful neoclassic town houses which escaped the mania of demolition which began at the end of the 19th century. The brick walls of the houses, their stone porticos with Doric or Ionic columns, the stoops and bay windows give us an idea of Washington Square in the 1840's.

Behind these houses, two picturesque alleys have survived, which originally served the stables and kitchens of the town houses. These two enclaves **Washington Mews** and **MacDougal Alley**, with their whitewashed walls, their gaslights (the only surviving ones in New York) and, the cobblestone pavement of the Mews attract artists, actors and writers who prize a commodity rare in New York : calm.

In the early 1900's MacDougal Alley was inhabited by the sculptress Gertrude Vanderbilt Whitney, the sculptor Jo Davidson and the actor Richard Bennett.

(From photo Seymour Linden.)

Washington Mews.

Lower Fifth Avenue. – In the vestibule of number 2 you can see a trace of the Minetta Brook, which still flows underground : a small fountain.

■ ADDITIONAL SIGHTS

Church of the Ascension. – *Northwest corner of 10th Street and Fifth Avenue.* This Episcopal church, built in 1841 in the Gothic Revival style, was later remodelled by Stanford White. It boasts a mural of the Ascension by John La Farge (1835-1910).

The New School of Social Research. – *66 W 12th Street (between 5th Avenue and the Avenue of the Americas).* The Nation's leading university for adults, was founded in 1919 by the economists Thorstein Veblen and Alvin Johnson, educational philosopher John Dewey and historian Charles Beard as a small informal center for adults where a broad range of economic and political issues would be discussed.

Today, the New School is the only university committed to meeting the intellectual and cultural needs of mature citizens. 85 % of all New School students are enrolled in its Adult Division which includes the Human Relations Center and the Institute for Retired Professionals. In 1934, the New School became a degree-granting institution when the Graduate Faculty of Political and Social Science was created. In 1965, the Center for New York City Affairs, the first institute devoted to the study and improvement of a single metropolis, was founded. In 1970, the Parsons School of Design became a division of the New School.

Among the scholars who have taught or lectured here are : Margaret Mead, Frank Lloyd Wright, Jacques Maritain, Aaron Copland, Archibald MacLeish, Thomas Mann and T.S. Eliot.

The building is decorated with frescoes by the Mexican artist José Clemente Orozco, and murals entitled *America Today*, painted in 1930 by Thomas Hart Benton, representing rural American life.

To visit contact the public relations office in advance at (212) 741-5668.

Distance : about 1 mile − Time : 2 hours.

Greenwich Village occupies approximately the area from Spring Street to the south to 14th Street to the north and from Greenwich Street to Broadway, but its heart is the relatively small area west of Washington Square. Here, Italian grocery stores, restaurants and coffee houses are interspersed with antique and craft shops, theaters and art galleries, housed in older buildings some of which have been converted into comfortable homes.

But, like Janus, Greenwich Village has two faces. During the day, a serene small-town atmosphere pervades, enlivened on Sunday afternoons by strollers who gather to hear street musicians or have their portrait painted then and there. The night reveals a countenance reminiscent of Montmartre and St. Germain des Prés in Paris : a cosmopolitan tourist crowd rubbing elbows with artists, intellectuals, students and Bohemians. People flock to theaters and movie houses, and folk, rock and jazz musicians perform in dimly lit night clubs and cafés.

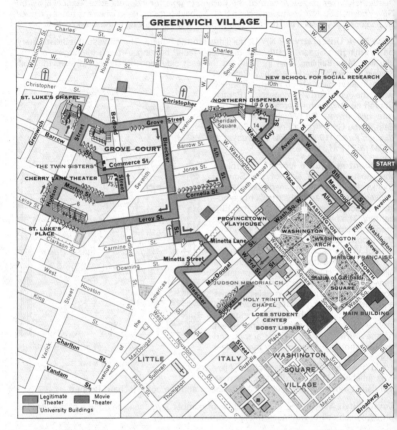

A BIT OF HISTORY

A Country Village. − At the time Henri Hudson arrived, the countryside, which was to become Greenwich Village, was covered with woods and streams abounding with fish, and sheltered an Indian settlement called Sapohanickan. Later, British colonists settled here and in 1696 a village sprung up which was named after the English town Greenwich (actually, the name "Greenwich Village" is redundant, since "wich" means village or town). Between rows of wooden houses ran Greenwich Street, then the main street of the village which overlooked the Hudson and its warehouses.

It is during the 18th century that wealthy landowners such as the De Lanceys and Van Cortlandts, Sir Peter Warren and Abraham Mortier had estates there. It became a settled and well-known area of the city : with its good taverns and even a road that led directly out of town.

Thomas Paine, the famous revolutionary figure and pamphleteer, lived in Greenwich Village for a time.

During recurrent smallpox and yellow fever epidemics ravaging the downtown New York area, New Yorkers sought the healthy country air of Greenwich Village. The present Bank Street, in the northern part of the Village, was named for the Wall Street banks which took refuge here, in 1822, along with other businesses.

In the 1830's, prominent families built town houses here, but they moved further north when industry developed near the waterfront. While the small Black community decreased, Irish and Chinese immigrants came to live in the Village ; "Little Italy" sprouted up around Bleecker Street. Lower rents attracted artists and writers, following the example of **Edgar Allan Poe** who had taken up residence at 85 West 3rd Street, in 1845, where he had written *Gordon Pym* and *The Fall of the House of Usher.*

Village Bohemia. – By the early years of the 20th century, Greenwich Village was largely identified with New York's Bohemia. The intellectual ferment was intense. In 1910, a young Dutchman named **Piet Vlag** founded *The Masses,* a publication which condemned the established order and symbolized the independent spirit of the Village. The favorite haunt of the Village rebels was the **Liberal Club,** frequented by such social critics as **Upton Sinclair.** At its headquarters, 137 MacDougal Street, the club organized cubist art exhibits, lectures and debates, and all-night dances called "Pagan Routs" ; there were soon so many Pagans that the festivities had to be moved to other quarters. Polly Holliday's restaurant, located below the Liberal Club, became the favorite meeting place of anarchists.

But not all the agitation was political. Walt Whitman, Mark Twain, Henry James were among the writers who found the intellectual climate of the Village stimulating. Theodore Dreiser, O'Henry, Stephen Crane came to live there for a certain time. Not surprisingly, the Village attracted the theater. In 1915, the **Washington Square Players,** later to become the Theater Guild, were founded at the Liberal Club. In the following year, the Provincetown Players made their New York debut on the ground floor of a bottling plant, after a summer season in Provincetown, Cape Cod. Among the members of the company was the poetess and playwright Edna St. Vincent Millay. It was here that Eugene O'Neill first gained recognition. The jazz age of the 20's touched off a wave of eccentricity with **F. Scott Fitzgerald** the main actor of the Lost Generation scene.

In our day, Greenwich Village is going through yet another phase. A number of struggling artists and would-be artists had to find cheaper quarters in the **East Village** (east of Washington Square). Scattered among the small houses in the winding streets, high-rise buildings accomodate New Yorkers who prefer the liveliness of the Village to the conventionality of suburbia or residence uptown. They are attracted by a community which welcomes talent, offers serious and light entertainment, caters to the bibliophile and to the gourmet and cherishes diversity of life style. They, as well as their neighbors, are deeply committed to preserving the character of their unique neighborhood.

VISIT

We describe a walk linking the most typical parts of the Village and advise you to visit it twice, once during the day and once at night.

Leaving Washington Square, first take Sullivan Street, and turn right on 3rd Street, with its restaurants and coffee houses, and then right again on MacDougal Street : at number 133 is the **Provincetown Playhouse,** one of the oldest off-Broadway theaters.

Continue on Washington Square West before turning right on MacDougal Alley *(see p. 77).* It was here in a converted stable that Gertrude Vanderbilt Whitney opened a gallery that was to be the precursor of the Whitney Museum *(see p. 51).* Then visit 8th Street, where a diversity of shops (jewelry, clothes, books, records) are interspersed with pizza shops and other restaurants. Turn left on Avenue of the Americas before going right on Waverly Place and right again to Gay Street. At number 14 lived Ruth McKenney and her sister, who inspired the best seller *My Sister Eileen,* later adapted for stage and screen. At the end of this little street, lined with brick houses, turn left on Christopher Street. At the next intersection is the **Northern Dispensary,** a brick building erected in 1831 for the Association of Physicians.

Follow West 4th Street, between Seventh Avenue and Avenue of the Americas ; it is jammed with a succession of restaurants, coffee houses and craft shops which offer handmade jewelry, gloves, etc.

Walk along Corneliat Street and Leroy Street, which becomes St. **Luke's Place***. This attractive row of houses from the 1860's is shaded by fine trees. It was here at number 16 that Theodore Dreiser wrote *An American Tragedy.* At number 6, the "Mayor's Lamps" indicate the former residence of Jimmy Walker. South of this area, near Charlton and Vandam Streets, was an elegant estate, Richmond Hill, which served as a headquarters for General Washington, and later as a residence of both John Adams and Aaron Burr.

Continue on Hudson Street and Morton Street to Bedford Street. Number 75 1/2 is reputed to be the narrowest house in the city. Edna St. Vincent Millay and John Barrymore are thought to have lived there. Number 77 is considered the oldest house in the Village (1799).

Other wooden houses can be found on Commerce Street. At number 38, an old barn has been used since the 1920's as an Off-Broadway theater ; the **Cherry Lane** has seen the American premieres of plays by Beckett, Ionesco and Edward Albee. Across the street are two handsome brick houses, "The Twin Sisters", it is said that these were built by a sea captain, for his two daughters, who could not live together under the same roof.

On Hudson Street, between Barrow and Christopher Streets, **St. Luke's Chapel,** built in 1822, still seems a country church. Turn right on Grove Street ; a few steps further, where the street turns a corner, you will discover the gate of **Grove Court★★** on the right. Its brick and grass covered area is surrounded by houses of wood or brick (1840). Another wooden house, unusual for New York, is on the northern corner of Grove and Bedford Streets. Grove, like Bedford, is a peaceful byway which seems miles away from feverish Manhattan.

The scene changes at **Bleecker Street,** one of the hubs of "Little Italy" and, with 8th Street and MacDougal Street, one of the most active commercially in the Village. Notice the overwhelming displays of fruits and vegetables, the specialized grocery stores and pastry shops, and the coffee house for espresso lovers.

A few more steps and you will enjoy the contrasting calm of Minetta Street and **Minetta Lane.** Return to Washington Square by taking Sullivan Street, another main artery of Little Italy.

Going to Europe ?
Then take the Michelin Green Tourist Guides : LONDON and PARIS.

Distance : about 1 mile − Time : 1 hour.

Typical of old New York, this section has remained unchanged for many years. Today it is a cosmopolitan neighborhood, with a predominantly white population. However, in the last few years, a number of artists "intellectuals and pseudo-intellectuals" have moved into the area, and restaurants, Off-Broadway theaters and antique shops have appeared : it is now sometimes known as the **East Village** (from Broadway to Tompkins Square).

■ ST. MARK'S-IN-THE-BOUWERIE

Starting at 14th Street, we go south on Second Avenue, cleared since 1941 of the noisy El. At the corner of 12th Street is the Eden Theater, an establishment given over to Off-Broadway productions.

St. Mark's Church. − *On the corner of 10th Street.* Miraculously, St. Mark's has remained a fieldstone country church for almost 200 years, surrounded by its now landscaped cemetery. The bust to the right of the portico is of Peter Stuyvesant and to the left is one of **Daniel Tompkins,** governor of New York State (1807-1817) and Vice President of the United States under James Monroe. Nearby Tompkins Square was named for him.

Entered by a portico added in 1835, the Georgian church appears very simple.

SECOND AVENUE-LAFAYETTE STREET

The interior, with its gallery on three sides, offers a stained glass window representing Peter Stuyvesant (the second on the lower right).

Now take Stuyvesant Street : on the right, the **Renwick Triangle** includes 16 town houses built by the architect Renwick in the middle of the 19th century.

Astor Place. − On either side of this place between Third and Fourth Avenues are the buildings of the Cooper Union for the Advancement of Science and Art, a privately funded tuition-free college. On the left is the red sandstone **Cooper Union Foundation Building**★, founded in 1859 by Peter Cooper (1791-1883) an industrialist, inventor and philanthropist who manufactured among other things, *Tom Thumb,* the first steam engine to run in the United States. It was in the Great Hall *(ground floor)* in 1860 that Abraham Lincoln made his famous "right makes might" speech, his first step towards the Presidency. The Cooper Union Forum, a series of free public lectures and cultural events are held here.

During the 19th century, the majestic Astor Place Opera House stood here. Opened in 1847, it was the scene, two years later, of a protest riot against the English actor William Macready, accused of stealing the limelight from local talent. Crying "Washington forever !", the mob tried to burn down the opera house where the unfortunate Englishman was playing but was dispersed by the Seventh Regiment, at a cost of 22 dead and 150 wounded.

Take Lafayette Street. Soon you will see on your right a series of Corinthian columns of Westchester marble. With their air of faded aristocracy, they have obviously seen better days. **Colonnade Row**★ was originally known as La Grange Terrace, after the name of the Château de la Grange, near Paris, which belonged to Lafayette. When built (in 1836), the group included 8 houses ; 4 of them remain. The maternal grandfather of Franklin D. Roosevelt once lived at number 426.

The monumental building across the street from Colonnade Row was the home of the Astor Library, opened in 1854 and later the nucleus of the present New York Public Library. About 100,000 volumes were available without charge, which was revolutionary at the time. The building now houses the Public Theater of the Shakespeare Festival, which gives free performances in Central Park in the summer *(see p. 99) ;* the building accomodates seven theaters which present entertainment ranging from fullscale productions of new plays to cabaret.

Turn left on 4th Street ; the Old Merchant's House is at No 29.

Old Merchant's House. − *Currently being restored, scheduled to reopen in 1979.*

The House was built in 1832-1833 for a prosperous hardware merchant, Seabury Tredwell. It is graced with handsome wrought iron grilles, and its entrance has a decorative arcade. The interior has kept its original decoration and furniture, in Chippendale and Empire styles.

The house nearby at 37 East 4th Street was the home of a leading businessman Samuel Tredwell Skidmore. Built in 1844-45 the house is characteristic of the Greek Revival period with an Ionic portico and a simple wood roof cornice.

Return to Second Avenue and continue south to Houston Street, the end of this walk.

Distance : about 1 1/2 miles – Times : 2 hours.

From Houston to Canal Steets and from Lafayette to Clinton Streets the lover of the picturesque or arresting sights may explore an area full of an atmosphere reflecting different ways of life.

■ THE BOWERY★

Paradise of the gay life in the 19th century and the heart of nocturnal frivolity, the Bowery has now become the Skid Row of New York from 4th Street to Chatham Square.

The Governor's Farm. –
Peter Stuyvesant (1592-1672) was the last Dutch governor of New Amsterdam, from 1647 to 1664. He was stern, even forbidding, and always wore black – his peg-leg replaced the one he lost when attacking St. Martin's Island in the Caribbean.

A colonizer to the core, he established a farm ("bouwerie" in Dutch) on the land of Indians he had helped to drive out, in the area between Broadway and the East River and the present 5th and 17th Streets.

To reach his farm, Stuyvesant laid out a broad straight road which is now the "Bowery". His own home was near a small chapel, rebuilt between 1795 and 1799 by one of his descendants ; this is the present Episcopal Church of St. Mark's-in-the-Bouwerie *(see p. 80).*

The Street of Ghosts. –
Above the squalid pavement of the Bowery hundreds of ghosts roam by night. Peg-legged Peter Stuyvesant, who laid out the street, leads the motley band of immigrants, theater and vaudeville stars, audiences and bandits...

Early in the 19th century, the Bowery was the refuge of newly arrived immigrants. Beerhalls were soon filled, catering particularly to the newly arrived Germans *(see details p. 25).* The first theater in the area, the Bowery Theater, opened in 1826, becoming the nation's first gaslighted play house ; it seated 3,000 persons.

But it was after 1840, when the opera house on Astor Place opened its doors *(see p. 82),* that the Bowery really blossomed as an entertainment center. In fact, except for that elegant establishment, the local theaters offered little comfort or propriety. If the prices were moderate (from a "top" of 50 cents down to 12), the seats were mere wooden benches, the lighting dim, the heating non-existent, and occasional rats joined the spectators. The public enjoyed habits rather too close to nature on occasion. A newspaper reporter claimed to have observed a man place his hat upside down on the floor. The neighbors just behind him found it a handy spittoon.

By the end of the century the simplicity of these quaint customs had

(From drawing, Museum of the City of New York.)

The Bowery. — A ball in 1871.

somewhat deteriorated. In 1864, Tony Pastor's Opera House made vaudeville fashionable, despite occasional racy interludes ; "chorus girls" in black stockings and tight costumes appeared in 1866, the "revue" or "passing show" caught on in the 90's. The cellar dives welcomed men in bowlers with hangdog looks and their molls without hats : these gang members, including the notorious "Bowery Boys", held up customers emerging from dance halls and saloons when they were not battling among themselves. The Bowery had become "the street of crime" under the propitious shadows of the El passing noisily at the level of the upper floors.

Charles Dickens described a number of Bowery characters in his works *(American Notes : Martin Chuzzlewit).*

Today. – Although the Bowery is popularly known for its bums - homeless alcoholics - it is now a commercial avenue active in such trades as restaurant and electrical equipment and chinaware.

Those who have called the Bowery their home since the days of the 3rd Avenue El have been joined by a new breed of derelicts – younger alcoholics and addicts – the chronically disturbed and the unemployed. Fleeing the more expensive West Village, artists have sought out the residential lofts above some of the shops and warehouses.

The city is now making efforts to improve the neighborhood with the establishment of a Men's Shelter, which provides food and extends social and medical benefits.

From Houston Street to Essex Street

A walk on the Bowery is not dangerous, but may make you feel uneasy. Derelicts lie on the sidewalks and in the doorways or wait for handouts. Some trade their meager possessions in the street.

Walk south along the middle of the Bowery from Houston Street, turn left on Grand Street.

Grand Street. – Grand Street is lined with small stores carrying home furnishings, clothing and fabrics. There are still some bridal shops of old fame. Here and there, street vendors hawk their wares.

From Essex Street to Mulberry Street

Essex Street Market. – This European-type market (located between Broome and Stanton Streets) is housed in a large brick building : notice the abundance of fresh produce, the display of specialties from many lands and the variety of languages spoken.

Delancey Street. – Delancey Street, which you will cross, is still very much the "Main Street" of the Lower East Side and of the Jewish section ; many shops here are open on Sundays since they are traditionally closed for the Jewish Sabbath.

The area between Delancey and Canal Streets was almost entirely occupied by Jews until recently. In the last few years, many of them have moved away ; Spanish signs tend to replace Hebrew letters, and Delancey Street is now also host to Latin Americans, Greeks, Italians and Orientals who shop here for inexpensive clothing and household articles.

Next, turn left into Rivington Street, lined with shops, and then left again into Orchard Street, which is crammed with stores offering men's, women's and children's clothing, some bearing brand names which are sought out by bargain hunters. It leads to **Canal Street** long known for its jewelers and diamond merchants.

Mulberry Street. – Mulberry Street also known as Via San Gennaro is the Italian "Main Street" : colorful shops offer national specialities such as pasta, salami, artichokes, olives and cheese.

■ ADDITIONAL SIGHTS

At the corner of Mulberry and Prince Streets, **Old St. Patrick's Church** was the first Roman Catholic Cathedral of New York. The original building, which dated back to 1809, was designed by the French architect Mangin *(see p. 84)* ; although it burned down in 1866, a part of its Gothic façade still remains.

The present Roman Catholic Cathedral, St. Patrick's, is located on Fifth Avenue *(see p. 47)*.

SoHo. – Designated in 1973 as a historic district, SoHo (for south of Houston Street) is bounded by West Broadway, Broadway, East and West Houston, Crosby and Canal Streets. It was originally an area zoned specifically for light manufacturing. This district is important because of the cast iron front buildings, unique in architecture. The cast iron building usually has iron columns lining the building fronts a different row on each floor. Precursor of the modern skyscraper, the cast iron front allowed the exterior continuity on a larger scale than had been possible before.

Modern artists and sculptors, working on a grand scale proved the need for studio space, outwith Chelsea and Greenwich Village, where rents had become prohibitive. In the early 1960's artists began to move into the SoHo district, being attracted, by the spacious lofts in the commercial buildings. With the legalization of residence within SoHo the area has become a flourishing artists colony, and a center of art galleries. The combination of small manufacturing artists, shops, boutiques, restaurants and bars makes the area exciting. Saturday afternoon is the time to visit when the art scene is going full strength.

NEW YORK IS FOR CHILDREN

Museums : American Museum of Natural History ; Brooklyn Children's Museum ; Chinese Museum ; Fire Department Museum ; Hayden Planetarium ; Junior Museum at the Metropolitan Museum of Art ; The Long Island Automative Museum in Southampton ; Whaling Museum in Cold Spring Harbor.

Walks : Central Park ; Jamaica Bay Wildlife Refuge ; Old Bethpage Restoration in Long Island ; Richmond Restoration in Staten Island ; South Street Seaport ; Stony Brook in Long Island.

Views : Circle Line Tour around Manhattan ; Empire State Building ; World Trade Center.

Amusement : Coney Island ; Jones Beach in Long Island ; Montauk State Park in Long Island ; Robert Moses State Park on Fire Island ; Sunken Meadow in Long Island.

Zoos : Bronx Zoo ; New York Aquarium ; Staten Island Zoo.

*Distance : about 3/4 mile –
Time : 1 1/2 hours.*

Like other "immigrant" neighborhoods, "Chinatown", the Chinese quarter of New York has not escaped the twin processes of Americanization and assimilation. Although, an overall oriental atmosphere pervades.

Smaller than its San Francisco counterpart, New York's Chinatown occupies a compact area roughly bounded by Baxter Street, Canal Street, the Bowery and Chatham Square. Numbering 10,000 some years ago the Chinese community has expanded substantially.

When the Lights were Low. – The first subjects of the Celestial Empire settled in this area after the Civil War. Most of them were Cantonese. The community had already grown to a substantial size when the Chinese Exclusion Act of 1882 cut off further immigration.

Like the nearby Bowery, Chinatown was then an area rife with debauchery and vice, the scene of "tong wars" fought by rival "tongs" to win control over opium dens, gambling haunts and houses of ill fame. Accounts were settled with hatchets (hence "hatchetman") or revolvers; there were so many "shooting affairs" at the corner of Doyers and Pell Streets that it became known as "the bloody corner". After 1910, Chinatown settled down.

Visit. – You should stroll at random around Chinatown, a city within a city with its pagoda, schools, cultural center, post office, Bank of China and theaters where Chinese films and occasional operas are presented. The main streets are Mott, Bayard, and Pell. Try to visit Chinatown on a Sunday, when many "out-of-town" Chinese come to visit friends and relatives, stock up on native specialties, or arrange weddings and funerals. But Chinatown really comes to life with a bang on the Chinese New Year (the first full moon after January 21) ; it may not be as noisy as Hong Kong, but for no more than the price of a subway token you can watch the fire (cracker)-breathing dragons and lions winding their way through the illuminated streets accompanied by masked dancers, while the evil spirits are driven off by a display of fireworks.

Meandering slowly, ever alert, will allow the visitor to appreciate all the local color of the area ; the handsome Chinese children wearing typically American school sweat shirts or ski suits, depending on the season, may appear more exotic to some than did the venerable sages of yore with their wispy beards, silk kimonos and

(From photo Éd. Sun, Paris.)

Chinatown phone booth.

pigtails. Notice the pagoda-like telephone booths, the many colored signs with their exotic letters, the "tea-shops" and "lunch-counters" where one suspects the most authentic Chinese food is served, the apothecaries with their herbs and roots, the grocery stores with their unfamiliar vegetables and Chinese mushrooms looking like strange marine plants, the inevitable ducks strung up as if in a shooting gallery. A number of souvenir shops offer silks, fans, "Chinese" lanterns, toys, prints, and other artifacts, often made in Japan. Finally, an abundance of restaurants reminds you of the refinement of Chinese cuisine : while most offer fairly standard Cantonese dishes, regional specialities from Shanghai, Peking and Szechwan may be sought out by the more gastronomically inclined.

Chinese Museum. – *8 Mott Street. Open from 10 AM to 6 PM. 50 cents (75 cents on Sundays and holidays).*

A visit to this museum, devoted to Chinese customs and culture, can round out your visit to Chinatown. It is more interesting than the gimcrack souvenir gallery and amusement arcade attached to it would lead you to believe. In particular, you will see models of a Buddhist altar and a market, a collection of musical instruments, documents and objects relating to rice growing, incense, printing and arts. For an extra 25 cents, you may see the snorting and cavorting Chinese dragon, a fellow of the famous denizen which romps through the streets symbolizing the force of Nature on the Chinese New Year : 18 feet long, he weighs a ton and a half.

Chatham Square. – Dominated by a memorial to the Chinese-American war dead, it marks the eastern side of Chinatown. At No 18 Bowery is the Edward Mooney House, a brick Federal building dating from the Revolutionary period and housing betting office which takes bets in Chinese and English. At No 6 Bowery is the Olliffe Pharmacy, said to be the oldest pharmacy in the United States. Remnants of the oldest Jewish Cemetery (1656) can be seen to the south.

Distance : 3/4 mile − Time : about 3 1/2 hours.

Located at the end of Brooklyn Bridge, the **Civic Center** is named for the main municipal administration buildings, grouped around **City Hall** and forms a breathing space downtown.

■ CIVIC CENTER★

Start from **Foley Square** which was once the location of The Collect, a large pond where John Fitch tried out his first miniature steamboat in 1796. It was drained and filled in 1811 when the canal was dug, giving its name to the present **Canal Street.**

Today, Foley Square is an administrative and judicial center, just north of City Hall. If you stand in the middle of the Square, you can pick out the different buildings. We cite the principal ones in counterclockwise order :

− Municipal Building, on the northeast corner of City Hall Park ; 40 stories high, this building, which dates from 1914, contains many city offices, including the marriage license bureau and the Municipal Reference Library. East of Center Street, Chamber Street, which runs under the center of the building through a series of arcades, has been repaved for pedestrians and extends on an overpass or plaza to the new police headquarters.

− United States Court House, seat of the Federal District Court, is a curious architectural mixture with a Corinthian façade and a modern style tower, crowned with gold leaf.

− New York County Court House, a neoclassic monument with a colonnade. The interior is imposing ; notice the rich polychrome marble floor, with copper medallions representing the signs of the zodiac.

− The 1966 Federal Office Building houses the United States Customs Court.

− The Hall of Records, home of the city archives which go back to 1643.

Walk south to City Hall.

City Hall★★. − Surrounded by a pleasant park, this handsome building with its pure lines is unfortunately somewhat dwarfed by the height of neighboring buildings. It contains the office of the Mayor and the City Council room.

The "New" City Hall. − The present building is the third New York City Hall. The Dutch established their "Stadhuis" in 1653 in a former tavern on Pearl Street (their city council comprised two burgomasters, a public attorney and five magistrates). During the eighteenth century, the English City Hall was at the corner of Wall and Broad Streets (the present site of the Federal Hall National Memorial, *see p. 91*).

Today's City Hall was built between 1803 and 1812. Its construction cost about half a million dollars. The French architect **Joseph F. Mangin** won the competition for its design, and a prize of $350. Mangin had emigrated at the time of the French Revolution, and started as an engineer for the fortifications of New York ; then, in 1795, he became city surveyor and published a map in 1803. He was assisted in the design of City Hall by the Scottish architect and decorator, John J. McComb, Jr.

(From engraving, photo City of New York.)

City Hall, early 19th century.

Solemnly inaugurated on May 15, 1812, City Hall has been the scene of many memorable events. In 1824 Lafayette was officially entertained here during his triumphal American tour. The first parades up Broadway for visiting dignitaries began at that time.

In the middle of the night of April 9, 1865, City Hall learned of Lee's surrender at Appomattox, and the next day the city was draped with flags. The gaiety was brief, for less than a week later, **Lincoln's** assassination caused general consternation. Lincoln's body lay in state at City Hall, where 120,000 grief-stricken New Yorkers filed past. Then, on April 25, the hearse, pulled by 16 black horses, proceeded slowly up Broadway to the Hudson River Railroad where the coffin was placed in a special train for Springfield, Illinois.

The 1860's witnessed less solemn and dignified proceedings at City Hall and nearby Tammany Hall (at the corner of Park Row and Frankfort Street). The Tammany political machine, founded by Aaron Burr at the beginning of the century, flourished under the leadership of "Boss" William M. Tweed. Their fierce tiger-head emblem came from one painted on the *Americus,* a fire engine, for Tweed rose to power from the ranks of the volunteer firemen. The pendulum swung against him during the 1870's ; discontented city officials, aided by the incisive cartoons of Thomas Nast, brought about his downfall and imprisonment. Tammany Hall, however, remained a powerful force in New York politics for many decades.

City Hall was restored in 1956 (at a cost of about $2,000,000) and recently redecorated. It remains the focus of welcoming ceremonies for visiting VIP's and the start of the ticker tape parades in which the hero of the day is deluged with tons of paper shreds : ticker tapes, torn up telephone books and whatever else is handy.

The Building. − *Open Monday through Saturday 10 AM to 3 PM.* The building was constructed of white Massachusetts marble, replaced by Alabama limestone, on brownstone − now Minnesota granite − foundations.

The architecture is balanced and dignified, in the French tradition of the Louis XVI style.

Majestic steps lead to the vestibule. Here rises a magnificent double stairway with a fine wrought iron railing. The stairway ascends to the City Hall Museum, comprising the **Governor's Rooms** and the Board of Estimate Room, which is also used by the City Council. The Governor's Rooms contain the original early 19th century furniture and decoration.

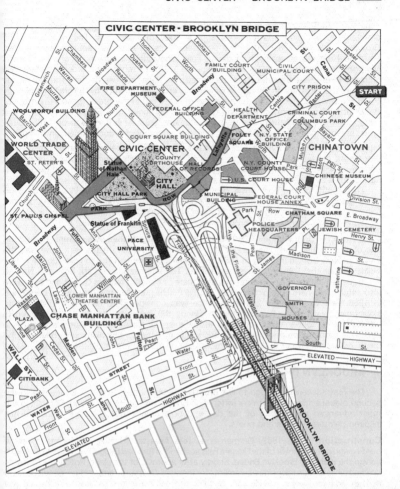

Side doors display civic symbols and there are portraits by John Trumbull of Alexander Hamilton, John Jay and De Witt Clinton. Notice the large mahogany desk where Washington drafted his first message to Congress. The desk reminds us that New York was briefly the capital of the United States in 1789. Washington's first "White House" was nearby at 1-3 Cherry Street, now covered by the Brooklyn Bridge pier.

The Park. – At the time of the Revolution, this area was a commons, planted with apple trees.

A patriotic group, the Sons of Liberty erected a series of Liberty poles on the Commons prior to the Revolution. Here, in July 1776, the Declaration of Independence was read solemnly in the presence of Washington, his troops and patriots. A crowd then surged down to Bowling Green to attack the statue of the King *(see p. 90)*.

When the English returned a few weeks later, the scene changed and the apple trees were converted into gallows. A statue, erected on the Broadway side of City Hall Park, commemorates one of the heroes of this period, **Nathan Hale**, a captain of 21, hanged for having spied on the English in the costume of a schoolmaster. His last words "I regret that I have but one life to lose for my country" have thus entered American History.

A statue of Horace Greeley and a plaque to Joseph Pulitzer are reminders that this was once the center of newspaper publishing in New York.

Pass in front of City Hall and turn left into Broadway.

Woolworth Building*. – *233 Broadway*. President Wilson opened the building in an original fashion on April 24, 1913 : sitting in his office in the White House, he merely pushed a button and 86,000 bulbs lighted up the highest skyscraper in the world at that time.

The imposing Woolworth Building, designed by Cass Gilbert, held the record for height until 1931, when the Chrysler and Empire State Buildings *(see pp. 69 and 44 respectively)* were completed. Enter the huge lobby ; notice the golden mosaics and carved caricatures of Woolworth and Gilbert, among others.

St. Paul's Chapel*. – A dependency of Trinity Parish, this grey stone chapel with a reddish tint is the oldest church building in Manhattan. It was built between 1764 and 1766 on a rectangular plan by the Scottish architect Thomas McBean, who was probably inspired by St. Martin in the Fields, in London. The spire and portico were built in 1794. At that time, Major Pierre L'Enfant, who later planned the layout of Washington, D.C., supervised the remodelling.

In this chapel took place the ceremony following Washington's first Inaugural *(see p. 91)*.

Exterior. – St. Paul's, surrounded by its old **cemetery**, is not only a rare example of colonial architecture, but also a picturesque spot in modern New York. The façade, on the Broadway side has a portico with a pediment. This gives it the appearance of a main entrance. Here, placed against a handsome Palladian window, is a memorial of Major General Montgomery, who fell in the Battle of Quebec in 1775. The monument, ordered by Benjamin Franklin in Paris, is the work of the French sculptor, Jean-Jacques Caffieri. The real façade overlooks the cemetery on the Church Street side, and is surmounted by the graceful spire.

In the peaceful cemetery, tombstones are scattered in the green grass. A number of British officers who attended services at St. Paul's are buried here. But near the Church and Fulton Street corner of the cemetery is a monument to **Béchet de Rochefontaine** (1755-1814), who served during the Revolution, and became a symbol of Franco-American friendship.

Interior. – Intimate and yet sparkling, the chapel, with its pastel walls and cream-colored woodwork contains fine Corinthian columns, symmetrically aligned wooden pews and benches, 14 Waterford crystal chandeliers (installed in 1802) and a cream and gold pulpit, surmounted by a gilded three-plumed crest and coronet.

To the left, on the north aisle, is the pew occupied by President Washington, who worshipped here after his election in 1789 ; on the south aisle you can recognize Governor Clinton's pew, with the arms of the state of New York painted on the wall behind.

St. Paul's Chapel : musical program at 12 : 10 PM every Thursday.

Park Row. – On the edge of City Park, Park Row was a fashionable promenade and the site of the popular Park Theater. By the 1850's and until the 1920's Park Row was the center of New York journalism. In 1887, the *Evening Sun* moved into the old Tammany Hall building, near the Tribune, Times, and World. The intersection of Park Row and Nassau Street became known as "Printing-House Square" : the print makers Currier and Ives were also established here. The old **New York Tribune Building** recalled this era until its demolition in 1966. Built in 1874, the 250-foot edifice was considered to be the first Manhattan skyscraper. Near the statue of Franklin stands the imposing façade of **Pace University** adorned by a cooper-relief sculpture. Inside this, the Civic Center Campus, there is a Japanese garden with pools and futuristic sculpture : the curving aluminum sheets of one piece, reflect the water and give an impression of moving metal.

■ BROOKLYN BRIDGE★★

The first suspension bridge to link Brooklyn to Manhattan, Brooklyn Bridge is also the second oldest bridge in New York (after High Bridge, on the Harlem River). Combining the most advanced engineering of the day and bold architecture, its dark silhouette has inspired painters, writers and poets.

Construction. – In 1869, German-born **John Augustus Roebling**, a pioneer in bridge building and chief engineer of the Niagara Falls suspended Railroad Bridge, was commissioned to design the plans for Brooklyn Bridge. Shortly after approval of the plans, Roebling's foot was crushed while he was taking measurements for the piers. Despite an amputation, gangrene set in and he died three weeks later. His son, Washington Roebling, carried on his work, adopting new methods in pneumatic foundations which he had studied in Europe.

To construct the foundations, workers used caissons immersed and filled with compressed air to prevent water from infiltrating. In order to adapt to the air pressure, the men had to undergo periods of gradual compression before going down to work, and decompression afterward. Despite these precautions, a few had burst eardrums or developed the « bends » which cause convulsions and can bring on partial or total paralysis. Washington Roebling himself was stricken with the "caisson disease" ; confined to his sickbed he continued to direct the operation from his window overlooking the bridge. Finished in 1883, the bridge cost $25,000,000.

History and Legend. – Brooklyn Bridge immediately became the busy thoroughfare its planners had foreseen. 150,000 people crossed the bridge on opening day. On sunny days, strollers enjoyed the one-mile walk along the pedestrian path. However, less than a week after inauguration by President Arthur, tragedy struck. A woman fell on the stairway ; her screams set off a panic killing 12 persons and injuring many more. Monumental and awe-inspiring, Brooklyn Bridge has fascinated, obsessed and haunted New Yorkers. Some people felt compelled to jump from the bridge, not all of them in despair. A character named Steve Brody who purportedly jumped off Brooklyn Bridge without harm, gained fame as an actor on Broadway.

Since the end of the 19th century, the bridge has provided an opportunity for confidencemen to fleece strangers to the city, by extorting exorbitant "tolls" (the original toll, now abolished, was one cent for pedestrians) or actually "selling" the Brooklyn Bridge to the gullible.

Characteristics. – The bridge, including its approaches, has a length of 6,775 feet with a central span of 1,595 feet ; the suspended section measures 3,450 feet in length and 85 feet in width. The vertical clearance above water is 133 feet. Two massive masonry towers, 272 feet high, serve to support the four huge cables. Each of these main cables, 15-3/4 inch in diameter, is composed of 5,700 wires.

Visit. – The best view of Brooklyn Bridge is obtained from the East River *(see p. 16)* but a stroll along the elevated pedestrian path is not without interest.

The bracing air, the tumult of the traffic below, the network of huge cables crisscrossing in all directions create a sense of unreality.

You can reach the bridge by taking the subway to High Street - Brooklyn Bridge.

Admire the superb **view**★★ of Manhattan, the skyscrapers of Wall Street or midtown, the Statue of Liberty and on the horizon, the Verrazano-Narrows Bridge. The sight is spectacular at nightfall as the city lights go on.

Distance : 1 1/4 miles — Time : about 4 1/2 hours (visits not included).

Gigantic skyscrapers, as close together as trees in a forest, are typical of the Financial District, feverishly busy during the week and deserted on weekends. Along with Broad Street, Wall Street is the most famous : its name symbolizes the financial power of the United States.

It is best to visit in the morning during the week.

A BIT OF HISTORY

New York's Dutch Days. — The general area we now call the Financial District was the center of Dutch power in the middle of the 17th century, when the town was still called Nieuw Amsterdam. The Dutch town occupied a limited area, protected to the south by a fort and to the north by a wooden wall (the origin of the name of Wall Street) from the Hudson to the East River.

About 1,000 persons occupied the 120 houses made of wood or brick, with characteristic Dutch gables and tile roofs. The windmill and a canal, "The Ditch", in the middle of Broad Street, made the town seem really Dutch. At the end of "The Ditch" on the East River where plumed Indians paddled their canoes, sailing ships anchored, sheltered by the tip of Manhattan. There was already a ferry between Nieuw Amsterdam and "Longe Eyelandt".

The inhabitants were of varied origins : in 1642, when the first Stadhuis (became City Hall in 1653) was buit at 71 Pearl Street, Nieuw Amsterdamers reportedly spoke no less than 18 languages.

Governing them all was first a commercial agent of the Company, and later a succession of governors. The most famous, Peter Stuyvesant *(see p. 81)* founded the noble body of chimney inspectors in 1648. Fires then, as now, were a constant concern of the municipal authorities.

Under the Cross of St. George. — When the British occupied Nieuw Amsterdam in 1664, the town changed very little. Pigs still roamed the muddy streets, haphazardly solving the garbage problem and occasionally biting passersby. But Breetweg became Broadway, the Ditch was filled in, the wall was torn down and, from the beginning of the 18th century, colonial Georgian houses *(see p. 28)* like Fraunces Tavern began to replace the narrow Dutch ones.

The press had its difficulties. Eight years after William Bradford founded the first New York newspaper, the *Gazette,* another printer, **John Peter Zenger,** started the New York *Weekly Journal* (in 1733), in which he attacked the Governor. The furious official had the offensive numbers burned by the sheriff's men in the middle of Wall Street, and Zenger was thrown into prison, where he languished for a year, still managing to publish his newspaper. Finally, the trial began at the colonial City Hall (at the site of the present **Federal Hall National Memorial**) : brilliantly defended by Andrew Hamilton, Zenger was acquitted. Fifty years before England, New York was well on the way to achieving a free press.

The Blacks, Africans or West Indians increased in numbers, forming a fifth of New York's population by the middle of the 18th century. A number of freed slaves settled at the end of Wall Street, near the slave market.

Two fires, in 1776 and 1835, devastated the area, without affecting its role in finance.

VISIT

■ THE WORLD TRADE CENTER★★★

The World Trade Center occupies a 16-acre site near the Hudson River. The idea of such a trade center was proposed in 1960 and legislation was passed in 1962 authorizing the Port Authority to realize such a project.

Plans were drawn up by the architects Minoru Yamasaki and Associates and Emery Roth and Sons ; construction started in August 1966. The first tenants of this great project opened their offices in late 1970 and it is estimated that 50,000 people will work here and a further 80,000 businessmen and other visitors will come to the center daily.

The role of the Trade Center is the advancement and expansion of international trade and it has already been called a "United Nations of Commerce". All international business services are concentrated here — exporters, importers, American and overseas manufacturers, freight forwarders, Custom House brokers, international banks, federal, state and overseas trade development agencies, trade associations and transportation lines — making this the central market of international trade.

THE BUILDINGS

The complex includes two 110-story high buildings, twin towers (1 and 2 WTC), a U.S. Customhouse (6 WTC), two plaza buildings (4 and 5 WTC) and an international hotel (3 WTC *completion late in 1979),* all surrounding a landscaped plaza. Featured also in the 6 subterranean levels are a new PATH (Port Authority Trans-Hudson) railroad terminal, parking for 2,000 cars, truck dock, storage areas, access to the New York subways (the BMT, IRT and IND lines) and 8 acres of shops and services on the concourse.

The Plaza. — This spacious five-acre plaza links the various buildings of the center and interconnects with other pedestrian systems in the area. Focal point of the plaza is the slowly revolving huge bronze sculptured globe by the German Fritz Koenig which is placed in the fountain-pool.

Plaza Buildings (4,5). – These two 9-story buildings flanking the main entrance in Church Street, serve as offices for the New York Cotton Exchange, the New York Coffee and Sugar Exchange, the Commodity Exchange and the Mercantile Exchange as well as product display areas, enabling world trade firms to show products to potential customers. *The visitors gallery is open 9:30AM to 4PM weekdays.*

U.S. Customhouse (6). – Bordering the northwest corner of the site this 8-story building consolidates all intricate customs functions relating to the movement of commerce in and out of the port, in one convenient location.

In the lobby there are changing exhibits related to the U.S. Customs Service. *Open 8:30 AM to 4PM Mondays through Fridays.*

Twin Towers (1, 2). – These two 110-story tower buildings, the second tallest buildings in the world after the Sears Roebuck Building in Chicago, soar upwards to 1,350 feet to add a new landmark, to the Manhattan skyline. The problem of laying foundations in wet landfill terrain without disrupting existing communications and surrounding buildings was solved by using the "slurry wall" foundation system, whereby an underground concrete wall was built around the site. With the wall in place, excavation work could start within this "bath tub" area, without danger of subsidence due to water pumping. The excavated material was used to create 23 acres of infilled land for the Battery Park City.

The conventional skyscraper is built with a maze of interior columns. In the towers, a new structural design was used, in which the exterior walls bear most of the load, providing the maximum of open column-free floor space. These outer walls consist of closely spaced vertical columns of steel, tied together by massive horizontal spandrel beams which girdle the towers at every floor. The columns are covered with a thin skin of aluminum, and separated by tinted floor to ceiling windows recessed 10 inches.

The introduction of the "skylobby" system minimizes the floor space occupied by elevator shaftways. Each building is divided into 3 zones : 1 – 43rd ; 44 – 77 ; 78 to 110th. The 44th and 78th are the skylobbies which are connected to the main ground floor lobby by large express elevators, traveling at 1,600 feet. per minute. A battery of local elevators then serves all floors within each zone. There are therefore three "locals" operating in each shaft.

One World Trade Center or north tower contains several of the special services offered by the Trade Center. In the lobby **Information Center** is **Interfile**, this is the first automated library of world trade information sources, designed to handle practical questions on international trade and commerce. The **Electronic Yellow Pages Service** is a constantly updated guide to the location and services of World Trade Center tenant firms. The **World Trade Institute** *(55th floor)* offers pratical courses in all aspects of world trade, as well as modern conference facilities.

Numerous public restaurants, buffets, bars and snack shops can be found in this complex : Windows on the World *(107th floor)*, a restaurant situated in One World Trade Center and snack-cafeteria facilities on the Observation Deck of Two World Trade Center, which is a glass enclosed deck *(107th floor)* offering a breathtaking **panorama**★★★ of the entire New York Metropolitan area. Take an escalator up to the 110th floor *(weather permitting)* – a quarter of a mile in the sky – to the rooftop "promenade". *(Open 9:30AM to 9:30 PM. Adults $1.70 ; children 85 cents.*

Return to Church Street before turning left into Cortlandt Street, which is overlooked by the striking building at One Liberty Plaza.

From Liberty Plaza to Hanover Square

One Liberty Plaza. – This 54-story building of dark blue-grey painted steel and tinted grey windows contains the headquarters of Merrill Lynch, one of the worlds' largest securities companies.

The surrounding plaza and Liberty Park to the south of Liberty Street, form an important link in the pedestrian system reaching from the World Trade Center eastward to the financial district.

An **Investment Information Center** *(main floor : entrance 165 Broadway ; open Monday through Friday 9AM to 5PM)* provides visitors with a wealth of information on securities, markets and the economy. **The Money Tree** exhibit explains the money flow in the United States.

Trinity Church★. – On Broadway, at the beginning of Wall Street, stands **Trinity Church**, now dwarfed by the surrounding buildings, but the highest building in New York for nearly 50 years. Around the church is a cemetery where a number of famous New Yorkers are buried.

The first Anglican Parish of New York. – An Episcopal church, Trinity was founded by a charter granted by William III in 1697. Influential local citizens aided in its construction. Among them was **Captain Kidd**, the famous pirate-privateer, who lived at nearby Hanover Square, and who was hanged for piracy in London in 1701.

The first church building looked like a country chapel with a spire and narrow spearshaped windows. In 1754, King's College, which was to become Columbia University *(see p. 107)*, occupied a schoolhouse next door to the church.

This first building burned in the great fire of 1776 and was replaced by another, whose roof collapsed in 1830. The present building was finished in 1846, except for part of the choir (1877), All Saints Chapel (1913) and the Bishop Manning Memorial Wing (1966).

Before the Revolution, Trinity was one of New York's most fashionable parishes.

The Church. – The most interesting part of the exterior is the bell tower (the bells date back to 1797) with its 280-foot spire, which towered above the nearby houses when it was built. Handsome bronze doors, inspired by those of the Baptistry at Florence, lead to the interior. To the left of the entrance is a model of the original church. Notice the highly colored stained glass windows, the white marble altar erected in 1877 and the wooden screen of the Chapel of All Saints (1913), at the right of the choir.

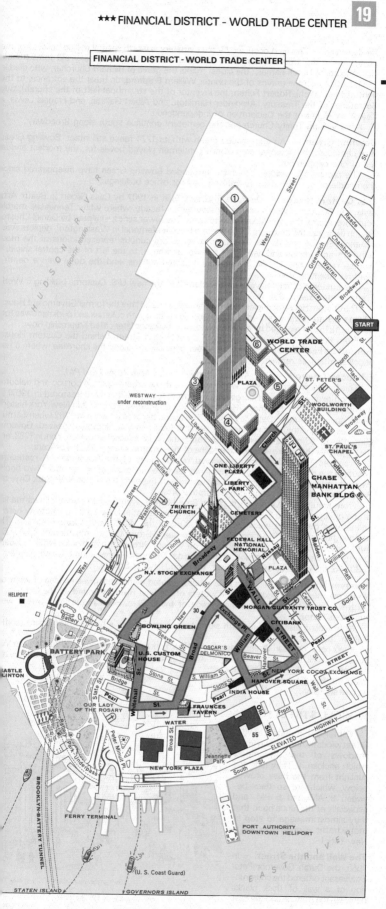

FINANCIAL DISTRICT - WORLD TRADE CENTER

HUDSON RIVER

Street

Reade St.

Chambers St.

Greenwich

Warren St.

Park Pl.

Murray St.

Broadway

Barclay St.

West St.

START

WORLD TRADE CENTER ⑥

Church St.

St.

St. PETER'S

WESTWAY under reconstruction

PLAZA

⑤

③

④

WOOLWORTH BUILDING

Liberty St.

Albany St.

Carlisle St.

Church St.

Ann St.

ST. PAUL'S CHAPEL

Fulton St.

ONE LIBERTY PLAZA

LIBERTY PARK

CHASE MANHATTAN BANK BLDG

Washington St.

Greenwich St.

Rector St.

TRINITY CHURCH

CEMETERY

Nassau St.

Maiden Lane

William St.

Platt St.

FEDERAL HALL NATIONAL MEMORIAL

PLAZA

Pine St.

Cedar St.

Gold St.

N.Y. STOCK EXCHANGE

West St.

Battery Pl.

HELIPORT

Broadway

New St.

30

Exchange Pl.

WALL STREET

MORGAN GUARANTY TRUST CO.

CITIBANK

Pine St.

Pearl St.

Gold St.

BOWLING GREEN

Beaver St.

OSCAR'S DELMONICO

William St.

Hanover St.

NEW YORK COCOA EXCHANGE

STREET

BATTERY PARK

U.S. CUSTOM HOUSE

State St.

Stone St.

S. William St.

Beaver St.

HANOVER SQUARE

Bridge St.

Stone St.

Pearl St.

INDIA HOUSE

ASTLE LINTON

OUR LADY OF THE ROSARY

Whitehall St.

Pearl St.

FRAUNCES TAVERN

WATER

Front St.

Broad St.

55

Pearl St.

NEW YORK PLAZA

Peter Minuit Pl.

Jeannette Park

South St.

ELEVATED HIGHWAY

Slip

Battery Park Underpass

BROOKLYN-BATTERY TUNNEL

FERRY TERMINAL

PORT AUTHORITY DOWNTOWN HELIPORT

(U.S. Coast Guard)

STATEN ISLAND

GOVERNORS ISLAND

EAST RIVER

The Cemetery. — This land occupied by the cemetery is worth several million dollars, for the going rate in the area is about $600 per square foot. There are many old tombstones including some Dutch names : the oldest marks the grave of Richard Churcher, who died in 1681. Notice also the graves of the printer William Bradford, Jr. (near the entrance, to the right of the church), Robert Fulton, the inventor of the steamboat (left of the church), two Secretaries of the Treasury, Alexander Hamilton, and Albert Gallatin, and Francis Lewis, a New York signer of the Declaration of Independence.

After visiting Trinity Church and the cemetery continue south along Broadway.

Bowling Green. — An egg-shaped green with its 1771 fence still intact, Bowling Green was named for the lawn where colonial gentlemen played bowls for, the modest annual fee of one peppercorn.

The prosperous residences which surrounded Bowling Green have disappeared since the middle of the 19th century, making way for office buildings.

U.S. Custom House. — *On Bowling Green.* Built in 1907 by Cass Gilbert in Beaux Arts style, the Custom House presents a monumental façade, where white Tennessee marble sculpture adorns the grey Maine granite walls. The lower series, sculpted by Daniel Chester French (who did the statue of Lincoln in the Lincoln Memorial in Washington), depicts Asia, America, Europe and Africa. The statues above are curious representations of the most famous trading cities and nations of the world : notice, to the left of the central shield, a woman representing Lisbon, by Augustus Saint-Gaudens, and the doge with a death's head representing Venice.

The customs offices have been transferred to the new U.S. Customs building 6 World Trade Center (see p. 88).

The Custom House occupies the site of an early fort and later the former Government House where the state governors resided : this majestic building with columns and pediment was torn down in 1815 and replaced by a row of handsome buildings later called Steamship Row.

From Bowling Green, continue south on Whitehall Street, behind the Custom House. Turn left on Pearl Street. This very old street originally ran along the shoreline, where a few neoclassic houses remain.

Fraunces Tavern★. — *Open Monday through Friday from 10 AM to 4 PM.*

This handsome brick house, with its slate roof and cream-colored portico and balcony, is a good example of neo-Georgian architecture. It was built in 1719 (restored in 1907) as the home of Etienne de Lancey. He was the first of a family prominent in New York history, which gave its name to Delancey Street. The house became a tavern in 1762 when Samuel Fraunces bought the building. He later became President Washington's steward. Governor Clinton (see p. 93) gave a dinner here, celebrating the British evacuation of New York in 1783, and the same year the tavern was also the scene of Washington's farewell to his officers.

Fraunces Tavern has been preserved by the Sons of the Revolution. A restaurant occupies the main floor. A wooden stairway leads to the museum on the upper two floors where permanent and changing exhibitions reflect the early history of New York City, the Revolutionary War and American decorative arts.

From Fraunces Tavern walk north on Broad Street, whose slight curve follows the line of the old canal. Broad Street used to be the main street in New York ; the activity here is still intense during the week. At number 30 was the *Wall Street Journal* building. The famous financial daily now located at 22 Cortlandt Street has a circulation of 1,500,000. Turn right on Exchange Place, and again on William Street for two blocks. Notice Oscar Delmonico, the modern version of the original Delmonico's restaurant which opened in 1830. Continue one block to the east, to reach Hanover Square.

Hanover Square. — This quiet little square, planted with trees, gives an idea of what old New York must have been like. The waters of the East River extended up the Old Slip, to lap the foundations of the southeast side of the Square. Here and in Pearl Street were numerous shops.

Note **India House**, on the south side of Hanover Square, a handsome classical edifice built in 1837.

Walk north on Pearl Street, passing the New York Cocoa Exchange, and turn left on Wall Street : you will be struck by the **view★★★** of the celebrated "canyon", which ends with the tiny dark silhouette of Trinity Church (see p. 88). Pearl Street follows the original shoreline.

■ **WALL STREET★★**

Center of high finance, Wall Street winds its narrow way in the shadows of the skyscrapers which enclose it. They hide the sunlight from the busy crowds below, which are so thick between 9 AM and 5 PM, and especially at the lunch hour, that they almost manage to stop all motor traffic – quite an exploit in New York !

The Wall and the Street. — In 1653, the Dutch Governor Peter Stuyvesant ordered the construction of a wall of thick planks between the Hudson and the East

(From engraving, Museum of City of New York)

Wall Street, early 19th century.

River to protect the town from marauding Indians. In fact, the protection was rather symbolic, since the inhabitants regularly dismantled the wall, taking the planks to shore up their houses or even to heat their homes.

Completely dismantled by the English in 1699, the wall was replaced by a new street, where the new City Hall was built on the corner of Broad Street. Wall Street became an administrative and residential street, with rows of wealthy homes ornamented with Georgian pilasters and porticoes.

After the Revolution, the east end of the street harbored a series of coffee warehouses and taverns. One of the most famous was the **Tontine Coffee House**, built in 1792 at the corner of Water Street ; it was the first home of the New York Stock Exchange.

Business takes over. – In the 1840's merchants, warehouses, stores and banks occupied buildings rapidly reconstructed after the 1835 fire, which destroyed 700 houses in the area.

But speculation flourished, especially after 1860. Thus **Jay Gould** (1836-1892) tried to corner the gold market with an associate, James Fisk ; when Fisk left him to work on his own, Gould sold out and brought about the financial panic of September 24, 1869, "Black Friday".

The father of 13 children, **Cornelius Vanderbilt** 1794-1877) was nicknamed "Commodore" because he was first interested in shipping. Beginning in 1862, he extended his activities to the railroads. First the owner of small lines (the Harlem, Hudson, and New York Central), in 1873 he launched the New York – Buffalo line.

J. Pierpont Morgan (1837-1913), a banker, financed the great new industries : steel, oil and railroads. Generous, but a ruthless businessman, the founder of the famous Morgan Library *(see p. 73)* was succeeded by his son John Pierpont Morgan, Jr., who was the target of an assassination attempt in 1920 ; on September 16, a bomb exploded in a cart near the bank, missing Morgan, Jr. but killing 38 innocent people caught in the noonday rush.

(From photo Andreas Feininger, New York.)

Wall Street today.

It replaced London as the world financial center, and has maintained this position despite the crash of 1929.

VISIT

From the intersection of Wall and Pearl Streets, continue toward Trinity Church. William Street on the right leads to the Chase Manhattan Bank *(see p. 92)*.

Citibank. – This financial establishment, dating from 1812, succeeded the first bank founded in New York by Alexander Hamilton ten years earlier. Its Wall Street branch occupies a massive building with a double colonnade.

Continuing west, you arrive at the intersection of Wall and Nassau Streets, with the Federal Hall National Memorial to the northeast, the Morgan Guaranty Trust Company to the southeast, and the New York Stock Exchange to the southwest.

Federal Hall National Memorial★. – Administered by the National Park Service, built of Massachusetts marble, reminiscent of a Doric temple, the Federal Hall Memorial occupies the site of one of the most important buildings in old New York. It was originally New York's City Hall and was later (in 1788) remodeled to serve as Federal Hall, the country's first capitol.

The first English City Hall was built in 1699 on land donated by Abraham de Peyster, and in 1703 the city government moved in. In front of it were placed the pillory where minor offenders were exposed to public derision, and the stake to which they were bound or flogging. The first City Hall also served as a courthouse and a debtor's prison. It was here in 1735 that John Peter Zenger was tried and acquitted of seditious libel *(see p. 87)*. The Stamp Act Congress met in the same place 30 years later to oppose English colonial policy.

Reconstructed in 1788-1789 under the supervision of **Major Charles Pierre L'Enfant**, the French engineer who designed the master plan of Washington, D.C., the building became Federal Hall, the first capitol of the United States under the Constitution. George Washington took the oath of office as the first President on the balcony of Federal Hall on April 30, 1789. The towering statue of Washington commemorates this event. The Federal government was transferred to Philadelphia the following year, and the building was used for state and city offices, to be sold for salvage in 1812 for $425.

The present building dates from 1842, and served as the New York City Custom House until 1862, when it became the United States Subtreasury. Later the site of a number of government offices, it was designated as an Historic Site in 1939, and a National Monument in 1955.

The **interior** *(open from 9 AM to 4:30 PM)* is arranged around a large dome resting on sixteen marble columns : mementoes of Zenger and Washington are displayed and there is also an exhibit on the Bill of Rights and freedom of expression .

Morgan Guaranty Trust Company. – The marble building which sheltered J. Pierpont Morgan and his fortune still shows the traces of the explosion of 1920. A huge crystal chandelier is visible through the ground floor windows of the 23 Wall Street building.

New York Stock Exchange★. – The façade, with its Corinthian columns and sculpted figures on the pediment symbolizing Commerce, is on the Broad Street side of the building. In front of the entrance, a tree recalls the buttonwood trée at Wall and William Streets where 24 brokers met to found the forerunner of the New York Stock Exchange in 1792. The traders dealt in stocks and bonds issued by the government and a few private companies ; a handshake or a tap on the shoulder sealed a bargain.

Today 1,366 Exchange members trade the shares of more than 1,500 leading companies which are listed on the Stock Exchange. These companies are the leaders of American industry and include virtually all of the automobile industry, 90 % of the steel industry and more than 80 % of the electricity producers. One American in eight is a shareholder.

The present seven-story **building** dates from 1903. *On the ground floor is the actual exchange where trading takes place from 10 AM to 4 PM. The public may visit the second floor exhibits, which show the history of the Stock Exchange, attend lectures or films explaining the workings of the Stock Market and the financial organization of companies listed. Open Monday through Friday 10 AM to 4 PM. Closed public holidays.*

The visitor's gallery at 20 Broad Street overlooks an apparently chaotic agitation ; receptionists explain some of the rules of the game.

Continue west along Wall Street, returning to Trinity Church.

■ CHASE MANHATTAN BANK BUILDING★★

Born of the merger between the Chase National Bank and the Bank of the Manhattan Company, the Chase Manhattan Bank has occupied, since 1961, a prestige building with a high shiny rectangular silhouette.

The Manhattan Company : from dolors to dollars. – In 1798, a yellow fever epidemic broke out in New York. The inhabitants (55,000 at that time) attributed it to polluted water. The following year, the Manhattan Company was founded to provide and distribute drinking water to the city. They laid down a network of hollow pine log pipes which still come to light occasionally during excavations.

At the same time, the Manhattan Company, with the encouragement of one of its founders, **Aaron Burr**, decided to expand its activities to the realm of banking and finance, a possibility included in the original charter of the Company granted by the State of New York. Thus, on September 1, 1799, the Manhattan Company opened its first office of discount and deposit. The extension of its activities was a serious blow to the outside financial interests of another founder, **Alexander Hamilton**, who was interested in the two banks then operating in New York. These financial differences were reinforced by political animosity, and Burr finally challenged Hamilton to the fatal duel of July 11, 1804.

The Chase National Bank : Salmon P. Chase, father of the modern banking system. – The Chase Bank was founded in 1877 by John Thompson and his son, who named it in honor of Salmon P. Chase (1808-1873). Chase, U.S. Senator and Governor of Ohio, was later Lincoln's Secretary of the Treasury and Chief Justice of the U.S. Supreme Court. He drafted a bill which was enacted by the Congress as the National Currency Act of 1863, establishing a national currency and the present Federal banking system. The portrait of Chase appears on the largest bill in circulation ($10,000).

THE BUILDING

Construction. – Originally, the Chase Manhattan Bank acquired a tract of land which was large, but unfortunately cut in two by a street. This problem was solved when the bank arranged to become owner of that part of the street by purchase and exchange with the city. On this land, the most expensive in the world, the Bank decided to build just one high-rise building, leaving two and a half acres of esplanade. Note Dubuffet's striking sculpture *Group of Four Trees* on the plaza.

Constructed of glass and aluminum on a steel frame, the building was completed less than five years.

A few figures. – One of the largest office buildings constructed in the last 30 years, the Chase Manhattan building is 813 feet high and contains 65 stories (including 5 below street level) and 8800 windows. About 15,000 people work there, half for the bank itself, which occupies the five basement floors (90 feet of foundations), the first 35 stories and the top floor ; the rest is rented to other firms. The interior telephone system links 6000 extensions.

Concourse. – To the left of the lobby, the Plaza Banking Office is curved around the Japanese water garden, where fountains play in the summer.

Bank vault. – Located in the fifth basement, it is reputed to be the world's largest : longer than a football field, it weighs 985 tons and has 6 doors, each 20 inches thick (four of them weigh 45 tons a piece and the other two 30 tons). This vault holds $43,000,000,000 in securities and the paltry sum of $3,000,000 or $4,000,000 in cash for current needs.

NEW YORK'S HISTORIC HOUSES

Distance : about 1 mile – Time : 2 1/4 hours (not including visit to the Statue of Liberty).

Battery Park, at the southern tip of Manhattan, and the Statue of Liberty, on Liberty Island, are among New York's favorite excursions. Here, visitors may enjoy one of the finest panoramas in the world.

A BIT OF HISTORY

The *Dauphine* had sailed from Rouen in May 1523 with three other ships to discover the legendary passage to India and at the same time to trade with the natives. Small and stubby, the modest fourmaster weighing about 100 tons was named in honor of the Dauphin, son of Francis I, born in 1518. The hazards of navigation caused the loss of her companion ships. After long delays en route, the *Dauphine* finally sighted the coast of Florida and headed north. In April 1524 the anchor was dropped near the island of Manhattan.

The fifty-man crew was commanded by Antoine de Conflans but the real head of the expedition was the pilot, **Giovanni da Verrazano**, a Florentine merchant who served France. Returning to Dieppe on July 8, 1524, Verrazano addressed a report to the French king ; four copies of this report still exist, one of them annotated in Verrazano's hand. He was to perish four years later on a voyage to the Caribbean, a victim of cannibals.

(From engraving, photo The French Book Guild, New York.)

Verrazano.

Today, a statue and the giant bridge which was opened in 1965 *(see p. 129)* commemorate the first recorded sighting of New York and its harbor, 85 years before Hudson's exploration.

■ BATTERY PARK★★

At the southern tip of Manhattan, against the background of the Financial District skyscrapers, Battery Park is an open area of 21 acres extending from Bowling Green *(see p. 90)* to the junction of the Hudson and the East Rivers. The view of New York Bay, animated by the constant movement of boats of all sizes, attracts large numbers of tourists.

Under Battery Park passes the **Brooklyn-Battery Tunnel** (about two miles long) which links Manhattan to Brooklyn.

Man-made Land. – During the 17th and 18th centuries, the shore followed the lines of Greenwich Street, Bowling Green and Pearl Street. The British built a fort in 1693 on a rocky island offshore.

Early in the 19th century the West Battery was built, giving its name to the present park, and in 1870 the land was filled in between the island and Manhattan proper.

VISIT

We suggest the following walk starting from Bowling Green, where you enter Battery Park.

This park is dotted with **commemorative monuments** among which is one dedicated to the memory of Emma Lazarus, author of the sonnet *The New Colossus,* written in 1883 to aid the fund-raising drive for the pedestal of the Statue of Liberty. From the entrance of Battery Park, there is an attractive view over green lawns and walks to the dark mass of Castle Clinton.

Castle Clinton National Monument. – Built on a small island from 1807 to 1811, Fort Clinton went the way of a number of fortifications since Dutch times ; it never had to be used for its original purpose.

In 1824 it was transformed into Castle Garden, and used for entertainment and opera. It could be reached from Manhattan by a covered foot-bridge. That same year a gala evening was held there in honor of **Lafayette.** James Fenimore Cooper described the occasion in an article : « nearly five thousand persons, it is estimated, were brought together... The General walked several times around the area and the galleries of the castle, receiving the eager pressure of fair hands...''.

On another grand occasion in 1850, Castle Garden was the setting for a concert by the Swedish Nightingale'', **Jenny Lind.** Tickets for the Lind concert were worth up to $225. It was here, also, that Morse demonstrated his new invention, the telegraph.

Between 1855 an 1890 the former fort and opera house was once more transformed, this time into an immigrant landing depot through which many immigrants passed.

Over 7 million of them passed through Castle Garden, eager for the Promised Land. Later the New York Aquarium – now in Coney Island *(see p. 130)* – occupied the building until 1941.

Today, after restoration, **Castle Clinton,** named for De Witt Clinton, governor of New York State in the early 19th century, is once more the severe circular red sandstone building of the last century. The eight-foot thick walls are pierced with gun-ports for cannons, and the entrance is framed by pilasters.

The interior contains a large courtyard, the very spot which served as a ballroom (roofed with a tent) when Lafayette was entertained. *Open daily 9 AM to 4:30 PM June through October ; November through May Sunday through Thursday 9 AM to 4:30 PM.*

To the left of the fort, the **statue of Verrazano** was erected in 1909 ; nearby is an air vent from the Brooklyn Battery Tunnel.

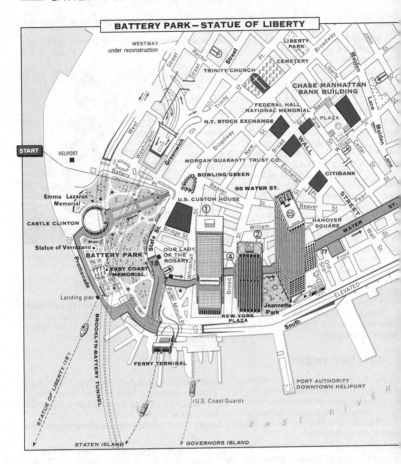

Walk. – From Castle Clinton to the Ferry Terminal, where the famous Staten Island ferries dock, the walk winds pleasantly along the shore of New York Bay. Sunny, thanks to its southern exposure, and protected from chill north winds by the buildings of the Financial District, it is an agreeable walk in winter. In summer, too, New Yorkers come to enjoy the sea breeze. It is here that you can take the ferry for the Statue of Liberty *(see opposite)*. Nearby is the **East Coast Memorial** commemorated to those who lost their lives in the Western Atlantic during the Second World War. The powerful statue of a landing eagle with outspread wings, the work of Albino Manca, faces Liberty Island. On either side leading down to the water there are four granite columns inscribed with names.

The **view**★★★ extends in three directions. The bay is animated by a constant succession of ferries and railroad barges, ocean liners and tankers, tugs and motor boats, while helicopters chop the air. From Jersey City on the right to Brooklyn, you will see in the foreground :

– **Jersey City** with its Colgate clock, one of the largest in the world. Despite the distance, you can easily read it.

– **Ellis Island.** The island was opened in 1892 as a processing center for immigration replacing Castle Garden. Between 1892 and the center's closing in 1954, an estimated twelve million people entered the United States through Ellis Island. The center vacated for over twenty years, has been opened to the public. *(Open May to November 9:30 AM to 4:30 PM ; ferry departs from Battery Park 9:30 and 11:30 AM and 1:30 and 5:30 PM. $2.50, children $1.25.)*

– **Liberty Island,** formerly known as Bedloe's Island, with the colossal Statue of Liberty.

– **Governors Island,** known in Dutch times as Nutten's Island, because of the many nut trees which grew there. The island which possesses spectacular views of Manhattan and Brooklyn, is the site of two pre-1800 structures : the Governor's House and Fort Jay. Another fort, Castle Williams, was built there at the beginning of the 19th century, at the same time as Castle Clinton. Since then, the island remained a military reservation. *Visits can be arranged, inquire at the U.S. Coast Guard Support Center by calling (212) 264-3780.*

– **Brooklyn,** with its docks at the foot of Brooklyn Heights.

Further in the background are Bayonne, New Jersey, with its oil refineries and its naval port, the hills of Staten Island, the Narrows and the cobweb of cables of the Verrazano Narrows Bridge, half hidden by Governors Island.

Continue to the Ferry Terminal, where ferries leave frequently for Staten Island. Returning in the direction of Bowling Green by State Street pass on the way, at No 7 State Street, the chapel and parish house of Our Lady of the Rosary, and at No 15, the **Seamen's Church Institute** which welcomes all sea farers. A maritime museum exhibits model boats and the bell of *S.S. Normandie,* a former transatlantic liner. In the auditorium the history of navigation is traced through the ages. *(Dining room and cafeteria open to the public.)* The part on the right was built in 1792 for one James Watson ; the graceful colonnade was added in 1806.

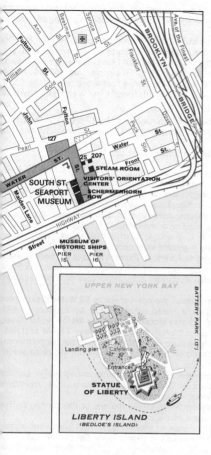

■ STATUE OF LIBERTY★★★

At the entrance to New York harbor stands the Statue of Liberty lighting the world. This symbolic gesture has warmed the hearts of countless numbers of immigrants. Stately guardian of New York, ''the grandest lady in the world'' majestically welcomes sea travelers...'' in her bronze dressing gown, with a candlestick in her hand'' (Paul Morand).

A BIT OF HISTORY

Franco-American Cooperation. –
In 1865, an idea was born in France : to give the American people a statue commemorating the alliance of France and the United States during the War for American Independence.

A committee was formed under the chairmanship of the historian Edouard de Laboulaye. A young Alsatian sculptor, **Frédéric-Auguste Bartholdi** (1834-1904), a member of the committee, was sent to America. He conceived the idea of a colossal statue of Liberty, which would be financed by a Franco-American committee. The French underwrote the statue itself, and the Americans the pedestal ; a private subscription of $250,000 was planned.

Bartholdi started work in 1874. Using his mother as a model, he made a plaster model 9 feet high, and another 36 feet tall. Finally the present dimensions were achieved.

On a framework designed by Gustave Eiffel, the French engineer who was to build the Eiffel Tower, more than 300 hammered copper plates were applied, representing a total weight of 90 tons.

Meanwhile, the American members of the committee were working on the pedestal. A site was chosen – Bedloe's Island, named after its first owner in the 17th century, Isaac Bedloe. It had been fortified in 1811.

Construction was started, but had to be interrupted due to a lack of funds. Thanks to a publicity campaign in 1885 led by **Joseph Pulitzer**, the famous editor of the *New York World*, the pedestal was completed by the end of that year.

The Statue itself arrived in New York in May, 1885. It had been dismantled and the parts shipped in 214 cases.

The dedication took place on October 28, 1886. President **Cleveland,** Bartholdi and Ferdinand de Lesseps, who had succeeded Edouard de Laboulaye, were there.

VISIT

Ferries leave from the Battery every hour from 9 AM to 4 PM in winter, (Labor Day through Memorial Day) ; every 1/2 hour from 9 AM to 6 PM in summer. Length of crossing : 15 minutes. Price : $1.50 round trip including the price of admission to the Statue and museum.

Information at the Circle Line (telephone : 269-5755).
The Statue is placed at one end of the island, above the old fort, and receives about 1,200,000 visitors a year.

Weighing 225 tons, it represents a crowned woman trampling the shackles of tyranny. In her left hand she holds a tablet representing the Declaration of Independence while her right hand raises the symbolic torch 305 feet above sea level. The torch and the crown are lighted in the evening. It is especially at the base of the statue that you will realize the enormous size of the monument.

The Statue is a National Monument administrated by the National Park Service. Entrance to the Statue is gained by walking up a landscaped mall to the main lobby. From there visitors may proceed directly to the Statue or to one of two exhibit areas : the **American Museum of Immigration** on the second floor of the pedestal, where drawings, photos, models and audio-visual aids describe the role played by each ethnic group of immigrants, in the development of all spheres of American life, or the

(From photo National Park Service, Washington, D.C.)

The Statue of Liberty.

Statue Story Room where a bronze plaque is engraved with the sonnet written by Emma Lazarus in 1883 "Give me your tired, your poor, your huddled masses yearning to breathe free...".

Take the elevator (10 cents) within the statue itself, which carries you up the first 10 stories, or 167 steps, without undue fatigue. Save your strength for the circular staircase which rises 12 stories (168 steps) inside the body and head of Liberty leading to her crown. From the platform at that level, which can hold 20 to 30 people, you will discover a magnificent panoramic **view★★★** of New York Bay. The views northward toward the tip of Manhattan and the Financial District, and southward toward the Verrazano-Narrows Bridge, are spectacular.

A few figures. — The statue is 151 feet high and the head is 10 by 17 feet. The right arm, holding the torch, measures 42 feet long with a diameter of 12 feet and the index finger is 8 feet long.

Leaving the ferry take State Street before turning right into Water Street.

Water Street★. — Since 1968 there has been a tremendous change in Lower Manhattan principally due to the creation of new office space. Water Street epitomizes the astonishing pace of development. Here progressive planning has re-established the human and recreational elements in the architectural landscape. Water Street, on land fill, is lined with new office buildings of a variety of shapes, colors and construction materials, greatly altering the skyline of this seafront area. Visit on a weekday.

The buildings of **New York Plaza**, Nos 1, 2 and 4, form a fascinating, highly varied grouping, linked by street level plazas and a ground level concourse lined with shops and restaurants. 2 New York Plaza, now known as American Express Plaza is the headquarters of the American Express Company. The 22-story red brick building of 4 New York Plaza with its narrow slit windows houses the electronic accounting unit of Manufacturers Hanover Trust.

Jeannette Park, a street level plaza continues the open space to **55 Water Street** where the two buildings, north and south, flank a raised plaza (access by escalator) which overlooks the East River. **Downtown Branch Whitney Museum of American Art** (55 Water Street, south building, entrance at plaza level, open Mondays through Fridays 11 AM to 3 PM, admission free). Exhibits vary in theme and feature some of the works from the permanent Whitney Collection. Sculptures are displayed on the plaza ; a view from the plaza across the East River to Brooklyn Heights.

Continuing along Water Street pass the television screens imbedded in cement columns, then the welcoming "fun" plaza of 77 Water Street where pools, fountains, sculpture, seats and tables have been thoughtfully provided.

The northwest corner of Wall and Water Streets, was the site of the Tontine Coffee House (see p. 91), which was the first home of the Stock Exchange.

Passing other elegant office blocks, continue to Maiden Lane, look westward up this street to catch a glimpse of the Twin Towers of the World Trade Center and the Chase Manhattan Building. 127 John Street with its digital clock, colored chairs, tables and awnings, provides a pleasant touch in the urban landscape (Tours available on request).

South Street Seaport Museum. — South of the Brooklyn Bridge a 33-acre site made up of 5 blocks has been set aside to be developed as a cultural center : restoration of historic 18th and 19th century buildings in the block bounded by Fulton (named after the designer of the first successful steamboat), Front, Beekman and Water Streets, and rehabilitation of the piers where the seaports fleet of vintage sailing vessels is docked.

South Street Seaport is the last vestige of the 19th century port that made New York City a world shipping center.

Ships, shops and galleries are open 11 AM to 6 PM. Closed Christmas, Thanksgiving and New Year's Day. Guided tours by appointement.

Schemerhorn Row. — On Fulton Street is a fine group of 19th century Federal-style brick buildings.

Visitors' Orientation Center. — 16 Fulton Street. This center gives a historical introduction to the area, describing the crafts once practiced here (chandlers, sailmakers, shipyard carpentry, etc.), the various trade routes specializing in different cargoes and the many types of ships which moored here.

At 25 Fulton Street is the Book and Chart Store ; nearby at 207 Water Street is the Model Shop and Gallery.

Steam Room. — 203 Front Street. On the ground floor of the South Street Seaport Office a collection of famous 20th century passenger and freighter models.

Other recent renovations are the New Fulton Market (3 Fulton and 200 Front Streets) and the Bowne & Co. Stationers and Printing Museum (211 Water Street).

Museum of Historic Ships. — Voluntary admission suggested : $1.50 ; students $0.75. All land exhibits are free. Moored at piers 15 and 16, off South Street is the fleet of old ships: the Ambrose, the first lightship to man New York's Ambrose Channel ; one of the oldest ships the Wavertree (1885) a square-rigger ; the Lettie G. Howard (1893), one of the last extant Gloucester fishing schooners ; and the Peking, a square-rigged, four-masted barque (1911).

You will find on pp. 16 to 19

two **suggested programs for a short visit** to New York,

depending on the time you have available.

Distance : 2 miles — Time : 2 hours. To save time you can take an 8th Avenue bus uptown.

This walk does not include any notable sights, but shows the visitor some characteristic aspects of New York activity, as well as some of the busiest public buildings in the city.

"Clothes make the woman". — The area between Broadway and Ninth Avenue, south of 40th Street, is devoted to the manufacture and finishing of clothing, especially for women ; it is known as the **Garment Center.** Workshops, ware houses and factories line the streets

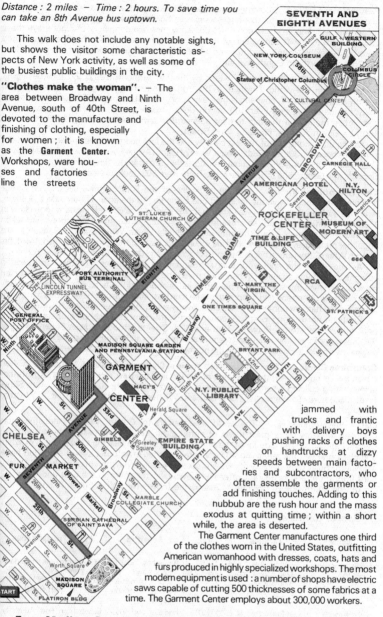

jammed with trucks and frantic with delivery boys pushing racks of clothes on handtrucks at dizzy speeds between main factories and subcontractors, who often assemble the garments or add finishing touches. Adding to this hubbub are the rush hour and the mass exodus at quitting time ; within a short while, the area is deserted.

The Garment Center manufactures one third of the clothes worn in the United States, outfitting American womanhood with dresses, coats, hats and furs produced in highly specialized workshops. The most modern equipment is used : a number of shops have electric saws capable of cutting 500 thicknesses of some fabrics at a time. The Garment Center employs about 300,000 workers.

From Madison Square to Columbus Circle

Leaving Madison Square *(see p. 122)* take West 25th Street. Along this street are second-hand stores selling sewing, button-making and overcasting machines and other tools of the trade. You pass the Serbian Cathedral of St. Sava, (1855) in English Gothic style.

Turn right and walk north on Seventh Avenue. On the cross streets, from 25th to 28th Streets, is the largest **Fur Market** in the world. By contrast, 28th Street is the scene of the wholesale **Flower Market** between Broadway and Seventh Avenue.

Madison Square Garden and Pennsylvania Station. — On this spot, from 1910 to 1963, stood the imposing bulk of the old Pennsylvania Station ; now "Penn Station" spreads out below street level, accommodating three railroads : Amtrak, Conrail and Long Island Railroad ; about 600 trains are scheduled daily, entering or leaving New York through tunnels under the Hudson and the East River. Above ground, a new group of buildings includes a high-rise office building along Seventh Avenue, the round Madison Square Garden Sports Center and other facilities.

The Madison Square Garden is the sports and entertainment capital for over five million people annually. Since its opening in 1968, the Madison Square Garden located on the upper five tiers of the nine-story complex has been a worthy successor to the three previous Gardens, beginning with the first at 26th Street and Madison Avenue in 1879. The Garden is the home of the New York Knickerbockers (basketball team) and the New York Rangers (ice hockey team), and the traditional headquarters for major attractions : the National Horse Show, the Westminster Club Dog Show, rock concerts, circus, etc.

Walk west on 33rd Street to Eighth Avenue, across from the General Post Office.

General Post Office. – Covering two square blocks, between Eighth and Ninth Avenues and 31st and 33rd Streets, this huge neoclassic building bears on its colossal Corinthian façade the well-known inscription : "Neither snow nor rain nor gloom of night stays these couriers from the swift completion of their appointed rounds". It is rather liberally adapted from the Greek historian Herodotus and, ideally, describes the workings of the post office.

Continue north on Eighth Avenue.

Port Authority Bus Terminal★. – Built by the Port Authority *(see p. 27)*, it is the largest bus terminal in the world. Finished in 1951, this functionally designed building is linked directly to the Lincoln Tunnel and is the daily "port" for more than 7,000 buses from some thirty companies. A two-year 160 million dollar expansion is underway to expand and completely modernize the bus terminal *(scheduled completion in spring 1979)*. Continue north on Eighth Avenue, crossing 42nd Street.

During the second half of the last century and the first quarter of the present century, the entire area between 30th and 58th Streets, west of Eighth Avenue, was known as Hell's Kitchen. This tenement area was rife with crime, serving as the home base for ferocious gangs such as the Gophers, the Gorillas and the Kitchen Mob. There were 500 Gophers alone in 1910.

The Triumph of Virtue. – At the beginning of the 20th century, West 42nd Street harbored a number of saloons, including one belonging to the prize-fighter **John L. Sullivan**, who was as feared as he was well-known. In his saloon a celebrated incident took place in 1901. **Carry Nation,** who led the crusade against intemperance and debauchery, had taken to destroying suspect establishments in the Middle West. When John L. Sullivan heard about her rampages, he declared that he would toss Carry in the gutter if she tried it with his saloon. When Carry Nation heard Sullivan's challenge, she decided to leave for New York.

A week later she appeared, was surrounded by newspaper reporters, and headed straight for Sullivan's saloon. When she arrived, he was calmly drinking a beer, but when he spied her face illuminated with righteous indignation and her hand brandishing a deadly instrument, he turned and fled, stopping to reflect on his humiliation only when he had barricaded himself in the furthest corner of the cellar. Sullivan never quite recovered from his retreat.

Continue north along Eighth Avenue, lined with inexpensive shops and second-hand book and record stores. Between 49th and 50th Streets, stood Madison Square Garden. Recently demolished, this renowned arena of sports events and meetings was so named for the original two buildings which stood on the northeast corner of Madison Square *(see p. 122)*.

Columbus Circle. – The circle boasts a **statue of Christopher Columbus**, erected in 1894 on a high rostral column. On the west side of the Circle is the **New York Coliseum** a large, rather uninteresting building where conventions and exhibitions are held. The annual Auto Show takes place here. To the north at One Gulf and Western Plaza stands the Gulf + Western Building.

Gulf + Western Building. – The world headquarters for Gulf + Western Industries, this gleaming 44-story rectangular tower of tinted glass, defends imposingly the entrance to Central Park West. The exterior of the first four floors of the building exhibit layers of white and black granite ; the remaining 40 floors are sheathed in an outer skin of silver and black aluminum. Solar grey glass windows are spaced evenly over the entire structure. On the 43rd floor a bar and restaurant offer fine views over the town to the east and west.

On the south side of Columbus Circle is the former New York Cultural Center.

Sports Centers

Name	Location	Tel.	Activities	Public Transportation
Madison Square Garden	Seventh Ave. and 32nd Street above Penn Station, NYC	(212) 564-4400	Basketball, hockey, track and field sports, games, ice shows, boxing, circus	IRT Seventh Ave. and Broadway lines, IND "A" or "E" train or BMT "N" or "RR" train to 34th Street Penn Station
Meadowlands Racetrack and Giants Stadium	East Rutherford, N.J.	(201) 935-8500 935-8222	Harness and Thoroughbred Racing football, soccer	Buses from Port Authority Midtown Terminal
Roosevelt Raceway	Old Country Road, Westbury, L.I.	(516) 222-2000	Harness Racing	L.I.R.R. from Penn Station to Minneola, from there bus to track. Buses marked "Trotters" from Port Authority Midtown Terminal
Shea Stadium	Flushing Meadow, Flushing, Queens	(212) 672-3000	Baseball, football	IRT Flushing Line to Willets Point
USTA National Tennis Center	Flushing Meadow Park, Flushing-Queens	(212) 592-8000	Public tennis courts, U.S. Open Tennis Championship	IRT Flushing Line to Willets Point
West Side Tennis Club	1 Tennis Place, Forest Hills, Queens	(212) 268-2300	Tennis tournaments, musical events	IND "E" or "F" train to Continental Ave. L.I.R.R. from Penn Station to Forest Hills
Yankee Stadium	River Avenue at East 161st Street, Bronx	(212) 293-6000	Baseball, other events	IND "CC" or "D" train ; IRT Lexington Ave, train No.4, both to 161st Street
Yonkers Raceway	Central and Yonkers Avenues, Yonkers	(914) 968-4200	Harness Racing	IRT Lexington Line No.4 to Woodlawn, from there bus No.20 to track or call New York Bus Service (212) 994-5500 Walter's Transit (212) 397-2626

Distance : 1 1/2 miles − Time : 2 1/2 hours.

A haven of greenery, light and air in the heart of Manhattan, Central Park covers 840 acres, and is 2 1/2 miles long and 1/2 mile wide. Framed by the silhouettes of surrounding buildings, its occasionally sparse vegetation forms a striking contrast.

A BIT OF HISTORY AND GEOGRAPHY

An Idea Takes Shape. − Foreseeing the need for open spaces in the growing city, the journalist and poet **William Cullen Bryant** launched the idea of Central Park in 1850 through a press campaign in his newspaper, the *New York Post*. With the aid of two well-known authors, Washington Irving and George Bancroft, he urged the city government to acquire, well beyond 42nd Street, where the city ended, a "waste land, ugly and repulsive". It was in fact a swamp inhabited by squatters who raised pigs and goats.

After acquiring the land, the city held a design competition, and the $2,000 prize was awarded to **Frederick Law Olmsted** and **Calvert Vaux**. Clearing began in 1857 with a labor force of 3,000 mostly unemployed Irish workers, and 400 horses.

In spite of fierce resistance of the squatters who bombarded the workers with stones, the project got underway and proceeded at a steady pace. A billion cubic feet of earth were moved, and after years of extensive drainage, planting, road and bridge building and ingenious landscaping, the park emerged essentially as we know it today. From its beginnings, Central Park enjoyed great popularity among New Yorkers.

Carriages, Horses, Bicycles. − Soon after its completion, Central Park became the testing ground for the finest equipages. On sunny afternoons, carriages lined up at the entrance to the park, avidly eyed by the populace. Victorias, broughams, phaetons and barouches carried high society ladies in elegant attire who pitilessly judged the rigs of their rivals.

Trotters were in great favor, and they whipped through the park to the speedways of Harlem. Around 1875, it became fashionable for gentlemen to drive their own four-in-hands. In 1876, Leonard Jerome, the maternal grandfather of Sir Winston Churchill, founded the select Coaching Club together with the financier and sportsman August Belmont.

Bicycle riding, which became the fad in the 1890's, was denounced as unbecoming for young ladies because of undue freedom of dress and movement. But the trend was too strong to resist, and before long the curved paths of Central Park were teeming with cycling women.

An Unfortunate Interlude. − In the early 1930's, Central Park served as a camping ground for victims of the depression ; the emptied Reservoir sheltered "Hooverville", a cluster of shanties.

Design of Central Park. − Covering an area of 840 acres, Central Park is one of the landscaped gardens held dear by the 19th century where the designers used nature as their main source of inspiration while skillfully blending natural and man-made elements to create scenic effects.

Central Park offers great diversity in design. Sparse vegetation in parts of the park, where the thin layer of top soil barely covers outcropping rocks, accentuates rather than hides the rugged character of the topography. In the northern part, hills and dales, rocky crags, trees, bushes and shrubs produce a landscape of great picturesque beauty ; wide open spaces and meadows where sheep grazed until 1934 give other sections a pastoral charm, unimpaired by asphalt-covered roads. 185 acres were set aside by the designers for lakes and ponds. A formal atmosphere prevails at the Mall and in the Conservatory Garden.

Despite the frequent police patrols, on horseback or by car, it is inadvisable to wander alone through the more deserted parts of the Park or to go there after nightfall (except for entertainment such as plays or concerts).

Recreation *(1).* − Central Park has two zoos, skating rinks, tennis courts, various athletic fields and other recreational facilities.

In summer the Parks Administration offers symphony concerts and a variety of light entertainment. One of the great attractions, the annual "Shakespeare in the Park" festival, is held at the Delacorte Theater.

In addition one can boat on the lake, ride horseback on the five miles of bridle paths, cycle on the several miles of bicycle paths *(you may rent a bicycle at the 72nd Street Boat House),* or play quieter games at the Chess and Checker House.

Park drives are closed to vehicular traffic to permit safe cycling : all year round, Saturdays and Sundays from sunrise to sunset ; Tuesday and Wednesday evenings from 7 PM to 10:30 PM in summer.

In addition to the stylish Tavern on the Green, there is a cafeteria at the Zoo, with tables outdoors, and a snack bar at the Loeb Boat House.

For children, there are the Children's Zoo *(admission : 10 cents)* donated by the late Governor Herbert H. Lehman ; pony rides *(15 cents per ride) ;* a marionette theater : fishing and other recreational facilities. There are lectures (dealing with such subjects as : environment and nature) at the Children's Zoo in the winter and, story telling on fine summer days, in front of the statues of Hans Christian Andersen, not far from the statue of Alice in Wonderland (and friends) on a giant toadstool.

You may hire a horse-drawn carriage for a ride in Central Park, at the southeast corner of the Park, near the Plaza Hotel ($10 less than half hour ; $14 about 45 minutes).

---

(1) For the program of summer activities, information is available at the New York City Parks Administration Central Park, 64th Street and Fifth Avenue (472-1003).

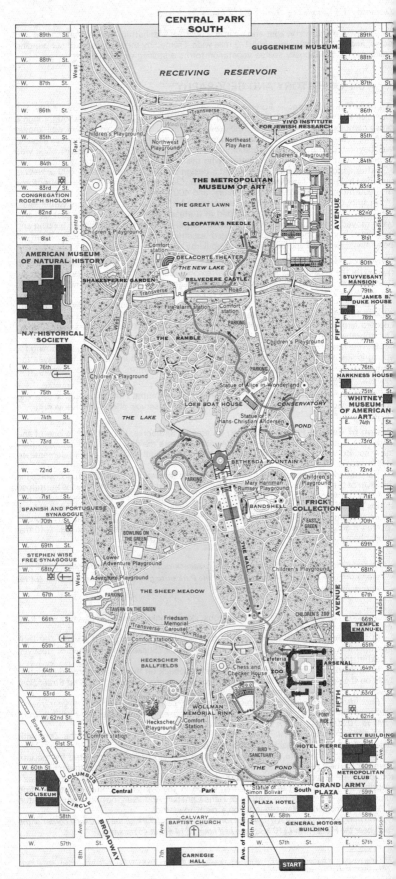

CENTRAL PARK SOUTH

W. 89th St.
W. 88th St.
W. 87th St.
W. 86th St.
W. 85th St.
W. 84th St.
W. 83rd St.
CONGREGATION RODEPH SHOLOM
W. 82nd St.
W. 81st St.

AMERICAN MUSEUM OF NATURAL HISTORY

N.Y. HISTORICAL SOCIETY

W. 76th St.
W. 75th St.
W. 74th St.
W. 73rd St.
W. 72nd St.
W. 71st St.

SPANISH AND PORTUGUESE SYNAGOGUE
W. 70th St.
W. 69th St.
STEPHEN WISE FREE SYNAGOGUE
W. 68th St.
W. 67th St.
W. 66th St.
W. 65th St.
W. 64th St.
W. 63rd St.
W. 62nd St.
W. 61st St.
W. 60th St.

N.Y. COLISEUM

COLUMBUS CIRCLE

Central
W. 58th St.
W. 57th St.
BROADWAY
8th Ave.
7th Ave.
CARNEGIE HALL

RECEIVING RESERVOIR

Transverse Road No. 2

Children's Playground
Northwest Playground
Northeast Play Area
Children's Playground

THE METROPOLITAN MUSEUM OF ART
THE GREAT LAWN
CLEOPATRA'S NEEDLE

Children's Playground

Comfort station
DELACORTE THEATER
THE NEW LAKE
SHAKESPEARE GARDEN
BELVEDERE CASTLE
Transverse Road No. 2
Fire-alarm station
Comfort station
PARKING

THE RAMBLE
Children's Playground
PARKING

Children's Playground
Statue of Alice in Wonderland
LOEB BOAT HOUSE
CONSERVATORY
POND
THE LAKE
Statue of Hans-Christian Andersen
PARKING

BETHESDA FOUNTAIN
Mary Harriman Rumsey Playground
Children's Playground
BANDSHELL
FRICK COLLECTION
EAST GREEN
BOWLING ON THE GREEN
Lower Adventure Playground
Children's Playground
Adventure Playground
PARKING
THE SHEEP MEADOW
TAVERN ON THE GREEN
Friedsam Memorial Carousel
Transverse Road No. 1
CHILDREN'S ZOO
Comfort station
HECKSCHER BALLFIELDS
Cafeteria
Chess and Checker House
ARSENAL
ZOO
WOLLMAN MEMORIAL RINK
Comfort Station
PONY RIDE
Heckscher Playground
Comfort station
BIRD SANCTUARY
THE POND
Statue of Simon Bolivar

THE MALL
East Drive
West Drive
Park Drive
Central Park West

GUGGENHEIM MUSEUM
E. 89th St.
E. 88th St.
E. 87th St.
E. 86th St.
YIVO INSTITUTE FOR JEWISH RESEARCH
E. 85th St.
E. 84th St.
E. 83rd St.
E. 82nd St.
E. 81st St.
E. 80th St.
STUYVESANT MANSION
E. 79th St.
JAMES B. DUKE HOUSE
E. 78th St.
E. 77th St.
E. 76th St.
HARKNESS HOUSE
E. 75th St.
WHITNEY MUSEUM OF AMERICAN ART
E. 74th St.
E. 73rd St.
E. 72nd St.
E. 71st St.
E. 70th St.
E. 69th St.
E. 68th St.
E. 67th St.
TEMPLE EMANU-EL
E. 66th St.
E. 65th St.
E. 64th St.
E. 63rd St.
E. 62nd St.
GETTY BUILDING
E. 61st St.
HOTEL PIERRE
METROPOLITAN CLUB
E. 60th St.
GRAND ARMY
GRAND PLAZA
E. 59th St.
PLAZA HOTEL
General Motors Building
E. 58th St.
E. 57th St.

FIFTH AVENUE
Madison Avenue

Park
South
Ave. of the Americas
6th Ave.
CALVARY BAPTIST CHURCH

START

VISIT

The Park is open every day from a half hour before sunrise to midnight. The section south of the Receiving Reservoir is the most interesting. The Park is most lively on Sundays.

From Central Park South to the Metropolitan Museum of Art

Enter the Park through the ''Artist's Gate'' across from Avenue of the Americas on Central Park South. The statue of Simon Bolivar overlooks this entrance. Turn right, taking the path leading down to the **Pond**, which winds among green shores. Continue around the Pond to your right, noticing the flocks of birds which enjoy this protected area, and head northwest to the Wollman Memorial Rink, which is also used for folk or square dances as well as ballroom dancing in the summer. Turn eastward to visit the Zoo.

Central Park Zoo★. – *Open every day from 11 AM to sunset. Admission 10 cents, children free.*

Full of children, the Zoo is a pleasant spot sheltered from the wind. Although rather small, it has an interesting collection of animals. The seals and sea lions would seem to be the favorites, but the elephants and lions also have their faithful public.

On the Fifth Avenue side of the Zoo is a severe massive building in grey stone, a former **Arsenal** of the State of New York, built in the 1840's in Gothic Revival style. It is now the headquarters of the New York City Parks Administration.

Turning your back to Fifth Avenue, continue a short distance to the northwest, to visit the Mall.

The Mall. – The Mall, the only formal area in the park, is a straight path lined with handsome elms and containing two rows of busts of famous men. It leads to the bandshell where orchestras and popular musicians play *(most summer evenings of the week at 8:30 PM)*; from the Mall, steps lead down to the Bethesda Fountain and the Lake.

The Lake. – Steps, banks and irregular shores make the lake seem almost transplanted from some far-off mountains. A graceful iron bridge to the west of Bethesda Fountain has been reproduced innumerable times in engravings and photographs.

Boats may be rented by people over 16 at the Loeb Boat House (at the east end of the Lake). Price : $2.00 per hour up to four people, and $10 refundable deposit.

Between the Lake and Fifth Avenue, Conservatory Pond is given over to young mariners. To the north of the

(From photo Andreas Feininger, New York.)

Central Park. — The Lake.

Lake, **the Ramble** is a heavily wooded hill with a number of hidden paths which seem to wind aimlessly. At the top of the Ramble is Belvedere Castle.

Belvedere Castle. – An imitation medieval castle complete with merlons and crenels, it overlooks the entire northern part of the Park. Just to the north are the New Lake and Delacorte Theater, next to **Shakespeare Garden**, originally planned to include every species of flower mentioned in the works of the Bard. Beyond are the vast reaches of the Great Lawn, which contains several playing fields, and the **Receiving Reservoir**, dug in 1862 to supply the city water system.

From Belvedere Castle walk northeast toward the Metropolitan Museum : its massive outline appears through the trees. West of the Met is **"Cleopatra's Needle"**, a pink granite Egyptian obelisk from Heliopolis, given to the City of New York in 1880 by the Khedive Ismaël Pasha. It is 77 feet high and bears its 3,000 years lightly.

The Metropolitan Museum of Art★★★ *(description pp. 54-63)* which rises on the ground of Central Park, marks the end of our walk.

Car trouble

If you have car trouble in New York City,

Call Police Emergency

Telephone : 911.

Arrangements will be made for authorized tow.

24-hour service 7 days a week.

Distance : 1/2 mile – Time : 2 hours.

At the intersection of Broadway and Columbus Avenue, the Lincoln Center for the Performing Arts, an integrated architectural group constructed between 1959 and 1969, comprises six buildings devoted to theater, music and dance in an area of 14 acres.

Just to the south of Lincoln Center, Fordham University has established a new campus *(see p. 119)*.

A BIT OF HISTORY

It was in 1955 that the original conception of a great cultural center where ballets, plays, opera, operettas and concerts could take place at the same time was first discussed. A committee under the chairmanship of John D. Rockefeller III was formed in 1956, and the following year the City of New York bought the necessary land in a poor and rundown neighborhood (between West 62nd and 66th Streets, Columbus Avenue, Broadway, and Amsterdam Avenue) ; 188 buildings were demolished and it was necessary to relocate 1600 persons.

In May, 1958, the committee chose the architects headed by **Wallace K. Harrison**, who had also participated in the design of Rockefeller Center, the United Nations and the John F. Kennedy Airport. Harrison began by creating an expert commission which was to visit 60 concert halls and theaters in 20 different countries to analyze their strong points and weaknesses.

In order to tailor the seats in the halls to their occupants, the architects even studied the dimensions of the average American, to find that the size of the hips, for example, had distinctly increased in the last 50 years. Harrison, remarking on this state of affairs, commented that it was too bad the volume of singers' voices had not progressed proportionately.

The total budget, an estimated $185,000,000, was largely met by private contributions ; public support accounted for only about a quarter of this sum.

Gifts ranged from $5 (for 118 bricks) to $5,000,000 (an entrance lobby) ; for $1,000 a donor could have his name inscribed on a seat in Avery Fisher Hall ; for $100,000 he could have his name on a plaque in the lobby.

■ THE BUILDINGS★★★

Avery Fisher Hall (formerly Philharmonic Hall), the New York State Theater, the Metropolitan Opera House, the New York Public Library ; the Vivian Beaumont Theater and the Juilliard School constitute a cultural unit which can accommodate 13,747 spectators at a time. The buildings are very classical in inspiration : rectangular floor plan, peristyle, flat or terraced roofs are reminiscent of antiquity, and are all covered with Italian travertine marble.

The interior is designed for maximum comfort and excellence in the performing arts.

Guided tours are available daily from 10 AM to 5 PM. $2.95.

For information, call : 874-4010.

Tours leave from the concourse level under the Metropolitan Opera House. Do not miss the Library and Museum, which are open without charge.

Bird's eye view of Lincoln Center.

① New York State Theater
② Metropolitan Opera House
③ Avery Fisher Hall
④ Vivian Beaumont Theater and Branch of the New York Public Library
⑤ Juilliard School

The Plaza. – Surrounded by three principal buildings of the Center, this pleasant flagged esplanade is decorated with an attractive fountain in black marble in the center.

A restaurant with a café terrace (summer only) borders one of the sides.

Free midday and evening performances in the summer.

Avery Fisher Hall. – Designed by Max Abramovitz, it was, in 1962, the first building finished. Somewhat resembling a Greek temple, it has a peristyle of 44 columns, seven stories high. The lobbies and corridors are decorated with works of art : a bust of the Austrian composer *Gustav Mahler* (1860-1911) by Rodin, a bust of *Beethoven* by Bourdelle and, suspended from the ceiling of the Grand Promenade foyer, two spectacular scintillating figures composed of polished metal strips : *Orpheus and Apollo*, by Richard Lippold.

The auditorium was totally reconstructed in 1976 by the architects Philip Johnson and John Burgee in association with Cyril M. Harris, acoustical consultant.

Seating 2,742 it includes the orchestra level and three balconies, called tiers. The stage, enlarged and reshaped for better sound projection, is framed by a proscenium adorned with gold leaf designs. The antique-white painted walls and ceiling, the oak floor and the velvet upholstery are in the classical tradition. A profusion of lights adds to the festive atmosphere of the hall.

Avery Fisher Hall is the home of the New York Philharmonic Orchestra, the oldest in America, which previously played at Carnegie Hall *(see p. 121)*. Zubin Mehta is Music Director of the New York Philharmonic, following such famous predecessors as Toscanini, Stokowski, Leonard Bernstein (also well-known as the composer of *West Side Story)*, Pierre Boulez and others.

New York State Theater. – Completed in 1964, the architect was Philip Johnson. The theater faces Avery Fisher Hall and is placed to the left of the Plaza. Behind its glass façade is a three-level foyer decorated with beautiful bronze grill work (executed by Meshekoff).

The ceiling is covered with 22 carat gold leaf.

The auditorium, which can hold 2,700 spectators, has five rounded balconies (called rings). Sculptures by Lipchitz, Nadelman, Johns, Higgins and Bontecou are displayed in the public areas.

The New York State Theater is the home of the New York City Ballet and the New York City Opera. The theater is owned by the City of New York and is operated by the City Center of Music and Drama, under whose aegis the Ballet and Opera companies operate.

*Cost of Philharmonic Hall : $17,000,000 ; New York State Theater : $19,000,000 ;
Vivian Beaumont Theater : $9,000,000 ; Metropolitan Opera House : $46,000,000.*

Metropolitan Opera House. – Opened in September 1966 with Samuel Barber's *Antony and Cleopatra,* it seats 3,800 persons. Designed by Wallace K. Harrison, it replaced the celebrated "Met" at the corner of Broadway and 39th Street, which closed on April 17, 1966, with a nostalgic farewell gala.

The façade, with a marble colonnade ten stories high, forms the background of the Plaza.

Inside, the huge stage is equipped with rolling platforms to change complicated sets. There are also 7 rehearsal halls, and space for scenery for 15 operas. Works of art include two large murals by Marc Chagall and significant sculptures by Mary Callery, Maillol and Lehmbruck.

The Metropolitan Opera Season is from mid-October to mid-April. Distinguished visitors, such as the American Ballet Theater or the Paris Opera appear during the other months.

Guggenheim Bandshell. – Located to the left of the Metropolitan Opera House, in Damrosch Park, this open-air theater with its bandshell is used for free concerts where 3,500 can be seated.

Beyond a plaza with Alexander Calder's steel sculpture *Le Guichet* and a rectangular reflecting pool displaying a bronze figure by Henry Moore, the Vivian Beaumont Theater appears.

Vivian Beaumont Theater and Mitzi E. Newhouse Theater. – Built according to plans drawn by the late Eero Saarinen shortly before his death, the Vivian Beaumont Theater was opened in 1965. It has an original architectural form with a projecting terraced roof. Seating 1,140, it is intended for repertory theater.

The Mitzi E. Newhouse Theater is a much smaller amphitheater with 270 seats.

New York Public Library at Lincoln Center. – This unique institution, a library and museum of the performing arts, is a true cultural center, as well as an attractive and ultramodern specialized library.

One can spend several hours enjoying the various free facilities provided here (films, concerts, exhibits, etc.).

Not included in the original plans, this intentionally unobtrusive building, designed by Skidmore, Owings and Merrill, houses a unique branch of the New York Public Library *(see p. 46)*. Containing both an extensive collection of circulating books and records and a Research Library on the Theater, Music and the Dance, it is a superlative cultural center which seeks to serve a public of various ages and interests.

Enter the building from the Plaza to the left of the Vivian Beaumont Theater ; on this level you will find a general presentation of the visual arts, and displays illustrating the history of New York theater.

Beyond these are temporary exhibits and the stairway leading to the Plaza Mezzanine Level. Here you will see the Children's Library, surrounding the Heckscher Oval, designed for puppet shows, children's films and story hours.

Turn left to browse in the Main Gallery, where you may also enjoy brief film shows or stereophonic recordings, thanks to audio drums near the armchairs. This mezzanine level also includes the Vincent Astor Gallery for temporary exhibits. (The Research Collections are on the floor above).

Take the elevator down to the Amsterdam Avenue Level : here is an art gallery, as well as an auditorium for 200 people, and small film projection or exhibit rooms.

The Juilliard School. – On the other side of 66th Street, the Juilliard building (designed by Pietro Belluschi, and Catalano and Westermann) is linked to the rest of Lincoln Center by a footbridge.

The Juilliard School moved here from its site at 120 Claremont Avenue, thus adding a center of training for musicians, actors and dancers.

Recitals, concerts, drama and dance events are presented in the four auditoriums of the school.

Alice Tully Hall. – Lincoln Center's smaller concert hall, is the home of the Chamber Music Society and is used by recitalists and chamber music groups.

For general information about Lincoln Center, call : 765-5100.
For box office information and ticket availability, call :

Avery Fisher Hall	874-2424	*New York Public Library*	799-2200
New York State Theater	877-4727	*The Juilliard School*	799-5000
Metropolitan Opera House	799-3100	*Alice Tully Hall*	362-1911

Outstanding institutions presenting natural sciences to the layman, the American Museum of Natural History and the Hayden Planetarium are located on Central Park West, between 77th and 81st Streets. Among the most venerated of New York establishments, they are especially popular with schoolchildren.

■ AMERICAN MUSEUM OF NATURAL HISTORY★★★

The Museum is one of the largest of its kind in the world.

The Building. – The construction of this colossus began in 1874, when General Ulysses S. Grant, then President, laid the cornerstone. It was formally opened three years later by his successor, Rutherford B. Hayes. Its architecture presents a curious mixture of styles, a result of a program directed by different architects. On the Central Park side is the main entrance, part of a majestic façade 700 feet long. The Ionic colonnade bears the statues of explorers and naturalists : Boone, Audubon *(see opposite)*, Lewis and Clark. Two other sides of the building more or less suggest a medieval castle while the fourth, on the Hayden Planetarium side, is modern.

(From photo Museum of Natural History.)

The American Museum of Natural History.

The Collections. – Before occupying its present site, the Museum was temporarily installed in the Arsenal *(see p. 50)*. The collections include more than 24,000,000 artifacts and specimens. There are 38 exhibition halls currently on view on four different floors. The displays, dealing with all facets of natural history, include life-size dioramas of animals from the five continents shown in their natural habitats : the ground and vegetation are faithfully reproduced, and the background scenes are effectively painted by artists using sketches made at the original sites. The lighting and occasional background noises and scents also contribute to the realism of the scenes.

Visit. – *Open weekdays from 10 AM to 4:45 PM : Wednesdays 10 AM to 9 PM ; Sundays and holidays : 11 AM to 5 PM. Closed Thanksgiving Day and Christmas Day. Discretionary admission fee.*

We mention only the most famous highlights, since a thorough visit of the Museum would require several days. *The Museum is often under renovation ; some halls may be closed.*

First Floor. – *Enter from West 77th Street.* In the foyer, you will see a seagoing war canoe from the Queen Charlotte Islands, in British Columbia, complete with suitable warriors. A section of this floor is devoted to the North American continent. Pause to visit the halls presenting Eskimos and Indians in lifelike groups (Indians of the Northwest Coast, with superb totem poles). You should also visit the halls of North American Mammals – from the bear to the bunny – and of North American Forests.

To the left of the 77th Street foyer is the unusually designed hall, Mollusks and Mankind ; it covers the many uses of mollusks and their shells by past and present cultures around the world. Further to the left is a hall depicting the Biology of Man, including exhibits illustrating human reproduction an area on human variation, and finally the section of meteorites Minerals and Gems with its 85,000 specimens including the Star of India.

Second Floor. – The Hall of Man in Africa shows the development of complex human culture on the African continent. The Hall of Mexico and Central America displays one of the finest pre-Columbian collections.

The most spectacular hall (African Mammals) is just west of the entrance foyer on Central Park West. In the center is an impressive herd of African elephants on the alert, and along the walls, groups of giraffes, zebras, antelopes, gorillas, lions, hippopotami and crocodiles are shown in their natural surroundings. In the galleries on the Third Floor level of this hall, other dioramas show different species of monkeys, rhinoceroses, leopards and hyenas.

Another attraction on the Second Floor is the Hall of Oceanic Birds, to the north of the Central Park West entrance. Overhead, a group of birds fly by, set off by the sky blue ceiling.

Third Floor. – The newest addition here is the fascinating Hall of Reptiles and Amphibians, featuring the world's largest living lizards : the Komodo Dragon. The Hall of the Biology of Primates displays animals from the same biological order as man, starting with the tree shrew. To the west of Primates are displays on the lifestyles of the Indians of the Eastern woodlands and plains, also of interest is the Hall of North American Birds where all the lifelike specimens are placed in natural settings.

Fourth Floor. – The Early and Late Dinosaur Halls form the most popular exhibit of this floor.

The dinosaurs, terrible giant lizards, divided into brontosaurs and diplodocuses, lived toward the end of the Secondary Era (Jurassic and Cretaceous periods) : the Museum possesses the skeleton of a huge brontosaur which must have weighed about 35 tons alive as well as a triceratops, a stegosaurus, and a tyrannosaur.

Dating merely from the Quaternary era, the mammoths resemble elephants with long hair and curved horns.

Beyond them, to the left, is the handsomely designed Rare Books and Manuscripts Room. Proceeding west past, this room is the John Lindsley Hall of Earth History, and beyond the Hall of Peoples of the Pacific, built under the guidance of Dr. Margaret Mead.

HAYDEN PLANETARIUM★★

Erected in 1935, the Hayden Planetarium is the astronomy department of the Museum of Natural History.

From the outside, the huge dome somewhat resembles an observatory ; inside are presented "Sky Shows" which clearly demonstrate the movements of the celestial bodies.

The Show *(time : 1 hour). – October through June, there are shows at 2 and 3:30 PM weekdays ; 1, 2, 3, 4 and 5 PM Saturdays, and Sundays ; July through September daily, at 1 and 3 PM ; Saturdays and Sundays, 1, 2, 3 and 4 PM. Wednesday evenings 7:30 PM all year round. Adults $ 2.35 ; children $ 1.35 (the fee includes admission on the Museum of Natural History).*

The Guggenheim Space Theater. – The space theater shows an exciting series, presented in sight and sound on the 360 degree space-screen covering such topics as the "Earth", "Moon", "Solar System" and "Rocketry".

The ceiling is an animated model of the solar system 40 feet in diameter. Around the central sun move six of the planets simultaneously rotating on their axes. They are the Earth, Mercury, Venus, Mars, Jupiter and Saturn with its rings ; Mars, Jupiter and the Earth are accompanied by their moons. The three outer planets, Uranus, Neptune and Pluto, are not represented, due to the huge distances involved and because they cannot be seen by the naked eye from the Earth.

The model is lighted so that each planet and satellite has "daytime" on the side facing the sun. A transcribed talk explains the movements of the solar system.

The Planetarium. – Go upstairs to the Theater of the Stars in which a new projector has been installed. The Sky Show is changed three times a year and features such subjects as "The Invisible Universe", "Spaceship Earth", "The Sky at Christmas", "Sol", "Between the Planets", etc.

The "screen" is the hemispherical dome 75 feet in diameter and 48 feet from the floor at its highest point. The spectators are placed all around the projector which weighs 2 1/2 tons and is 12 feet long. At either end are large globes which project images of the fixed stars : one globe can project the stars of the northern hemisphere and the other the southern hemisphere. The sun, moon and planets are projected from the cylinder which supports the globes.

On the second floor is the "Hall of the Sun" devoted entirely to the sun it includes how the sun affects our planet, the sun in the universe and a mini-theater with a short film of the sun.

Surrounding Corridors. – Two galleries, on the same floors as the Space Theater and the Planetarium itself, contain exhibits, such as Astronomia, illustrating the history and progress of astronomy. You will notice cases displaying old scientific instruments. Among astronomical murals is the recently completed 35-foot, scientifically accurate representation of the surface of the Moon, rockets, artificial satellites and a collection of meteorites, one of which, the largest displayed in the world, weighs 68,085 pounds.

■ NEW-YORK HISTORICAL SOCIETY★★

At 170 Central Park, between 76th and 77th Streets, the New-York Historical Society Building built in 1908, contains the museum and library of the most important local historical society.

Visit. – *Open Tuesdays through Fridays, 11 AM to 5 PM, and Sundays from 1 to 5 PM ; Saturdays 10 AM to 5 PM. The library : Tuesdays through Saturdays, 10 AM to 5 PM. Admission free.*

First Floor. – The first floor exhibits 17th, 18th and 19th century objects in silver, mainly by New York craftsmen, as well as sculptures by John Rogers, a highly regarded 19th century artist who specialized in genre groups. In some of the 1st floor galleries the Society holds temporary exhibits on New York history.

Second Floor. – 19th century travel toys, exhibited in the hallway, tell the story of New York's early transportation in miniature. As part of the exhibit "Moving in the City, Three Centuries of Transportation in New York", Dexter Hall displays the historical Beekman Coach as well as memorabilia related to transport in past centuries. This floor also contains colonial American period rooms and an installation of American 18th and 19th century decorative arts. Of great interest is the selection of original water colors by **John James Audubon**, the naturalist of French origin who painted the magnificent *Birds of America*. Changing displays of rare historical documents are held in the Library.

Third Floor. – This floor is devoted to folklore and applied arts (a handsome collection of fashion plates and posters).

Fourth Floor. – Amidst other furniture and paintings, two rooms are furnished in the style of the early Dutch settlers. Note also the collection of American portraits, landscapes (Hudson River School) and genre paintings.

Basement. – "Moving in the City, Three Centuries of Transportation in New York" is the theme of a vivid permanent exhibit displaying carriages, coaches and fire trucks as well as prints, maps and photographs which depict the various modes of transportation used by New Yorkers in the last three centuries, an extension of the second floor exhibit.

Distance : 1 1/2 miles — Time : 2 1/2 hours.

This walk, which leads us from Church to University, two pillars of American life, is relatively brief. But it will allow you to visit the area known as Morningside Heights, originally called **Harlem Heights**. The Battle of Harlem Heights took place here in 1776, when, for the first time, American troops commanded by Washington successfully resisted the British.

■ CATHEDRAL CHURCH OF ST. JOHN THE DIVINE★

The Cathedral Church of the Episcopal Diocese of New York rises impressively on Amsterdam Avenue at West 112th Street. "The largest Gothic cathedral in the world" can welcome 10,000 worshippers at any one time.

Model of the Cathedral
as it will appear when completed.

A challenging task. — The idea of building the largest religious edifice in the United States originated with the sixth Episcopal Bishop of New York (1861-1887), **Horatio Potter**. However, it was only in 1892 that his nephew and successor, Henry Codman Potter, bought the necessary land ; the cornerstone was laid on December 27 of that year, the Feast of St. John.

The first architects, Heins and La Farge, were inspired by the European Romanesque style, which is reflected in the existence of a narthex and, above all, in the choir and sanctuary. However, beginning in 1911, the Gothic style was adopted, and has come to dominate the present conception of the cathedral. The crossing, the choir and the sanctuary were completed in 1916.

In 1924 a national campaign raised $15,000,000, including $500,000 donated by John D. Rockefeller, Jr., although he was a Baptist. A year later, the foundation stone of the nave was laid. The first service in the completed nave was held in March, 1939.

At the present time, nearly one third of the Cathedral is yet to be completed : the towers of the West Front, the north and south transepts, the central dome and tower, the Chapter House and the Sacristy building. Also the carving of the figures of the central and south portals of the West Front remains to be done.

THE CATHEDRAL★ *(Visit : 1/2 hour)*

Exterior. — The wide West Front (207 feet) is flanked by two towers which will be 266 feet high when completed (the towers of Notre Dame in Paris are 225 feet high). They will relieve the impression of heaviness which now strikes the visitor.

The five portals, corresponding to the five interior naves, have not yet been entirely finished ; however, Burmese teak doors are installed in four of them. The central portal has bronze doors, cast and fabricated in Paris by Mr Barbedienne, who also cast the Statue of Liberty ; each door weighs about 3 tons and contains scenes from the Old and New Testaments. The central pillar bears a statue of St. John the Divine ; above, in the tympanum is the Majestas, a carving representing the Lord in Glory. The great rose window above the main portal measures 40 feet in diameter and contains 10,000 pieces of glass.

Interior. — Enter the narthex, which contains two of the finest stained glass windows in the Cathedral ; on the left is the Creation, and on the right scenes symbolizing elements of Christian doctrine. Note also the Greek icons and a Virgin and Child (15th century).

Taken together, the naves are 150 feet wide and 250 feet long ; the central nave is as wide as 112th Street. The arches rise 124 feet above (Notre Dame : 115 feet high.). The floor, known as the Pilgrims' Pavement, is decorated with medallions representing great Christian pilgrimages and episodes from the life of Christ.

At the crossing, the pulpit of Knoxville marble is also decorated with scenes from the life of Christ ; figures of Isaiah and John the Baptist are placed on the newel posts. Notice the large dimensions of the crossing which is surmounted by an impressive dome.

The Romanesque sanctuary is enclosed by a majestic semicircular arrangement of eight granite columns, each 55 feet high and weighing 130 tons. Notice the choir stalls in carved oak and the episcopal throne. This is surrounded by a white marble Historical Parapet. Niches are provided for statues of notable figures of the Christian Era, from St. Paul to Washington and Lincoln ; the 20th century is temporarily represented by a stone block to be carved. Behind the high altar of white Vermont marble is the tomb of Horatio Potter.

To the north of the choir, the baptistry is considered to be the most beautiful in the New World. It has a vaulted dome and octagonal lantern. In eight niches are figures from the history of the Netherlands, including Peter Stuyvesant *(see p. 81)*. The font is a copy of that from the baptistry of St. John in Siena, a work by Jacopo della Quercia (15th century).

Works of art. – Among the old tapestries hung in the Cathedral, we should mention the Scenes from the New Testament (17th century), after a design by Raphael. In the north transept a model of the completed cathedral is displayed. In the ambulatory you may admire paintings of the 16th century Italian school, a glazed terra cotta Annunciation (della Robbia school, 15th century) and a 16th century cloth embellished with an Adoration of the Magi. The central chapel of the Savior contains interesting icons.

Leading from the south transept, a passage takes you to a large room where contemporary art is displayed. On the Cathedral grounds are a Biblical Garden containing only trees and plants mentioned in the Bible and several Gothic buildings which serve as offices, the Bishop's House, the Cathedral school and the Synod house.

Leaving the cathedral, take 113th Street to the east. On the north side of this street is St. Luke's Hospital (600 beds), administered by the Episcopal Church. You will reach **Morningside Drive**, which follows the crest of the hills above Harlem ; the slopes are arranged in gardens known as Morningside Park. Between 114th and 115th Streets in the Grotto Church of **Notre Dame**, a Roman Catholic church in Corinthian style with portico and dome, built in 1915, where services have occasionally been conducted in French ; its unusual sanctuary is composed of a reconstitution of the grotto of Lourdes.

Continue on Morningside Drive to 116th Street ; at the northwest corner is the residence of the President of Columbia University, where General Eisenhower lived for several years.

COLUMBIA UNIVERSITY★

(Visit : 1 hour)

Enjoying a worldwide reputation, Columbia University is one of the oldest, largest and richest private universities in the United States, occupying a large area along 114th and 121st Streets and Broadway and Amsterdam Avenue.

A BIT OF HISTORY

From King's College to Columbia University. – Founded in October 1754, by charter from His Gracious Majesty George II, King's College was first established close to Trinity Church *(see p. 88).*

At the beginning of the Revolution, during the battle of Harlem Heights, the British were repulsed by Washington's troops after a struggle which took place on the present site of the campus of Barnard College on September 16, 1776 in what was then a buckwheat covered field.

In 1784, King's College reopened under a new name – Columbia College. A hundred years later, the college had but 80 and 1,600 students ; in 1897 it moved to the present site after 40 years at a Madison and 49th Street location.

CATHEDRAL OF ST. JOHN THE DIVINE — COLUMBIA UNIVERSITY

University Buildings

A galaxy of celebrities. – Among the first graduates of King's College were a number of noted public figures : **Alexander Hamilton,** aide de camp to General Washington, one of the authors of *The Federalist* and later Secretary of the Treasury ; **John Jay,** also a co-author of *The Federalist* and first Chief Justice of the United States ; **Robert R. Livingston,** the Chancellor of New York State who administered the oath of office to Washington in 1789 and was later U.S. Minister to France, negotiating the Louisiana Purchase ; **Gouverneur Morris,** also Minister of the United States to France, where he remained during the Reign of Terror. Another great administrator and alumnus of Columbia was **De Witt Clinton,** untiring promoter of the Erie Canal, opened in 1825, while he was governor of New York State.

More recently, both **Theodore** and **Franklin D. Roosevelt** attended Columbia Law School, although FDR left before graduation to begin his political career.

It was a Columbia Professor, **Harold C. Urey,** who discovered heavy water, earning a Nobel Prize in 1934. Finally, we should mention that General Eisenhower was President of Columbia University from 1948 to 1952.

Profile. – Encompassing a variety of academic disciplines, Columbia University is particularly known for its Law and Medical Schools, Teachers College, the School of International Affairs, the School of Journalism, Columbia College for men, and Barnard, an affiliated liberal arts college for women.

The coeducational private university has a student population of 16,900 and a teaching and research faculty of about 4,000.

The School of General Studies admits students with or without college credits or, in some cases, a high school diploma, who are 21 years and older and show promise of commitment and competency. Students under 21 who work and cannot study full time are also admitted. More than 1,000 liberal arts courses are offered each year. The average age is 29, but highly motivated students of all ages attend.

Campus sports facilities are supplemented by Baker Field, the Columbia University athletics complex for intercollegiate competition, located at the northern tip of Manhattan.

Columbia has an endowment of approximately $450 million and currently receives an annual rent of about $10 million from the property it owns at Rockefeller Center.

VISIT

You may stroll about the campus as you like. However, free guided tours are available which enable you to see the interior of many of the buildings at 10 AM and 2 PM during the summer vacation, and at 3 PM during the academic year ; they leave from 201 Dodge Hall, corner of 116th Street and Broadway.

Campus. – The green lawns and paths form a harmonious open space between **Butler Library** to the south, and **Low Memorial Library**.

Low Memorial Library. – Originally the University library, now occupied by administrative offices, this monumental edifice with its colonnade and 130-foot tall dome is built on a Roman mold ; it was designed by Charles McKim. In front of the majestic staircase stands the statue of the Alma Mater. The central rotunda serves as an assembly room or for exhibitions ; nearby is a reconstitution of a room from King's College.

(From photo Constance M. Jacobs, New York.)

Low Memorial Library.

St. Paul's Chapel. – Used for religious services and organ recitals, the chapel is predominantly neoclassic in style, with a dome and a rotunda. Inside, note the finely crafted woodwork. Next to Low Memorial Library, **Earl Hall**, also neoclassic in inspiration, serves for functions held by student groups and religious organizations.

Law Building. – An attractive building, finished in 1961, it now houses the Law School. In front of the building has been placed the monumental Lipchitz bronze *Bellerophon Taming Pegasus*.

Also departing from the traditional style is the Engineering Center Seely W. Mudd Building, located at the corner of 120th Street and Amsterdam Avenue.

The School of International Affairs including the renowned Russian Institute and other regional institutes occupies the modern building at 118th Street and Amsterdam Avenue.

Butler Library. – This building houses the central university library and the School of Library Service, the oldest in the country. The university libraries possess a distinguished collection of over 4,500,000 volumes.

Ferris Booth Hall. – A modern building, it serves as a student union and recreation center providing rooms for relaxation or informal discussion, lecture and reading rooms, bowling alleys, shooting galleries and ping-pong rooms.

The campus has recently been enriched by a modern building of striking originality the Sherman H. Fairchild Center for the Life Sciences, designed by a Columbia architecture professor.

Pupin Building. – Across the terrace of the Marcellus Hartley Dodge Physical Fitness Center is the 13-story red brick Pupin Physics Laboratories (1927). It was here that the maser (forerunner of the laser) was invented, heavy water was discovered, properties of atomic nuclei were explained and the development of atomic energy in this country – the Manhattan Project – was begun. A total of 14 Nobel Prizes have gone to Pupin Laboratory researchers.

Barnard College. – Founded in 1889, Barnard College is an independent college for women. It has its own campus, across Broadway from Columbia, ranging in architecture from the late 1880's to 1967. Barnard was among the pioneers in the late 19th century crusade to make higher education available for young women. A part of Columbia University, Barnard remains an independent liberal arts college for women, with its own campus and faculty.

Barnard's anthropology department, founded during World War One is one of the oldest in the U.S. Perhaps the department's best known student and scholar is Margaret Mead who began her field work in Samoa in the mid-20'ies.

Distance : about 1 mile − Time : 1 hour (not including the visit to the Museum).

This walk combines the pleasures of nature in Fort Tryon Park and the artistic joys of the treasures displayed in The Cloisters.

To reach The Cloisters take Bus No. 4, "Fort Tryon Park − The Cloisters", on Madison Ave or the Subway "190th Street − Overlook Terrace" (A line), and the No. 4 bus or walk.

Fort Tryon Park★★. − Covering 62 acres of wooded hills above the Hudson, this park is peaceful (except Sunday) and green, and gives the visitor the impression of being miles away from the bustle of the heart of the city. Although fairly small, the terrain is varied, with its hills and dales, and cleverly arranged terraces overlooking the Hudson. In the 19th century, this area was covered with farms and pastures, replacing earlier Indian camps.

Enter Fort Tryon Park from the south. The footpath leading to The Cloisters follows the crest of the hill, which slopes steeply down to the Hudson to the west.

To the left, and slightly lower, is a small botanical garden, with rare plants and flowers.

About halfway to The Cloisters, a lookout built upon the site of Revolutionary Fort Tryon caps a hill 250 feet above the river. The fort was named for William Tryon, last English civil governor of New York. Fort Tryon was the northern outpost of Fort Washington which was the last to resist the British invasion of Manhattan. It was here that Margaret Corbin replaced her husband killed in action, and fought until severely wounded. With the fall of Fort Washington on November 16, 1776, the British occupied all of New York City, which remained in their hands for seven years.

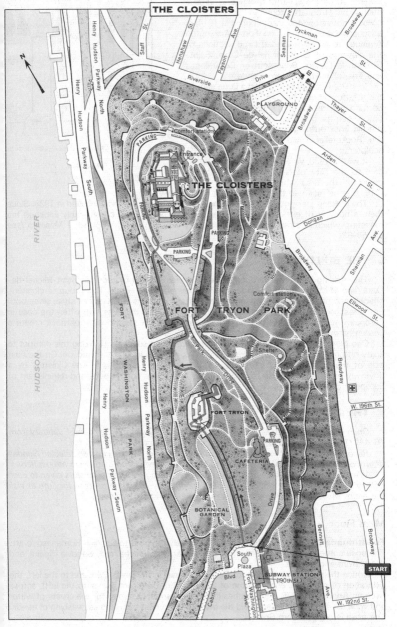

THE CLOISTERS

Not long ago. It was still possible to find cannon balls and Revolutionary buttons and belt buckles.

Now the fort serves as a lookout point, with a magnificent view of the Hudson and the George Washington Bridge to the west, and the East River to the east.

Continue to The Cloisters along the path which offers a superb **view** of the river and Palisades Park.

THE CLOISTERS★★★

Isolated on a hill in Fort Tryon Park, The Cloisters looks like a fortified monastery, a part of the Old World transplanted to the New where the lover of medieval art will find unrivalled collections.

A BIT OF HISTORY

Rockefeller to the rescue. – **John D. Rockefeller, Jr.** was largely responsible for this extraordinary institution : The Cloisters.

The core of the collection is made up of medieval sculptures and architectural remains assembled by the sculptor **George Grey Barnard** during his frequent trips to Europe. The collection was opened to the public in 1914, in a special brick building on Fort Washington Avenue ; it already included large sections of the cloisters of Saint-Michel-de-Cuxa, Saint-Guilhem-le-Désert, Bonnefont-en-Comminges and Trie, all from southern France.

In 1925, Rockefeller donated a large sum to the Metropolitan Museum to purchase the Barnard collection and to improve its presentation. When the first Cloisters opened in 1926 in the old brick building as an annex of the Met, the Rockefellers also added a number of sculptures.

(From photo Metropolitan Museum.)

The Cloisters.

It was in 1930, when Rockefeller decided to give to the City of New York an estate he owned in the area which is now Fort Tryon Park, that he reserved the northern part for the new Cloisters.

The building, designed in 1935 by **Charles Collens** of Boston, was finished in 1938. Since then, a number of gifts and an active purchasing policy have considerably enriched the museum, which has remained administratively a part of the Metropolitan Museum *(see pp. 54-63)*.

■ THE BUILDING★

The building is arranged around a square tower inspired by those of Saint-Michel-de-Cuxa *(see Michelin Green Guide to the Pyrénées, in French only)*. This group of cloisters, chapels and halls resembles an ancient monastery. There is little unity of style, since both Romanesque and Gothic elements are incorporated, but this was also often the case in European monasteries and the weathered stone and the felicitous proportions create a certain harmony.

One part of the construction is a rampart wall. You should walk along this parapet to enjoy different views of the building, as well as of the park and the Hudson. On the east side of the building is the entrance, a kind of postern gate, leave The Cloisters by a driveway paved with Belgian blocks, originally from New York streets, and reminiscent of European cobblestones.

■ THE MUSEUM★★★

Open every day, except Monday, Thanksgiving and Christmas Days and 1 January from 10 AM (1 PM Sundays and holidays) to 4:45 PM. Voluntary admission fee.

Recorded concerts of medieval music daily. There are live concerts on selected Sunday afternoons. These musical events help to create a peaceful and meditative atmosphere.

We give a suggested itinerary following the chronological order. The stars given to each gallery will permit you to see at least the highlights if you are too pressed for time to visit the entire Museum. A complete visit would require almost two days.

Main Floor

Fuentidueña Chapel★. – This "chapel" is largely devoted to Spanish Romanesque art. The apse comes from the church of San Martin at Fuentidueña, near Segovia (Spain), and dates from about 1160.

Notice the illustrative capitals (to the right, Daniel in the Lion's Den, and to the left, the Adoration of the Magi) and a statue of Saint Martin, Bishop of Tours (to the left), across from an Annunciation. The two niches in the wall probably served for the cruets of water and wine used in the Mass, and held the ewer for the priest's ceremonial washing of hands. The apse is on loan from Spain.

THE CLOISTERS

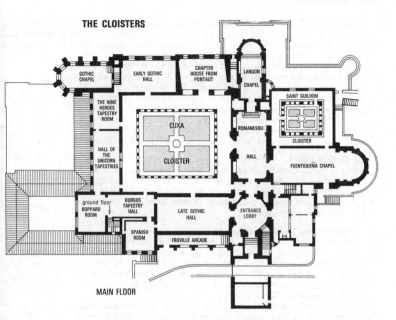

MAIN FLOOR

The semi-dome bears a fresco of the Virgin and Child with the three Magi and the archangels Michael and Gabriel. This originally was in the apse of a small Catalan church, San Juan de Tredos (Spanish Pyrenees).

Three recent acquisitions have been placed in the nave of the chapel. In 1965, an Italian Romanesque doorway from San Leonardo al Frigido in Tuscani (Italy) was installed. It was carved from Carrara marble in about 1175 and has the peculiarity of dissimilar jambs. Just to the left of the doorway is a cream-colored marble holy-water font, also from Tuscany, probably depicting a local saint, Raynerius, who lived and performed miracles in Pisa in the 12th century. It would seem that the font was carved in about 1160, the year of his death.

Romanesque Hall. – The entrance doorway has a round arch, a characteristic feature of the Romanesque style. On the left side the capitals are carved with graceful birds feeding upon acanthus plants. On the right side capitals, imaginary animals are surmounted by a delicate acanthus motif. The doorway is believed to come from Poitou in France.

The most noteworthy features of the Romanesque Hall itself are two early French portals. The one on the right, which leads to the Saint-Guilhem Cloisters, comes from a church in Reugny, in the upper Loire valley, and dates from the late 12th century ; the other, leading to the Langon Chapel, is 13th century Gothic : it was the entrance to a transept of the former abbey of Moutiers-Saint-Jean, in Burgundy. Notice the statues representing, on the left, Clovis, the first Christian French King, and on the right Clothar, who protected the abbey after its foundation by his father at the end of the 5th century.

On the right wall can be found the Torso of Christ (12th century), a fragment of a Crucifixion, whose head is one of the treasures of the Louvre in Paris.

Saint-Guilhem Cloister★★★. – This cloister contains a magnificent series of columns and capitals from the Benedictine abbey of Saint-Guilhem-le-Désert, near Montpellier (France). It was founded by Guilhem, count of Toulouse, in 804, and served as a stop on the pilgrimage route to St. James of Compostella in Spain. The property was sold during the French Revolution, and eventually some of the columns were used to support grape vines. George Barnard acquired them in 1906.

You will admire the vigor and freedom of execution of the capitals (12th to 13th century), with the intricate carving of plants and figures ; a number of the capitals bear the mark of Roman inspiration. Several columns are also carved with geometric patterns or vegetation.

The fountain in the center of the cloister was once a Romanesque capital in the church of Saint-Sauveur in southwestern France. The grotesque corbels to support the ribs and cornice of the vaults are from the abbey of Sauve-Majeure, near Bordeaux.

Langon Chapel★. – The original parts of this chapel came from the choir of the Romanesque church of Notre-Dame du Bourg at Langon, near Bordeaux, used as a Jacobin Club during the French Revolution, and later a dance hall and moving-picture theater. A 12th century Italian marble ciborium (tabernacle) symbolically protects a poignant Romanesque Virgin in walnut. This Virgin and Child from the Auvergne and an angel from the Cathedral of St. Lazare in Autun are among the few surviving wooden sculptures of the Burgundian school of the 12th century.

Chapter House from Pontaut★★. – Notre-Dame-de-Pontaut was first a Benedictine and later a Cistercian abbey in Gascony (France). The Chapter House, where the monks met every morning to discuss community affairs, in an example of the late Romanesque style and the transition to Gothic. On the other side of the open arches the lay brothers gathered in the cloister to follow the debates, while the monks were seated along the wall. The capitals are particularly worth noting for the simple but forceful carving of ornamental geometric or plant forms.

Cuxa Cloister*. – Although the largest cloister in the museum, it is composed of only about half the elements of the original. It was part of the Benedictine monastery of Saint-Michel-de-Cuxa, near Prades, in the French Pyrenees, one of the most active centers of art and learning in that area (the Roussillon). Abandoned during the French Revolution, the monastery was sold in three parts ; during the 19th century, its elements were widely scattered. In 1913, Barnard was able to bring together about half of the original Romanesque capitals, 12 columns, 25 bases and 7 arches. Rose-colored Languedoc marble was cut from original quarries to complete the restoration. Notice the vigorous carved capitals, with their plants, grotesque personages and fantastic animals possibly inspired by motifs from the Near East ; curiously, there are very few which bear a clear religious significance.

(From photo Metropolitan Museum.)
The Rheims Angel.

Early Gothic Hall*. – Here are a number of interesting statues, including a 13th century Virgin from the former choir screen of Strasbourg Cathedral, with its original paint. This is also true of the Virgin and Child (Ile de France, 14th century). Here we should also note two graceful angels recalling the famous "Rheims smile" and three 15th century alabaster sculptures.

The Nine Heroes Tapestry Room.** – Here is a large part of a set of tapestries which is among the oldest known, along with the Apocalypse tapestries at Angers (France). The theme of the nine heroes, very popular in the Middle Ages, includes 3 pagans (Hector, Alexander, Julius Caesar), 3 Hebrews (David, Joshua, Judas Maccabeus) and 3 Christians (Arthur, Charlemagne, Godfrey of Bouïllon). Their feminine counterparts were the Nine Heroines.

The Cloisters tapestries show 5 of the 9 Heroes. You can recognize David with a golden harp, Joshua, Alexander, Caesar and King Arthur : the three crowns on his banner represent England, Scotland and Brittany. A number of lesser personages escort the heroes : musicians, courtiers and warriors, cardinals and bishops.

The arms of Berry, with golden fleurs-de-lis on the tapestries depicting the Hebrew heroes, indicate that the set may have been woven for Jean, Duke of Berry, a well-known patron of the arts and brother of the French king Charles V. The tapestries have a style and technique similar to the Apocalypse set at Angers, which was designed by Nicolas Bataille.

From this same room, go downstairs to the Ground Floor, to the Gothic Chapel.

Ground Floor

Gothic Chapel*. – Inspired by a chapel in the church of Saint-Nazaire at Carcassonne and by the church at Monsempron, this modern setting forms the perfect background for an interesting collection of tomb effigies and slabs. Among the former are the effigy of Jean d'Alluye (13th century) and four Catalan sarcophagi of the Counts of Urgel (13th-14th century). The apsidal windows are now glazed with 14th century Austrian stained glass, mostly from the pilgrimage church of St. Leonhard in Lavanthal.

Bonnefont Cloister.** – On two sides this cloister is bordered by twin columns. Their double capitals in grey-white marble are from the cloister (13th-14th century) of the former abbey in the French Pyrenees. The other two sides of the cloister are terraces with a view on Fort Tryon Park and the Hudson. A medieval garden of herbs and flowers adds to the charm of this spot.

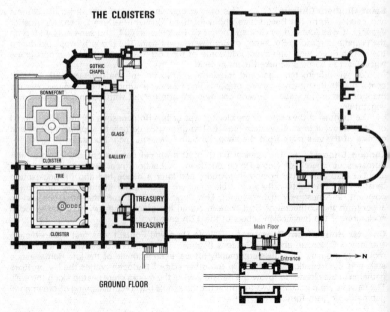

THE CLOISTERS

GOTHIC CHAPEL

BONNEFONT

CLOISTER

TRIE

CLOISTER

GLASS

GALLERY

TREASURY

TREASURY

Main Floor

Entrance

N

GROUND FLOOR

Trie Cloister**. – Of all the cloisters in the museum, this is the one which best recalls the intimacy and meditation of a monastery because of its reduced size. Its capitals, dating from the late 15th century, are decorated with coats of arms or religious scenes ; notice particularly those on the south arcade which illustrate the Life of Christ. In the center, the fountain bears a cross with, on one side, Christ between Mary and John, and, on the other, Saint Anne with the Christ Child and the Virgin.

Glass Gallery*. – This room is named for the roundels and panels of stained glass (15th-16th centuries) representing scenes from the Old and New Testaments. A fine group of 15th and 16th century statues is displayed here. However, the most curious feature, at the end of the gallery, is the Abbeville woodwork which came from the courtyard of a 16th century house in Abbeville.

Treasury***. – In three rooms reminiscent of medieval cathedral treasuries are gathered some of the most precious works of art in The Cloisters.

First Gallery. – Admire first the group of carved wooden panels believed to have been part of choir stalls, probably from the royal abbey of Jumièges in Normandy (early 16th century), decorated with scenes from the life of the Virgin, and then the Nativity and Vision of the Magi, painted on an altarpiece by a follower of Rogier van der Weyden (Flanders, second half of the 15th century).

Second Gallery. – The most outstanding object is the early Christian Chalice of Antioch in silver openwork enriched with gilding over an undecorated silver cup : dating from the 4th or 5th century, it is decorated with a series of grapevines in which appear birds (doves) and small figures of Christ and the Apostles. It is believed to be the earliest known surviving Christian chalice. Another admirable chalice is signed by its artist "Bertinus me fecit" (Bertinus made me), and dated 1222. You will also be interested in a rosary bead of boxwood, with a tiny representation of the Passion inside (Germany, 15th century) and the *Belles Heures* (a book of hours) of the Duke of Berry.

Main Floor

Boppard Room. – This hall is named for the town of Boppard on the Rhine, where the six stained glass panels were created for the Church of the Carmelites (late 15th century). There is also a handsome Spanish alabaster retable (15th century).

Hall of the Unicorn Tapestries***. – Finely executed, realistic in expression and attitude, precise in detail, harmonious in color, the Unicorn tapestries are among the most exceptional of the golden age of tapestry, at the end of the 15th century and the beginning of the 16th century.

The set includes seven tapestries which hung in the Château of Verteuil in Charente (southwestern France), the home of the well known La Rochefoucauld family, when they were bought by John D. Rockefeller, Jr. in 1920.

Burgos Tapestry Hall**. – The tapestry displayed is a Glorification of King Charles VIII of France, after his accession to the throne in 1483. The young king appears at least five times, and can be identified by his crown. His sister, Anne de Beaujeu, the regent during his minority, and his fiancée, Margaret of Austria, are also represented. Other scenes in the complicated iconographic scheme include the story of Esther and Ahasuerus, the Emperor Augustus, the three Christian Heroes, and Adam and Eve.

Spanish Room**. – This room, so named because of the painted Spanish ceiling, has been furnished with medieval domestic objects in order to recreate the atmosphere of that period : table and benches, bronze chandelier, and 15th century iron birdcage, (the only one known to have survived from the Middle Ages).

Above the chest is the famous **Annunciation altarpiece***** by Robert Campin, sometimes called the Mérode triptych, after the family who previously owned it.

The central panel represents the Annunciation, with a number of pleasing details. The side panels depict the donors, on the left, and on the right St. Joseph in his workshop : notice the mousetrap on St. Joseph's workbench, and the painstaking details of the town square in the background.

Late Gothic Hall*. – This large gallery, designed to resemble a monastery refectory is lighted by four 15th century windows from the convent of the Dominicans at Sens. There is a remarkable Spanish retable, or altarpiece, carved and gilded, dating from the early 15th century.

You will also admire the pure lines of a Virgin kneeling (Italy, late 15th century), the adoration of the Three Kings (Ulm, Germany, late 15th century) and the Brass Eagle Lectern (Belgium, 16th century).

Leave the Cloisters through the **Froville Arcade**, a series of Gothic arches.

Cloisters are covered passages round an open space connecting the church to the chapter house, refectory and other parts of the monastery ; and are generally south of the nave and west of the transept.
The plan of the New York City Cloisters was developed around architectural elements (12th to 15th century) from :
    Saint-Guilhem-le-Désert - Benedictine abbey ; founded in 804 ; intricate carved capitals and sculptures.
    Saint-Michel-de-Cuxa - Benedictine monastery ; founded in 878 ; vigorously carved capitals.
    Bonnefont-en-Comminges - Cistercian abbey ; founded in 1136 ; double carved capitals.
    Trie - Romanesque convent ; destroyed in 1571 (Wars of Religion) ; decorated capitals.
    Froville - Benedictine priory ; founded in 1091 ; arcade (14th-15th century).

Distance : 1 mile — Time : 1 hour (not including visits to the museums).

From the Museum of the City of New York to the Cooper-Hewitt Museum, Fifth Avenue passes from unassuming dwellings to the splendid residences of millionaires.

Museum of the City of New York★★. — The Museum recreates in a most effective way the history of New York from its discovery by Verrazano to our times. It is housed in a Colonial building, completed in 1932.

Open Tuesdays through Saturdays, from 10 AM to 5 PM, Sundays and holidays from 1 PM to 5 PM. Admission free. Acousti-guides available.

MUSEUM OF THE CITY OF NEW YORK COOPER-HEWITT MUSEUM

CENTRAL PARK

Children's Playground · The Mount · CONSERVATORY GARDENS · START · NEW YORK MEDICAL COLLEGE · MUSEUM OF THE CITY OF NEW YORK · NEW YORK ACADEMY OF MEDICINE · EAST MEADOW Children's Playground · MOUNT SINAI HOSPITAL · Children's Playground · RECEIVING RESERVOIR · INTERNATIONAL CENTER OF PHOTOGRAPHY · JEWISH MUSEUM · COOPER-HEWITT MUSEUM · Fifth Avenue · Madison Avenue

Ground Floor. — A gallery is devoted to fire fighting in New York.

Main Floor. — Maps, models and dioramas illustrate the history and growth of the city from its earliest beginnings through Dutch, English and Revolutionary times. In the Dutch Gallery you will find an engraved map of the city in 1660 and a model of the Nieuw Amsterdam fort in the center of a circular panorama.

In the cityrama room where a history of New York is presented in sight and sound, are to be found fragments of the first boat built in New York, the *Tiger,* a horse drawn omnibus and the only remaining box from the old Metropolitan Opera House.

Second Floor. — The Museum's fine collection of old New York silver is installed on this floor together with the J. Clarence Davies Gallery of New York prints and paintings. One section traces the history of the Stock Exchange *(see pp. 91-92)* with lifelike miniature dioramas. Another devoted to the port of New York, exhibits models of ships, from the 17th century to our time. Lastly the interior decoration of Old New York homes and the costumes worn by the first New Yorkers, live in dioramas depicting a Dutch living room, a colonial home of the 18th century (bedroom and living room) and parlors dated 1830, 1850 and 1900.

Third Floor. — This floor houses the toy and communications galleries together with a sampling of the Museum's furniture and portrait collection. Special exhibit galleries present rotating shows.

Fifth Floor. — You will be impressed by the luxury and beauty represented by the bedroom and dressing room from the house of John D. Rockefeller at 4 West 54th Street. Particularly striking are the mother-of-pearl encrusted woodwork in the dressing room and the ebony furniture with sandalwood marquetry.

Conservatory Gardens. — An enclave in Central Park, these formal gardens, donated by the Vanderbilt family at the end of the last century, are peaceful and harmoniously designed. A handsome wrought iron grille opens onto the main lawn of the gardens.

Opposite 106th Street, is the site of McGown's Pass where the Americans temporarily deterred the British in their move toward Northern Manhattan on September 15, 1776.

Cooper-Hewitt Museum, The Smithsonian Institution's National Museum of Design★. — *Fifth Avenue at 91st Street. Open Tuesday through Sunday, 10 AM (noon Sunday) to 5 PM (9 PM Tuesdays ; free).* $1.

This treasure house of the decorative arts is located in the beautiful renovated Carnegie Mansion. The collection, divided in terms of medium and technique, provides visual information for the study of design ; it is a "working museum" meant to serve as a design reference center.

Included are original drawings and designs for architecture and the decorative arts : 15th to 20th century drawings and prints - note especially the drawings of Frederic Church, Winslow Homer, Thomas Moran and other Americans. Fabric woven, printed and embroidered allows us to study textiles in all their mediums dating back as far as 3000 years ago. The decorative arts include silver, bronze and wrought iron metal work ; examples of jewelry and goldsmith's work ; wall paper and bandboxes ; porcelain, glass and earthenware ; furniture, woodwork (18th century panelling) and hardware (18 th and 19th century birdcages and splendid clocks).

The museum library includes a picture reference section and archives of color, pattern, textiles, symbols and interior design.

HARLEM★

Harlem, the largest Black community in the United States, seems a world apart, although physically only another section of Manhattan. Here are crowded in almost 50 percent of the 2 million Blacks who live in New York. Other concentrations are on the West Side and in Brooklyn, which has nearly 400,000 Black inhabitants.

The Dutch governor Peter Stuyvesant *(see p. 81)* founded the village of New Harlem ; its church was located between the present 124th and 125th Streets, to the west of First Avenue.

Harlem then was completely rural, with farmhouses dotted among the greenery. Later it became more residential. During the second half of the 19th century, elegant country cottages could be reached by tree-lined streets. By 1830 it was connected to the city by boat and by the Harlem Railroad, whose terminus was on Fourth Avenue, between 26th and 27th Streets. Trotting races on Harlem Lane were all the rage ; by 1900 the bicycle craze took over.

During the early years of this century, especially after the First World War, a number of Blacks, who were attracted to the north by higher wages and a somewhat more tolerant atmosphere, started to rent in the area north of Central Park, where speculators had over-extended the building boom of the 1890's. Harlem became the Mecca of gaiety and pleasure celebrated by visitors during the 1920's, such as the writer Carl Van Vechten. Gone is the time when night-owls finished the evening at the Cotton Club and similar establishments over bootleg liquor while listening to jazz stars, such as Duke Ellington and Cab Calloway.

Today, Harlem extends approximately from 110th Street to 162nd Street, and from Morningside Avenue to the East and Harlem River. The area contains a few historic districts, including "Striver's Row", several blocks of uniformed and distinguished homes at West 138th and 139th Streets, between 7th and 8th Avenues.

On its eastern fringes, along Park Avenue, is "Spanish" Harlem, now largely inhabited by Puerto Ricans. Near East 116th Street, from Lexington Avenue to the East River, and in the vicinity of Amsterdam Avenue, is what remains of "Italian" Harlem, although many Puerto Ricans also inhabit this area. The most lively areas in Harlem are along 125th Street between 5th Avenue and Broadway and along 116th Street between Park and Lexington Avenues. Travel through these areas during the day. Further north, Edgecombe Avenue, Hamilton Terrace and the surrounding area are inhabited by members of the Black middle class.

For guided tours of Harlem, apply to the Penny Sightseeing Company at 303 West 42nd Street, telephone : 247-2860.

Park Avenue Market★. – The hundreds of stands of this huge retail market, also called La Marqueta, extend from 111th to 116th Streets, an overcrowded and predominantly Spanish neighborhood in the shade of the New York Central Railroad. There, you may inspect a colorful array of goods ranging from children's and ladies' fashions to household articles, curios and knick knacks. Fresh vegetables and tropical fruits such as avocados, papayas and mangoes abound, meat is stacked high and the smell of fish wafts over the whole area. The atmosphere is reminiscent of the old-time market. In summer, sidewalk bands entertain with rumbas, mambos, merengues and guarachas. Visit the market in the morning, at its busiest.

The Schomburg Center. – *103 West 138th Street. Open Monday through Wednesday noon to 8PM ; Thursday through Saturday 10AM to 6PM.* Endowed with a reference and research library, this unique center is dedicated to the study of black culture and is noted both for the quality of its works and wide variety of subjects covered. On display are ivory, wood and metal art objects, paintings and African arms.

The Abyssinian Baptist Church. – *132 West 138th Street.* This oldest Black church in town is built of New York bluestone with a Tudor-Gothic window in its façade. In the interior, which takes the form of an amphitheater, the altar stands on a white marble dias. The memorial room traces the life history of Adam C. Powel, a former pastor of the church and Congressman.

Hamilton Grange. – *287 Convent Avenue at 141st Street. Open Monday through Friday 9AM to 4:30PM.* Built in 1801-2 by the architect John McComb *(see p. 84),* this Federal style two story frame house was the country home of Alexander Hamilton. Moved several hundred yards to this location in 1889, the house is scheduled to be fully restored to its original appearance.

Morris-Jumel Mansion★. – *Open daily 10AM to 4PM. Closed Monday. 50 cents.*

Located in a prosperous Black section (at 160th Street and Edgecombe Avenue), this handsome, Georgian house, formerly "in the country", is one of the few surviving reminders of colonial New York.

It was built in 1765 for Roger Morris a grandson of Sir Peter Jackson and was first known as Mount Morris. Ten years later in 1775, Colonel Morris left for England, where his loyalist sentiments were more appreciated. During the Battle of Harlem Heights in the Fall of 1776, the Mansion served as General Washington's headquarters.

(From photo Washington Headquarters Association.)

Morris-Jumel Mansion.

MANHATTAN - Additional Sights

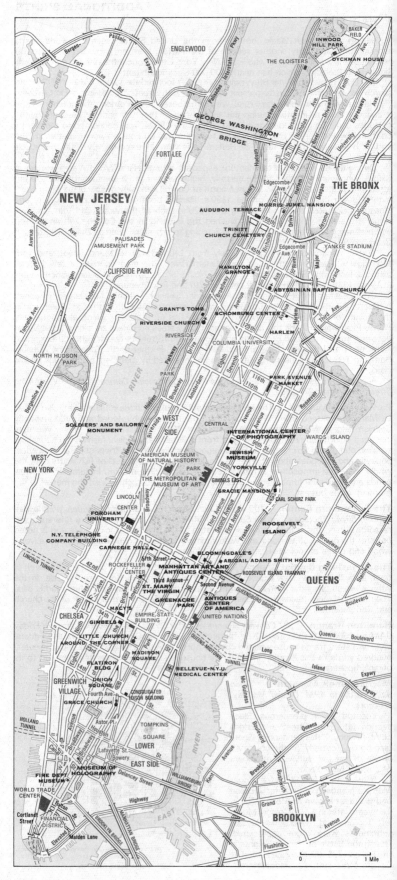

In 1810, a wealthy wine merchant of French origin, **Stephen Jumel,** bought the estate for his wife Eliza, and restored it to its original beauty. The Jumels made a number of trips to France during which they acquired some fine Empire furnishings and traveled in Napoleonic circles. In 1815 they offered the Emperor the use of their ship, *The Eliza,* to travel to America. He declined the invitation but legend has it that he gave his trunk and a carriage to the Jumels in gratitude. In 1820, Joseph Bonaparte, Napoleon's elder brother, may have visited the house. A year after Stephen Jumel's death in 1832, Madame Jumel married Aaron Burr *(see p. 92),* third Vice President of the United States.

Surrounded by a garden with a view overlooking the Harlem River the Morris-Jumel Mansion is an almost bucolic enclave in Manhattan. The house is built of brick, encased in wood.

The wide boards and wooden corner quoins, and the two-story colonnade and portico, although typical of the 19th century are part of the original structure and date back to 1765.

The interior of the house has been restored and furnished in excellent taste. In the first floor reception room, where Aaron Burr and Madame Jumel were married, are twelve chairs and a sofa and a French chandelier that belonged to Madame Jumel. The dining room table is set with Madame Jumel's china, and the grandfather clock that chimes in the hall told her the time.

On the second floor is Madame Jumel's bedroom containing furniture that once belonged to Napoleon and Queen Hortense of Holland, Empress Josephine's daughter. Aaron Burr's bedroom has in it his office desk and his trunk. On the desk in Washington's study is a box that belonged to Silas Deanes, first United States Ambassador to France.

Roosevelt Island. — Roosevelt Island, formerly known as "Welfare Island", is located at the East River 300 yards off the shore of Manhattan. The Island, politically part of the borough of Manhattan, is 2 miles long, 800 feet wide at its broadest point and 147 acres in size. It is linked to Manhattan by an "aerial tramway" which provides a three-minute ride across the East River with views in each direction.

The tramway station is located on Second Avenue and 60th Street, and the fare each way is a New York City subway token (50 cents) which can be purchased at the station. The tramway departs every 15 minutes on the quarter hour from 6 AM to 2 AM. From the tramway station on the Island one can take a free minibus to the heart of the new community. The Island can also be reached by car from the borough of Queens across the bridge at 36th Avenue. Because automobile traffic is restricted on the Island, all cars are required to park at the Motorgate Garage, just across the bridge on the Island. From there take the minibus.

The new community, built by the New York State Urban Development Corporation, was designed by the noted architectural firm of Johansen and Bhavnani, and Sirt, Jackson and Associates, based on a master plan by Philip Johnson and John Burgee. The new community contains housing for 2,148 families of various income levels, retail shops, schools, two city hospitals, parks and other recreational facilities. Two of the Isle's seven landmarks have been restored ; they are : the Chapel of the Good Shepherd, built in 1889, and the Blackwell Farm House, built shortly after the Revolutionary War and one of the oldest farm houses still standing in New York City. A water front promenade on both sides of the new community affords good vantage points for viewing river traffic and the Manhattan skyline.

■ MONUMENTS, CHURCHES

Riverside Church and Grant's Tomb★★. — Near the most picturesque part of Riverside Park, a pleasant strip of greenery overlooking the Hudson, Riverside Church and the tomb of President Grant are close neighbors.

Riverside Church★ is an interdenominational, interracial and international Christian church, historically linked to the American Baptist Churches in the United States and the United Church of Christ. It is also a community cultural center, with its own FM radio station, lecture series, clubs for persons of various ages, professions and interests, sports center and language courses, as well as regular concerts of religious music and theater performances.

Built in the late 1920's in Gothic Revival style *(see p. 28),* the building was inspired in part by the Cathedral of Chartres. John D. Rockefeller, Jr. contributed to the cost of the 400-foot tower (Chartres "Clocher Neuf" measures about 330 feet). The carillon is composed of 74 bells. *(You may visit the tower and its carillon on weekdays and holidays : 9:30 AM to 4:30 PM ; on Sundays : 1 PM to 4:30 PM ; interesting view of Manhattan. Admission : 25 cents.)*

The West Portal, facing Riverside Drive between 120th and 122nd Streets, is worth a pause to admire the large statues on the columns : prophets from the Old Testament to the left, and New Testament figures to the right ; the tympanum bears a seated figure of Christ and the symbols of the Four Evangelists.

Pass through the West Portal and enter the portico. Notice the four stained glass windows depicting the Life of Christ, made in the 16th century for Bruges Cathedral. From the portico you enter the nave, which is 100 feet high and 215 feet long, with room for 2500 worshippers. The nave clerestory windows are copies of those at Chartres. The inlaid "maze" design of the chancel floor is a reminder of medieval times, when penitents followed the winding lines on their knees. The chancel screen is decorated with 80 figures of men and women whose lives illustrated Christian moral principles : Luther, Milton, Lincoln and Pasteur, among others.

A passage from the portico leads to Christ Chapel, in 11th century Romanesque style. A stairway nearby leads down to the Cloister. In a waiting room next to the Cloister are hung two handsome tapestries from Reims Cathedral : one depicts the Christian King Clovis (Arras, 15th century) and the other a feast (France, late 16th century).

On the east side of the church is a *Madonna and Child* by Sir Jacob Epstein, modelled after an Indian woman and her son. The statue was exhibited at the Museum of Modern Art *(see p. 38)* until 1959, when it was presented to Riverside Church. Another work by

Sir Jacob Epstein is mounted on the rear wall of the nave. It is entitled Christ in Majesty. The metal casting hangs in Llandaff Cathedral in Wales. The figure spans approximately 19 1/2 ft. by 6 ft. It has been finished in gold leaf.

General Grant National Memorial★, popularly known as Grant's Tomb, is the final resting place of Ulysses Simpson Grant (1822-1885), commander of the Union Army during the Civil War and President from 1868 to 1876.

A granite-paved plaza leads to the monument on the west side of Riverside Drive, on the hill overlooking the Hudson River. Once thronged with reverent crowds. It is now visited less. The building was started in 1891 and dedicated on April 27, 1897, the 75th anniversary of Grant's birth ; 90,000 people contributed to the building fund of $600,000.

(From phto Éd. Sun, Paris.)

Grant's Tomb.

The grey granite monument, 160 feet high, somewhat resembles a Roman mausoleum, topped by a dome. A pediment on the south side bears two handsome classic figures and an inscription of Grant's plea : "Let us have peace". A majestic stairway, flanked by two eagles, leads to the entrance portico.

The interior *(open daily from 8:30 AM to 4:30 PM ; closed Monday and Tuesday October through March ; admission free)* with its white marble walls is lighted by translucent alabaster panels, whose half-light contributes to the solemnity of the monument. In the center, an open crypt similar to Napoleon's Tomb at the Invalides in Paris contains the sarcophagi of General Grant and his wife, Julia Dent Grant. In surrounding niches there are busts of Grant's comrades-in-arms : Sherman, Sheridan, Thomas, Ord, and McPherson. On the level above the crypt are two trophy rooms illustrating Civil War campaigns.

Soldiers' and Sailors' Monument. – *Riverside Drive at West 89th Street.* This white marble monument, with a peristyle of 12 corinthian columns, overlooking the Hudson River, was built in 1902 to commemorate those who lost their lives in the Civil War.

Grace Church. – *802 Broadway at 10th Street.* This Episcopal church was built between 1843 and 1846 in Gothic Revival style *(see p. 28)* by James Renwick Jr., who later designed St. Patrick's Cathedral. Founded by Trinity Church *(see p. 88)*, Grace Church has been and is one of New York's important parishes.

In 1863 **Barnum** managed to persuade the rector to marry two midgets from his circus, Charles S. Stratton, better known as Tom Thumb, and Lavinia Warren.

The church is an outstanding example of Gothic Revival ; notice the elegant spire. To the left of the church there is a garden in front of the rectory.

The Little Church Around the Corner (Church of the Transfiguration). – On 29th Street, not far to the east of Fifth Avenue, the charming "Little Church Around the Corner", with its peaceful garden, seems even smaller than it is, compared to the surrounding skyscrapers, especially the Empire State Building.

Built of red sandstone in the middle of the 19th century, this Episcopal church earned its nickname in 1870. That year, the pastor of a nearby church refused to hold funeral services for an actor since that profession was then still looked upon as performed by Satan's henchmen. The cleric did, however, suggest that the actor's friends try "the little church around the corner", where a monument still commemorates its pastor's charitable decision. Since that time, it has remained a favorite parish for theater people, and also one where many weddings are held.

The church constructed in 14th century Gothic style, is sometimes known as "Cottage Gothic".

The stained glass windows are dedicated to great New York actors : notice the one of Edwin Booth as Hamlet, designed by John La Farge and the one in the vestibule leading to the south transept which is studded with raw diamonds. It is dedicated to the memory of the Spanish actor José Maria Munoz. On the high altar reredos is the Transfiguration designed by Frederick Clark Withers.

Church of St. Mary the Virgin. – Situated at 139 West 46th Street this Episcopal Church with its Neo-Gothic façade merits a stop. Note in the left side aisle the Madonna and Child, a porcelain bas-relief from a workshop in Florence. In the Lady Chapel the murals represent the Annunciation and the Epiphany and there is a small statuette of Christ as a young boy. In the baptistry admire the wooden font cover which has seventy-three delicately carved figures. The Chapel of Our Lady of Mercy has a black marble altar and a 15th century plaque showing the death of St. Anthony.

■ HOSPITALS, BUILDINGS

Bellevue - New York University Medical Center★. – Along the East River, from 23rd to 34th Streets, is a modern hospital group, including a Veterans Administration Hospital, Bellevue Hospital and the New York University Medical Center.

The **Medical Center,** part of New York University, includes six buildings finished between 1961 and 1963. They are the University Hospital, the Medical School, a Rehabilitation Institute for the Physically Handicapped, an Institute of Experimental Physiology, Surgery and Pathology, Alumni Hall and a Hall of Residence with rooms for 300 students.

On the left is the Hospital ; the original building stood at 300 East 20th Street and dated back to 1882. Since its foundation, its medical and social role has been particularly significant : the first hospital infants' ward, the first therapeutic use of X-rays and the first research on blood transfusion were among its accomplishments. The new hospital, 18 stories in height and built at a cost of $25,000,000, has 626 beds and 14 operating rooms ; its dermatology and cancerology departments are especially well-known.

The Medical School, founded in 1841, then counted 239 students and 6 professors. Today 550 students are instructed and administered by some 1,500 persons. Thanks to one of its professors, Dr. Paine, the "Bone Bill" was voted in 1854, making dissection legal.

More recently, it was here that Jonas Salk and Robert Sabin discovered the first polio vaccine. You can enter the Medical School and Alumni Hall ; in the lobby is a model of the hospital group.

Bellevue Hospital, an even older institution, was established in 1736 and is the oldest public hospital in the United States. After an epidemic of yellow fever had caused the deaths of 700 New Yorkers during the summer of 1795 alone, the city then bought land at a spot named Bellevue, three miles north of town, on the banks of the East River, and constructed a pavilion for contagious diseases. However, the hospital itself was not finished until 1826.

The annals of Bellevue are linked to those of American medical history : in 1808, first ligature of the femoral artery by Dr. Hosack ; first ambulance service in 1863 ; first school of nursing in 1873 ; and first women medical students in New York in 1888. The concepts for open-heart surgery were developed at Bellevue.

A new modern 25-story Bellevue began accepting in patients in 1975. Completely air conditioned, it has transformed Bellevue into a modern setting. New York University Medical Center supplies the Medical House Staff for Bellevue as well as for University Hospital and the Veterans Administration Hospital.

Among the other major medical units in New York are the New York Hospital, Cornell Medical Center and the nearby Rockefeller University of Medical Research (on the East River between 63rd and 71st Streets); the New York Hospital is the oldest in New York, chartered in 1771 ; Mount Sinai Hospital of Fifth Avenue at 100th Street (member institution of the Federation of Jewish Philanthropies); and the Columbia-Presbyterian Medical Center on 168th Street between Broadway and Fort Washington Avenue, the largest voluntary hospital in the world.

New York Telephone Company Building*. – Located on Tenth Avenue, between 53rd and 54th Streets, this white building was finished in the 1960's, Windowless, its internal lighting is artificial.

Fordham University at Lincoln Center. – *60th Street and Columbus Avenue.* Fordham University founded in 1841 has two major campuses. The original Campus is at Rose Hall in the Bronx while the new campus at Lincoln Center was founded in 1968 on a seven-acre site, situated beside the Lincoln Arts Center. Among the several colleges, all of which are co-educational, housed in the campuses' two buildings, are the graduate Schools of Law, Social Service, Education and Business Administration. The undergraduate College at Lincoln Center, situated in the fourteen story Leon Lowenstein Center provides a liberal arts education for over 3,000 students.

■ MUSEUMS

Museum of Holography. – *11 Mercer Street. Open Wednesday through Sunday noon to 6 PM (9 PM Thursday). $1.50 adults ; 75 cents children.*
This museum located in the SoHo District *(see p. 82)*, is the only one showing holography – also known as lasar photography. By using lasar light, three-dimensional images, called holograms, are made. These illuminated images are so realistic that the viewer is tempted to reach out and touch the objects.

The International Center of Photography. – *1130 5th Avenue at 94th Street. Open Wednesday through Sunday 11AM to 5PM (8PM Tuesdays). $1.00 adults ; 50 cents students.*
The center, located in an elegant early 20th century townhouse, exhibits major works by photographers and photojournalists and offers audiovisual presentations and educational programs. The center also operates a bookshop.

The Jewish Museum*. – *1109 Fifth Avenue. Open Mondays through Thursdays, from noon to 5 PM, Sundays from 11 AM to 6 PM. Closed Fridays and Saturdays. $1.75.*
The Jewish Museum occupies the former mansion of Felix and Freida Warburg.
The permanent collection of Jewish ceremonial objects includes a blue mosaic 16th century Persian wall, a 17th century gold Kiddush cup and part of a Torah Ark from the 12th century. The collection also contains contemporary art, textiles, archaeology from the Holy Land and Hebrew coins.
In addition to the permanent collection the Museum has frequent exhibits *(on a rotating basis)* of sculpture, paintings and photographs as well as special events, films and lectures.

Audubon Terrace*. – *Open daily except Monday and holidays from 1 to 5 PM.*
On Broadway, between 155th and 156th Streets several museums and cultural institutions are grouped around a plaza where the naturalist Audubon *(see p. 105)* once had a country house named Minniesland. The present buildings, erected at the beginning of the 20th century in Italian Renaissance style, contrast with the unpretentious neighborhood.

119

The **Museum of the American Indian★★**, *(open Tuesdays through Sundays 1 to 5 PM. Closed Mondays and holidays ; $1.00)*, comprises three floors recently renovated, of exhibits related to the Indians of the American continents. The first floor features Indians of the Northeast Woodlands, the Plains, Great Lakes and Southeastern areas, displaying costumes, basketry, wood carving utensils, weapons and ritual objects. On the second floor are the Indians of the Northwest coast, the Southwest and Eskimo ethnology. In an adjoining hall is a display of North American archeology. The third floor houses a comprehensive presentation of pre-Columbian art and exhibits of South American ethnology.

The **Hispanic Society of America**, *(open Tuesdays through Saturdays 10 AM to 4:30 PM ; Sunday 1 to 4 PM ; closed on Mondays)* with a library and a museum, offers a panorama of Spanish civilization from pre-Roman times to the present century. A hurried visitor should at least visit the interior court (portraits by Goya, Renaissance tombs and a collection of furniture), and the upper gallery (earthenware, paintings by El Greco, Velazquez and Goya).

The **American Numismatic Society★**, *(open weekdays except Mondays 9 AM to 4:30 PM, Sundays, 1 to 4 PM. Admission free-ring the bell)* is the largest private museum of its kind. It includes two modern exhibition galleries ; the one on the right displays medals of historic or artistic interest ; the other, on the left, is devoted to topical exhibits.

The **American Academy** and the **National Institute of Arts and Letters** are the nation's highest honor societies, with a membership of 250 of America's foremost artists, writers and composers. Recurrent art and manuscript exhibitions *(Tuesday through Sunday 1 to 4 PM)*.

Fire Department Museum. – *Open Mondays through Fridays from 9 AM to 4 PM (9 AM to 1 PM on Saturdays).*

At 104 Duane Street, this firehouse contains a small museum which tells the history of fire fighting in New York.

The three floors exhibit a variety of fire fighting apparatus, hoses, helmets, fire engines, pumpers and hose carriages hand-drawn, horse-drawn and motorized. Don't miss "Chief" the dog who won an award for saving a cat from a fire !

Abigail Adams Smith House. – *421 East 61st Street. Open Monday through Friday from 10 AM to 4 PM. Closed in August.*

This Federal style stone building was originally built, around 1799, as the coach house and stable to a manor house on the country estate of Colonel Smith and his wife Abigail Adams, daughter of the President John Adams. The manor was destroyed by fire in 1826 while the stable subsequently became a hotel, then in 1833 a private house before being restored in 1924.

The house is maintained by the Colonial Dames of America.

■ DEPARTMENT STORES

Most of the large department stores are located on Fifth Avenue *(see pp. 45 to 48)* or on 34th Street between Lexington Avenue and the intersection of Avenue of the Americas and Broadway. The largest are R. H. Macy and Gimbel Brothers.

Macy's. – *34th Street and Broadway.* Macy's Herald Square is the world's largest store, with 2,151,000 square feet of floor space, as many as 10,000 employees in 168 selling departments.

Macy's stocks over 400,000 different items including fashions for the family and complete furnishings for the home. The store also provides all sorts of services such as eye-glass prescriptions, watch and jewelry repair, interior decorating, carpet cleaning and custom drapery and upholstery.

To help foreign visitors there are bilingual employees who speak a total of over thirty languages.

Macy's promotional activities include their annual Flower Show and the famous Thanksgiving Day Parade, which is seen by more than 65 million people across the country on television.

Gimbels. – *Broadway and 33rd Street.* Opened in 1910, the 9-story department store was later remodeled by Raymond Loewy. Besides a wide range of household furnishings and furniture, Gimbels carries contemporary fashions for men, women and children, fabrics, major appliances and such specialized items as foreign stamps and coins. There is a post office and an American Express branch. Entertaining and informative special events are frequently presented throughout the store, free to the public.

In 1972, Gimbels opened a new store, **Gimbels East**, at Lexington Avenue and 86th Street. Specialized boutiques carry high style fashion, accessories and gift items. Gimbels East operates a gourmet shop and a cooking school.

Bloomingdale's. – On Lexington Avenue between 59th and 60th Streets, Bloomingdale's is one of the most comprehensive fashion stores.

Founded in 1872 the store was originally sited at 938 Third Avenue, on the East Side, an unusual site at the time. The arrival of the Third Avenue Elevated ensured Bloomingdale's success and subsequent expansion necessitated a three block move to its present site.

Today, having passed its centennial this vast store has a wide range of departments, including many designer clothes boutiques for men, women and children, the famous food shop, a Health Food Restaurant and on the main floor, Cul-de-Sac, a shop with merchandise from all around the world.

A popular meeting place is near the eight digital Bulovas (clocks) which are recessed into a column, standing inside the Third Avenue entrance. One clock on each side shows New York time while the others give the hour in Paris, Rome, London, Tokyo and Rio de Janeiro.

WALKS

George Washington Bridge★★. – The George Washington Bridge was for a number of years the longest bridge in the world ; it links West 179th Street in Manhattan to Fort Lee, New Jersey.

Designed by O.H. Ammann (an American engineer of Swiss origin, also the designer of the Verrazano-Narrows Bridge) and the architect Cass Gilbert, the bridge was opened on October 25, 1931 and cost about $ 59,000,000. In 1959, the growing volume of traffic required the construction of a lower level, opened in 1962. At the same time, an intricate system of interchanges was installed.

A tremendous feat of engineering, the George Washington Bridge spans the Hudson River in one pure line 3,500 feet long. The towers are 604 feet high and the supporting cables have a diameter of 36 inches. Eight lanes of traffic can cross the upper level, 205 feet above the river ; the lower level can take six lanes of traffic.

It is a toll bridge *(round trip toll : $1.50 per passenger car)* and the world's only 14-lane suspension bridge. In 1977 more than 78 million vehicles used the bridge.

The best view of the George Washington Bridge may be had from the sightseeing boats *(see p. 16)* which circle Manhattan, or from the Henry Hudson Parkway, along the river. Notice the Little Red Lighthouse, on Jeffrey's Hook, a point of land on the Hudson near 178th Street ; there is a little park here, and the Lighthouse is a favorite with children.

Part of one of the bastions of Fort Washington can still be found near the Bridge in Bennett Park, Fort Washington Avenue and 183rd Street.

Yorkville-Gracie Mansion★. – Between Second and Third Avenues, 86th Street is the "Broadway" of Yorkville, still a largely German section although highrise apartment buildings and department stores have recently changed the scenery. The name "Yorkville" originally denoted a country village which sprang up here in the late 18th century. Toward the end of the 19th century, part of New York's German population moved here from Tompkins Square, especially after the elevated railroad went up in the 1870's. Today, restaurants, some with music from the old country, cafés, delicatessen, "wurst" stores, and pastry shops give some original flavor to the area. The Middle European atmosphere is further reflected in the Viennese, Hugarian and Czech restaurants found nearby.

Gracie Mansion. – *Not open to the public.* The first house on the banks of the East River dating from 1770 and belonging to Jacob Walton, was destroyed by gunfire in 1776. In 1798, the property was bought by Archibald Gracie, who built a new house and left it his name.

The Gracies entertained many public figures, including John Quincy Adams, Louis Philippe of Orleans, the future French king, and the writers Washington Irving and James Fenimore Cooper.

Located in **Carl Schurz Park** on East End Avenue and East 88th Street, Gracie Mansion is a handsome country house with verandas running around three sides. After housing the Museum of the City of New York *(see p. 114)*, it became the Mayor's official residence. The best view of the Mansion may be had from the excursion boats which circle Manhattan *(see p. 16)*.

Fulton Street. – Fulton Street which used to run from the Hudson to the East River, is now bounded to the west by the World Trade Center. Restaurants, snack bars and small shops line this narrow street.

Nassau Street which crosses Fulton Street, is closed to vehicular traffic during the middle of the day, to accommodate thousands of shoppers ; it has developed into a major shopping street in the area.

Fulton Street, along with Cortlandt Street, Wall Street and Beekman Street, was among the first to acquire gaslights (in 1830). Schermerhorn Row at the foot of Fulton Street in South Street Seaport *(see p. 96)* dates from the first half of the 19th century and illustrates the Federal-style.

Cortlandt Street-Maiden Lane. – Cortlandt Street, running from the Hudson River back to Broadway, was an area of sailor's dives and more or less dubious hotels during the 19th century. Today it is a shopping area convenient for office workers, particularly animated at lunch time.

Maiden Lane, the extension of Cortlandt Street to the east, still boasts several jewelers. Since the building of the World Trade Center, many restaurants have opened on Greenwich Street.

57th Street. – Fifty-Seventh Street is one of the city's few wide cross streets that runs from the East to Hudson River, unbroken by parks or buildings. It is an elegant and animated thoroughfare still possessing a few of the aristocratic town houses which graced it early in the century.

To the east of Fifth Avenue, 57th Street offers a succession of decorators and art galleries and some of New York's finest stores displaying home furnishings, tableware and decorative accessories.

Second and Third Avenues between 50th and 57th Streets harbor numerous antique shops and a few print sellers. On 56th Street at 1050 Second Avenue is the **Manhattan Art and Antiques Center** where 60 art and antique dealers present attractive displays (porcelain, jewelry, furniture etc.). The **Antiques Center of America** located at 415 East 53rd Street includes some hundred shops and showcases and a permanent antiques fair on the main floor. West 57th Street is dense with art galleries, at least 30 between Fifth and Sixth Avenues.

At the corner of Seventh Avenue, **Carnegie Hall**, which miraculously escaped demolition in the 1960's is universally know in the world of music. It was built under the auspices of Andrew Carnegie, the steel magnate and philantropist. Carnegie Hall opened in 1891, with a concert conducted by Tchaikovsky. The hall, which seats 2,784 persons is highly reputed for its acoustics.

PARKS

Inwood Hill Park*. – At the northwestern tip of Manhattan, Inwood Hill Park i separated from Fort Tryon Park by a ravine dotted with a few apartment houses. Woode and hilly, it seems to have changed very little since the Algonquins inhabited the spot, the known as Shora-Kapkok. You may still find caves used by them. During the Revolutior British and Hessian troops were quartered there and it was the site of Cox Hill.

During the week the park is quite empty and it is unwise to walk there alone, but o Sundays many New Yorkers like to picnic here.

Not far from the park, to the northeast, along the Harlem River, is Baker Field, th playing field of Columbia University *(see p. 107)*.

To the east of Inwood Hill Park, between West 204th Street and West 207th Stree **Dyckman House** *(open from 11 AM to 5 PM every day except Monday ; admission free)* is th only 18th century Dutch Colonial farmhouse in modern Manhattan. Restored and furnishe with period furniture, it evokes the atmosphere of the past, and a little garden adds to th pleasure of the visit.

Greenacre Park. – *51st Street between Second and Third Avenues.* One of the ve pocket parks. Greenacre is a haven of calm, away from the noise, dust and hustle bustle c the New York streets.

Union Square. – Once the scene of large, sometimes unruly political gatherings, a Ne York equivalent of London's Hyde Park where political radicals and others indulged in soa box oratory. Union Square is now no more than a busy crossroads between Broadway ar Park Avenue South and 14th and 17th Streets.

In 1836 the garden in the center of Union Square was enclosed by iron grillwork an locked at night. This was then the northern frontier of the city, but about 20 years later became a fashionable address, rivalling Astor Place. The park was then full of Englis nannies and French governesses supervising the offspring of New York's finest families

As the city spread northward, wealthy residences gave way to theaters, the Academ of Music (an opera house), commercial establishments such as Tiffany's and Brentano and restaurants like Delmonico's and Luchow's.

During the last years of the 19th century and the early years of the 20th, Union Squa witnessed mass demonstrations such as the one on August 22,1927, when Sacco ar Vanzetti were executed in Boston. A number of participants were wounded in the fray

Today, the park harbors two interesting statues : Washington, on horseback, by Hen Kirke Brown, and Lafayette, on foot, by Bartholdi, better known as the sculptor of th Statue of Liberty *(see p. 95)*. "Sweet Sounds in Union Square" an outdoor summer conce takes place every Wednesday *(12:30 to 1:30 PM from May to October ; free)*.

Walk a few steps to the east.

The **Consolidated Edison Building** (4 Irving Place at 14th Street) is the headquarters of th company which provides gas, electricity and steam for most of New York City.

Across the street, at 110 East 14th Street, stands **Luchow's** one of the olde restaurants in New York (1882), where you can dine on hearty Germanic fare to the strai of Viennese waltzes.

Return to Park Avenue South, known for its second-hand and rare book stores ; hea south to Grace Church *(see p. 118)*.

Madison Square. – Like Union Square, Madison Square was first an almost ru promenade where, in about 1845, the first baseball games of the city were played und the auspices of the Knickerbocker Club. From 1853 to 1856 the Hippodrome, a kind circus, drews as many as 10,000 spectators at a time to the Square. Later, during th second half of the 19th century, Madison Square became a luxurious residential area, a then a center of expensive shops. The Hoffman House was celebrated for the mural (painted Bouguereau) over its bar ; it was often filled with gay young blades. In 1884, the arm of the Stat of Liberty, complete with torch, was exhibited in the middle of the Square.

Madison Square gave its name to the famous Madison Square Garden, now located Eighth Avenue *(see p. 97)*. At the end of the last century, an ornate sports arena with roc for 8,000 spectators was built on the northwest corner of the Square. It was designed Stanford White, architect and man about town, who was killed on the garden roof by jealous husband who resented White's attentions to the actress Evelyn Nesbitt.

Today Madison Square is a spot of greenery, still visited but no longer at the height its glory. On the south side of the square is an unusual triangular Renaissance st building. One of the first New York skyscrapers, the **Flatiron Building*** adopted its nicknan as its official title. Built in 1902 by the Chicago architect Daniel H. Burnham, its 20 stori are 286 feet high.

At the northeast corner of 25th Street, the elegant Corinthian building (1899) in wh marble is the Appellate Division of the Supreme Court of the State ; the roof balustra depicts great legal experts of the past. Formerly on the far right the Mohamed statue h been removed at the request of the Moslems of New York, since their faith forbids t corporeal representation on the Prophet. The vestibule inside has a gilded ceilir supported by yellow marble columns.

To the north of the Appellate Division, the Manhattan Club dates from 1859 ; slightly la Jeannie Jerome, the mother of Winston Churchill, spent a few childhood years there. On northeast corner of the square, where the "Garden" once stood, is the New York Life Insurar Building designed in Louis XII style, complete with impressive gargoyles.

To find the description of a point of interest which you already know by name, please consult the **index**, pp. 145 to 148.

The only New York borough which is on the mainland, the Bronx has 1,385,351 inhabitants. The number of residents, predominantly of central and Eastern European extraction, has steadily declined, while Black and Puerto Rican residents have increased in number. Its southern part is mainly inhabited by lower income groups, while to the north more prosperous sections are found. To the east is the largest park in New York, Pelham Bay Park (**CXY**) with its popular sandy beach, Orchard Beach.

This borough was named after Johannes Bronck, a Danish emigré who was the first to settle (in 1639) beyond the Harlem River. The Bronx developed after the mid 1800's around the village of Morrisania (**AZ**), which now forms one section of the Bronx around Third Avenue and 161st Street. Two members of the Morris family, for whom Morrisania is named, were prominent during the Revolutionary period : Lewis Morris, a signer of the Declaration of Independence and Gouverneur Morris, penman of the U.S. Constitution. The borough is linked to Manhattan by 12 bridges, and 6 subway tunnels.

The Bronx was a part of Westchester County until 1898, when it was incorporated in New York City.

MAIN SIGHTS

The Bronx Zoo★★★. – *Open 10 AM to 5 PM ; 5:30 PM Sundays and holidays ; 4:30 PM November through January. Admission free Tuesday, Wednesday and Thursday. Adults $1.50, children 75 cents on the other days. Subway : get off at East Tremont Ave (2,5 lines) to reach the main entrance of the Zoo (on the south).*

The Bronx Zoo is located in Bronx Park, laid out at the end of the 19th century where the windmills of "West Farms" turned, on the banks of the Bronx River. On 252 acres, 3,500 animals of more than 700 species live in indoor and outdoor exhibits : the visitor can watch the animals cavort a few yards away, separated only by a moat in most of the exhibits.

Visit. – We recommend that you take the tractor train *($1.00 adults, 60 cents children)* to ride around the zoo or the skyfari *(50 cents)* which offers fine views of the zoo. You can also walk about, following the adjoining maps.

Through 38-acres of hilly, wooded land passes the Bengali Express monorail *($1.00 adults, 50 cents children)* for a journey into **Wild Asia** *(closed in winter)*. Over 200 rare and endangered animals, can be observed in large, natural habitat exhibits.

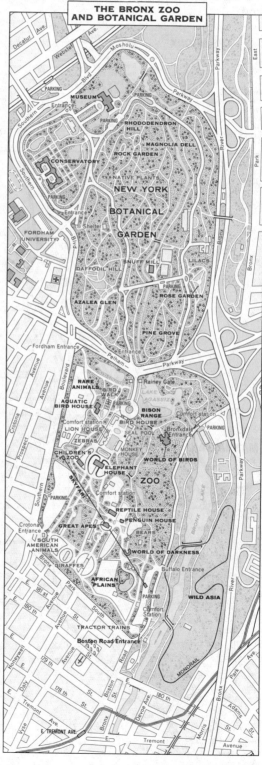

THE BRONX ZOO
AND BOTANICAL GARDEN

Among the animals not to be missed are the American and European bison (Bison Range), the Mongolian wild horses and the Pere David deer which have the feet of a cow, the neck of a camel, the tail of a donkey and deer antlers.

Visit also the African plains with their wild animals "at liberty" : the Reptile House ; the Penguin House and the Aquatic Bird House ; the World of Darkness *(night animals 10 cents)* and the World of Birds where hundreds of exotic birds can be observed in natural surroundings.

In the Children's Zoo, youngsters can see and touch a variety of animals from rabbits and goats to reindeer, donkeys and harmless snakes.

In the Great Apes Building may be found "the most dangerous animal in the world !"

see p. 123

New York Botanical Garden**. – *Open 8 AM to 7 PM May through September; 10 AM to 5 PM the rest of the year. Admission free. Open Tuesday through Sunday 10 AM to 4 PM in the Conservatory; $1.50.*

Subway : IND - Take the ''D''train to Bedford Park Boulevard ; IRT - take either a 2 or 5 line train to 149th Street and Third Avenue and continue by bus.

The Botanical Garden covers 250 acres, about the same size as the Zoo to the south. Founded in 1891, the Botanical Garden is always an inviting place to walk ; many thousands of flowering trees, shrubs and plants are at their peak in spring and early summer.

Among the favorite attractions are the rose garden, with 700 bushes of 400 different varieties ; the rhododendron hill ; the magnolia dell ; the azalea glen ; the rock garden ; the pine grove ; a native plant garden and a herb garden.

Beds of iris, lilies, hardy and tropical water lilies and lotus surround the Conservatory. The Museum Building houses the Exhibit Hall, featuring changing exhibits : ecology, environmental studies, botany and horticulture. The Building also houses the Library *(open to the public),* the Herbarium with dried plant specimens and fossils and the Auditorium.

Yankee Stadium★ (AZ). – *Subway : 161st St (4, D, CC lines).* This famous haven of the national sport is located at 161st Street and River Avenue. The stadium underwent a massive remodeling program from 1974 to 1975. The new ultra-modern stadium-complex has been designed to seat 54,000 spectators, to cater for various sports and other events. Major features of the stadium include new sets of escalators serving all upper tiers of the grandstands, an unobstructed view of the playing field, an increased capacity of concession facilities, a cafeteria for 500 people, and a new electonically-controlled scoreboard, etc.

Yankees : Babe Ruth and friends. – Yankee Stadium was built in 1923 for the baseball team of the same name. The stadium's first years were the heyday of Babe Ruth, who hit 60 home runs in 1927, still the world's record for a 154-game season. When he died, in 1948, 100,000 fans paid their respects. A bronze plaque commemorates : Babe Ruth, Lou Gehrig, Edward Grant Barrow, Joe Di Maggio, and Mickey Mantel.

■ ADDITIONAL SIGHTS

Valentine-Varian House (BY D). – *3266 Bainbridge Avenue at East 208th Street. Open Saturdays from 10 AM to 4 PM and Sundays from 1 to 5 PM. $1.00. Subway : IND ''D'' line to 205th Street ; Lexington Avenue 4 line to Mosholu Parkway.*

This fieldstone house originally stood on the opposite side of the street. The land was acquired in 1758 by Isaac Valentine and was the scene of many skirmishes during the Revolution. The ground was then bought in 1791 by Isaac Varian a prosperous farmer who was to become the 63rd Mayor of New York.

The house, situated on its present site since 1965, now contains the Museum of Bronx History with a fine collection of prints, lithographs and photographs.

This is also the headquarters of the Bronx County Historical Society.

Poe Cottage (AY B). – *Open Wednesday through Friday and Sunday 1 to 5 PM. Saturday 10 AM to 4 PM. 50 cents. Subway IND ''D'' line to Kingsbridge Road ; Lexington Avenue 4 line to Kingsbridge Road.*

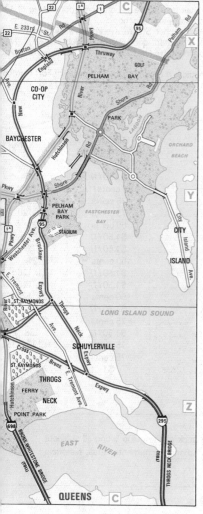

In this little wooden house, built in 1812, Edgar Allan Poe, lived two years (1846 to 1848) away from crowded New York City, paying John Valentine $100.00 yearly rental, towards the end of his life (he died in Baltimore in 1849). He was hoping to save his wife Virginia Clemm from tuberculosis. She died in 1847.

Poe wrote *Annabel Lee* and *The Bells* as well as *Ulalume* and *Eureka* in this cottage. Inside are displayed memorabilia and manuscripts.

Van Cortlandt Mansion Museum* (AX A). – *Broadway and West 246 Street. Open daily 10 AM to 5 PM ; Sunday 2 to 5 PM. Closed Monday and February. 75 cents.*
Subway : Van Cortlandt Park (IRT 1 Line).

Located in the southwest corner of Van Cortlandt Park, this 18th century colonial manor (built in 1748) is admirably preserved by the City and by the National Society of Colonial Dames in the State of New York.

The furnishings in the colonial style have been restored with utmost care : in the nine rooms open to the public, notice the Dutch room, the kitchen, and one of America's oldest doll houses in the nursery.

The mansion reflects a refinement and style of living typical of the New York gentry.

Washington is said to have slept here and to have used the house as headquarters before entering New York in triumph in November, 1783.

Bronx Museum of the Arts. – *Open Monday through Friday from 9 AM to 5 PM ; Sunday 12:30 to 4:30 PM. Admission free.*
Subway : 161 St-River Ave (4, D, CC lines).

Installed in the rotunda of the Bronx County Building (AZ), this museum presents about ten art exhibitions with different themes, each year.

Bronx Community College (AY). – *Subway : Burnside Ave (IRT 4 line).* Founded in 1891 as the Bronx campus of New York University *(see p. 77)* this group of eighteen buildings, now occupied by the Bronx Community College, stands on the calm banks of the Harlem River.

The **Hall of Fame** (C) *(open daily 9 AM to 5 PM, call 367-7300 for further information , admission free.)* reflects Stanford White's conception of an American pantheon in an outdoor colonnade, 630 feet in length surrounding three buildings in an imposing Beaux Arts style complex.

This unique sculpture museum honors Americans outstanding in many fields. Candidates chosen at least 25 years after their deaths are selected by a committee of 100 distinguished Americans representing each state in the nation.

Among those so honored are : Harriet Beecher Stowe, George Washington Carver, Edgar Allan Poe *(see details above)*, Walt Whitman, John James Audubon *(see p. 119)*, Henry Wadsworth Longfellow, Washington Irving *(see p. 139)*, Presidents Ulysses S. Grant, Thomas Jefferson, and Abraham Lincoln.

South of the Hall of Fame, on the campus, is a mound marking the site of Fort Number 8, one of a series of fortifications built in the vicinity by the Americans in 1776.

Toll Tunnels and Bridges		
Name	Toll Rates (per passenger car)	See map page
Bayonne Bridge	$1.50 *(1)*	136
Bear Mountain Bridge.	50 cents *(1)*	138
Bronx-Whitestone Bridge	75 cents	21, 125, 135
Brooklyn-Battery Tunnel	75 cents	21, 128
Cross Bay Parkway Bridge	50 cents	21
George Washington Bridge	$1.50 *(1)*	21
Goethals Bridge	$1.50 *(1)*	136
Henry Hudson Bridge	50 cents	21
Holland Tunnel	$1.50 *(1)*	21, 128
Lincoln Tunnel	$1.50 *(1)*	21, 128
Marine Parkway Bridge	50 cents	21, 129
Outerbridge Crossing	$1.50 *(1)*	136
Queens-Midtown Tunnel	75 cents	21, 134
Tappan Zee Bridge	$1.50 *(1)*	138
Throgs Neck Bridge	75 cents	21, 125, 135
Triborough Bridge	75 cents	21, 124, 134
Verrazano-Narrows Bridge	$1	21, 136

You will find an **index** at the back of the guide listing all subjects referred to in the text or illustrations (monuments, sites, historical and geographical items, etc.).

(1) Charge paid only on eastbound crossings.

Southwest of Long Island *(see p. 141)*, Brooklyn (Kings County) extends over 70 square miles from the East River to Coney Island and from the Narrows to Jamaica Bay.

The population of Brooklyn is about 2,400,000 making it the most heavily populated borough of New York City.

A long and rich past. – Brooklyn was founded in 1636 by Dutch settlers who called it Breukelen ("broken land") after a small town near Utrecht.

What is now the borough of Brooklyn was made up of six towns. One of the original settlements was located on Wallabout Bay, near the area where the Brooklyn Navy Yard was located until 1966.

Later, the town of Brooklyn spread westward along the coast, below the foliage of Brooklyn Heights. By the 18th century, there was a regular ferry service to Manhattan ; Long Island farmers crossed to sell their produce in Lower Manhattan.

By the end of that century Brooklyn was a pleasant residential area where many rich New Yorkers had country places. A French émigré, Moreau de St-Méry, recounts that even then many financiers commuted to Wall Street in the summer. At that time, most of the houses were still built of wood.

In 1834, Brooklyn became an incorporated city ; there were already 30,000 inhabitants. Incorporated into New York City in 1898, though not without a struggle, Brooklyn absorbed a number of villages whose names still mark various sections of the borough.

By 1883, the Brooklyn Bridge formed the first direct link with Manhattan, Williamsburg Bridge followed in 1903, and Manhattan Bridge in 1909. The first subway connection dates from 1905. More recently, the Brooklyn Battery Tunnel, completed in 1950, and the Verrazano-Narrows Bridge opened in 1965, further facilitate communication with the other boroughs.

A special world. – Although Brooklyn can hardly be considered isolated today, with the numerous Brooklynites who commute to Manhattan, the borough has retained its own personality, illustrated by Betty Smith in her book *A Tree Grows in Brooklyn*.

Furthermore, a number of writers have enjoyed living in Brooklyn, especially in Brooklyn Heights area, from Walt Whitman who wrote for the now defunct *Brooklyn Daily Eagle* in 1846, to Truman Capote, as well as Herman Melville, Arthur Miller, John Dos Passos, Thomas Wolfe, Norman Mailer and others.

For the visitor who passes through Brooklyn, the first impression is its huge size, and its labyrinth of streets and avenues lined with straight rows of houses.

However, a closer look reveals the variety of sections and inhabitants : Brooklyn Heights, residential and still the refuge of a few "old families" ; Williamsburg containing both Hassidic Jewish and Puerto Rican communities ; Flatbush, with handsome private houses ; and Bedford-Stuyvesant, an area with a number of handsome homes where a substantial proportion of Brooklyn's Black families reside.

The borough has many ethnic groups within its boundaries including Black, Italian (the tenor Mario Lanza was from Brooklyn), Jewish, Greek, Scandinavian Polish (the Dolly Sisters were daughters of a Brooklyn Pole) as well as a sizeable Caribbean population.

MAIN SIGHTS

Brooklyn Heights**. – Heavily fortified during the Revolution, Brooklyn Heights was the headquarters of General Washington during the Battle of Long Island. This section of Brooklyn was built up in the middle of the 19th century, and its calm is reminiscent of a small provincial town. Artists and authors, such as Thomas Wolfe, have lived here. Its narrow streets lined with town houses and brownstones are often shaded by trees, a luxury in New York. A number of the streets are named for fruits, and others for old Brooklyn families.

Visit *(about 1 1/2 hours).* – We suggest that you take this walk at dusk.

Leaving the Clark Street subway station (IRT 2,3 lines), take the street of the same name toward the East River. You will pass in front of the St. George Hotel and reach the esplanade above the expressway and port : from here, a magnificent **view***** of the Manhattan skyline ; the spectacle is impressive when the lights come on

BROOKLYN HEIGHTS

across the river. Behind the terrace is a series of attractive houses with miniature gardens. This is the approximate site of Fort Stirling, the first revolutionary fort built on Long Island and named for the American General, Lord Stirling.

Walk to the end of the terrace, and turn left on Remsen Street ; then take Henry Street to the right.

Just to the left, off Henry Street, is **Hunt's Lane,** a picturesque mews, where former stables and coach houses have been transformed into homes. Just south of here at about Hicks and Joralemon Streets was the country home of Philip Livingston, a signer of the Declaration of Independence. It is reported that on August 29, 1776 General Washington met here with his chiefs of staff to plan the evacuation of his army *(for more history see pp. 22-23).*

Next, take Joralemon Street to the Civic Center, a contrast to the residential section, with its massive public buildings, such as Borough Hall, the former Brooklyn City Hall and the massive Romanesque Revival Central Post Office.

Further down Fulton Street is Brooklyn's "downtown" including two famous department stores : Abraham & Strauss and Martin's.

Finally, return to Henry Street and the Clark Street station via Montague Street, with its unusual two-story shops, reminiscent of old Boston.

Long Island Historical Society
(see plan p. 127). − *Open Tuesday through Saturday from 9 AM to 5 PM. Closed August. Admission free.*

Located at 128 Pierrepont Street at the corner of Clinton Street, the Long Island Historical Society is the major resource of Long Island and Brooklyn History.

The Society contains the largest collection of books, documents and artifacts on Brooklyn and holds special features, concerts and tours.

Verrazano-Narrows Bridge★★★
(AZ). − *Subway : 95 St.-4 Ave (RR line).* The spider web silhouette of the Verrazano-Narrows Bridge, the longest suspension bridge in the world (Tancarville Bridge in France : 4,592 feet span) links Brooklyn to Staten Island *(see p. 136),* above the Narrows, the entrance to New York Harbor. It bears the name of the explorer of Italian origin who discovered the site of New York *(details p. 93).* At the Brooklyn entrance to the bridge, a monument has been erected, composed in part of stones from the castle of Verrazano, in Tuscany, and from the beach of Dieppe, the French port from which he sailed.

The Triborough Bridge and Tunnel Authority began construction of the bridge in January 1959.

The project cost $305,000,000. On November 21, 1964, the opening took place ; Governor Nelson Rockefeller and the bridge's engineer, O.H. Ammann, who also designed the George Washington Bridge *(see p. 121)* officiated.

A few figures. – Here are a few detailed figures :
Total length : 13,700 ft. – Main span : 4,260 ft. – Height of the towers above the high watermark : 690 ft. – Diameter of main cables : 3 ft.

The bridge which is high enough to allow the largest ocean liner to pass, has two levels of traffic (six lanes each) but no sidewalk for pedestrians. A toll bridge *($1 a car)*, it shortens the trip from Staten Island to the other boroughs.

Shore Parkway★★ (ACZ). – From Bay Ridge to Queens and the Kennedy Airport, this panoramic drive follows the coast.

There are successive views of the Verrazano Bridge and Staten Island, the U.S. Navy airport, the Rockaways and Jamaica Bay.

On a bright sunny day, the glittering water, the broad horizons and the bracing air combine to make this drive a complete change from citified Manhattan, despite its proximity.

Coney Island★★ (BZ). – *You can reach Coney Island by subway (B, N, F, QB, M, D lines).*
To the south of Brooklyn, Coney Island, bathed by the Atlantic, combines a popular beach with a wealth of other attractions.

On fine summer Sundays, the atmosphere is uproarious and not recommended to those lacking the gregarious spirit.

The air is overburdened with cries, laughter and music, while the smell of hot dogs and sticky candy pervades the air, and rows of bodies are streched out on the sand.

From Rabbits to Frock Coats to Bikinis. – In Dutch times there was nothing but a sandy island inhabited only by rabbits, who left it their name (Konijn Eiland – Rabbit Island). This title was soon transformed to its rough English "sound-alike", Coney Island.

In the 1830's the broad beaches on the island first began to be visited, principally by the well-to-do ; Coney Island was then embellished by elegant hotels, hippodromes, casinos and ice cream parlors.

Then, fifty years later, the resort became an area of popular entertainment and the clientele changed. The first roller coasters appeared in 1884, followed some years later by a huge Ferris wheel (George W.G. Ferris, an American engineer, built the first one for the Chicago World's Fair in 1893) and a merry-go-round. One hotel assumed the form of a 100 foot tall elephant.

By 1900, a hot summer Sunday drew 100,000 people to the beach.

The resort. – Coney Island has a fine sandy beach (about 3 1/2 miles long) and a boardwalk parallel to it, with a broad view made lively by the boat traffic in and out of New York Harbor.

But the great attraction of Coney Island is its amusement parks, where scenic railways, loop-the-loops roller coasters and Ferris wheels compete with phantom trains, sputniks and interplanetary rockets, merry-go-rounds and shooting galleries. The star attraction was the **parachute jump,** still standing but out of action, erected during the World's Fair of 1939-1940 ; the lover of thrills could drop in a chair attached to a parachute – but guided by cables.

Every year some 50,000,000 people visit Coney Island.

(From photo Nester's Map and Guide Corp., New York.)

Coney Island.
The former parachute jump.

The New York Aquarium★★ (BZ). – *Open daily from 10 AM to 6 PM (7 PM Saturdays, Sundays and holidays). $2.00 adults, 75 cents children. Subway : W 8 St. (IND F, M, D lines).*
The New York Aquarium has been located at the corner of the Boardwalk and West 8th Street since its move from the Battery *(see p. 93)* in 1957. In large outdoor pools, marine mammals, seals, sea lions, dolphins, turtles and penguins go through their paces ; feeding time *(in morning 10:30 to 11:45 AM ; afternoon 1:45 to 4:15 PM)* is particularly lively.

The indoor tanks, decorated with coral, harbor more than 200 varieties of fish. Notice the sharks who seem to get along with sleek mackerel, the peaceful white whales which are hand fed and the electric eel, which gives a charge of up to 650 volts when tickled by a keeper.

In summer dolphin show 11:30 AM, 2:30, 4:00 and 5:30 PM ; sea lion show half an hour before.

Brooklyn Museum★★ *(see plan opposite).* – *Subway station : Eastern Parkway (2,3 lines). Open Wednesday through Saturday from 10 AM (noon on Sundays) to 5 PM, holidays 1 to 5 PM. Admission free.* A huge building, complete with peristyle and pediment, a typical design of McKim, Mead and White, the Brooklyn Museum displays, on its five exhibit floors, comprehensive and rich collections which are too often overlooked.

First Floor : Primitive Arts. – Galleries of art objects from Africa (handsome wooden statuettes, masks and totems, witchdoctor's wands...) ; Oceania, American Indian civilizations (golden pre-Columbian jewelry) ; Peru (zoomorphic pottery).

Second Floor : Middle and Far East. – China (bronzes, jades, porcelain, paintings) ; Korea and Japan (sculpture, ceramics, paintings, metalwork, prints) ; India, Nepal, Tibet and Southeast Asia (sculpture, paintings) ; Middle East (paintings, ceramics, metalwork, carpets, textiles).

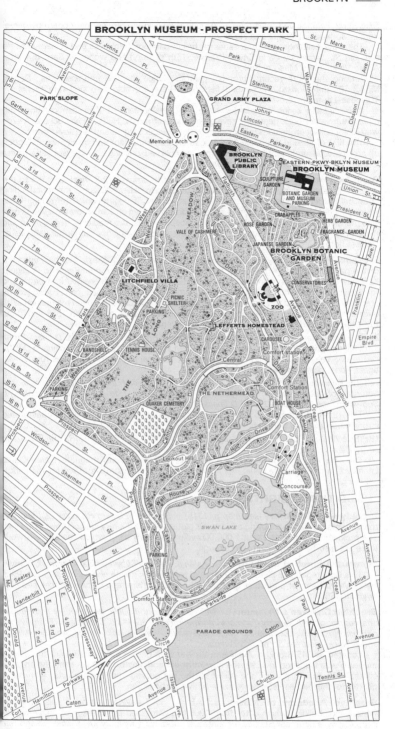

BROOKLYN MUSEUM · PROSPECT PARK

Third Floor : Mediterranean, Near Eastern and Coptic Antiquity. – The outstanding Egyptian galleries trace the development of the Nile civilization : notice the bust of Ptolemy and a sarcophagus in rose-colored granite from the Fourth dynasty (2500 B.C.), as well as a curious sarcophagus for a sacred ibis in gilded wood and silver, and small precious objects in alabaster or stone. You will also notice a few exhibits from Greek and Roman antiquity (vases, mosaics, jewelry) and twelve bas-reliefs from Assurbanipal's Assyrian palace at Nimrud.

Fourth Floor : Furniture, Decorative Arts and Costumes. – The most interesting displays on this floor are an excellent series of American interiors from the 17th century to the present : parlors, sitting rooms and dining rooms from both modest and wealthy homes, including an old Dutch home moved from a Brooklyn Street. The rest of the fourth floor features furniture, glass, silver, pewter and ceramics.

Also the Costumes galleries which contain outstanding fashions of the past and present.

131

Fifth Floor : Painting and Sculpture. – Among the sculpture, notice the modern by Barye, Rodin, Modigliani, Lipchitz and Nevelson.

The early paintings include a series of Italian painters, primitives and Renaissance : a splendid *St. James* by Carlo Crivelli (Venice, 15th century) and works by Sano di Pietro, Alvise Vivarini and Maso di Banco.

Among the more recent European painters notice the fine Impressionists : Degas, Monet, Berthe Morisot, Sisley and Pissarro. There are also two first-rate works by Toulouse-Lautrec.

A fascinating series of galleries trace the development of American painting with representative portraits, genre and several landscapes from the Hudson River School. A large watercolor collection includes major works by John Singer Sargent and Winslow Homer.

The first of its kind, the museum has gathered an important and fascinating collection of architectural ornaments salvaged from demolished buildings, in the **sculpture garden** *(behind the main building beside the parking)*.

Brooklyn Botanic Garden★★. – *Subway : Eastern Parkway (2,3 lines)*. Located to the east of Prospect Park, and to the south of the Brooklyn Museum, this outstanding botanical garden covers 50 acres with a great variety of vegetation. A refreshing oasis which includes three Japanese gardens, a Children's Garden and an arboretum. We should also mention the rose garden, the rows of crabapple trees, the medicinal herb garden and the garden for the blind (Fragrance Garden). Greenhouses enclose numerous varieties of tropical flora.

Prospect Park★. – *Take the Subway to Eastern Parkway (2,3 lines)*. The main entrance of the park is at Grand Army Plaza, a majestic oval plaza with a monument to President Kennedy and a triumphal arch dedicated to the Civil War dead. A network of paths and roadways winds through the park. The harmoniously landscaped park, designed by Frederick Olmsted and Calvert Vaux, extending over 526 acres, has been maintained in its original state. The City purchased the land in piecemeal fashion between 1859 and 1869, from the Litchfield family. We list the principal centers of interest below.

Zoo★. – *Open daily from 11 AM to 5 PM. Subway : Prospect Park (QB, M, D lines)*. Small but well designed, the zoo buildings are grouped around a semi-circular esplanade ; in the center is a seal pond. Around the perimeter of the seal pool are the houses for camels, tigers, lions, bears, as well as the bird house.

Lefferts Homestead. – *Open Sunday, Wednesday, Friday and Saturday (except 2nd Saturday of each month from November to May) from 1 to 5 PM ; closed holidays. Subway : Prospect Park (QB, M, D lines).*

This 18th century colonial farmhouse was moved to the park in 1918 and transformed into a museum, with period furniture.

Litchfield Villa. – *Open Monday through Friday 9 AM to 5 PM. Subway : IRT line 3 to Grand Army Plaza.*

The villa was built in 1855 by A.J. Davis, for the railroad magnate Edwin Clarke Litchfield, in the Italianate style. It is now used as an administrative office for the park.

■ ADDITIONAL SIGHTS

Brooklyn Public Library *(see map p. 131)*. – *Subway : Eastern Parkway (2,3 lines)*. A monumental building occupying a triangular plot, the Public Library was completed in 1941. The main library contains about 1,000,000 volumes nearly all of which can be borrowed there are also 58 branches in the borough.

Plymouth Church of the Pilgrims *(see plan p. 127)*. – *Subway : Clark Street (2,3 lines)*.

This Congregational Plymouth Church, a simple brick meetinghouse, dates from 1849 Henry Ward Beecher and other abolitionists preached here, and Lincoln worshipped here twice in 1860.

Brooklyn Children's Museum (BX M). – *Open to the public on weekday and Sunday afternoons ; closed Tuesday (for more information call 735-4432). Subway : IRT 7th Avenue Express No 2 (New Lots train) to Kingston Avenue ; walk 1 block west to Brooklyn Avenue and 6 blocks north to St. Mark's Avenue.*

Located at 145 Brooklyn Avenue in Brower Park on the same site where the original museum was launched in 1899, the new museum contains exhibits covering the areas of cultural and natural history, the sciences, the performing and creative arts. A museum geared to children, all its exhibits invite active participation.

Brooklyn Academy of Music (BX A). – *30 Lafayette Avenue*. This imposing Renaissance building which dates from 1906 has witnessed the passage of many famous people. It was here that Stanley recounted in public his meeting with Livingstone and that Enrico Caruso gave his last performance. Other well known names are associated with the Academy, such as Arturo Toscanini, Isadora Duncan and Sarah Bernhardt. Acting as a cultural center the BAM offers a varied program of dance, theater, music and lectures.

Park Slope *(see map p. 131)*. – Just west of Prospect Park, this is one of the finest residential areas in the town. Wide streets bordered with trees and uniform lines of apartment blocks punctuated by church spires showing Brooklyn as it existed in the 19th century The architectural style is typical of the period between the Civil and First World War.

Fort Greene Park (BX). – The 32 acre park, located off Myrtle Avenue and Washington Park in a community of elegant 19th century residences, was designed by Frederick Law Olmsted and Calvert Vaux. It contains the Martyr's Monument, designed by Stanford White. The monument commemorates the death of men and women who fought for the American cause and were confined in British prison ships moored off what is now the Brooklyn Navy Yard.

Queens is the largest borough of New York City, covering 108 square miles on Long Island. It is the next door to Brooklyn, extending from the East River in the north to Jamaica Bay in the south. A cluster of manufacturing plants in the Long Island City area gives way to more residential sections to the southeast, such as Forest Hills, Jamaica, and Flushing.

It is in Queens, which was named after Catherine of Braganza, the wife of Charles II, that two World's Fairs took place and that the United Nations General Assembly met before the completion of its permanent headquarters. The borough also contains two major airports (John F. Kennedy and La Guardia) and, for sports fans, Aqueduct Racetrack (CZ), Shea Stadium (BX) and West Side Tennis Club of Forest Hills (BCY), where the U.S. Open had been played. (The U.S. Open expects to move *(summer 1978)* to their future Flushing Meadow home, the National Tennis Center.)

■ SIGHTS

Jamaica Bay Wildlife Refuge. – *Open daily from 8AM to 6PM (9PM in summer). Subway : A train to Broad Channel.*

Adjacent to JFK Airport, is a peaceful wildlife refuge, a major migratory haven for birds, where a wide variety of waterfowl, land and shore birds can be found. Now part of Gateway National Recreation Area, it is the nation's largest urban park. The refuge lies off Cross Bay Boulevard.

Jamaica Arts Center (CZ). – *Open weekdays from 10AM to 5PM. Admission free. Subway : 160 St. (5 line).* The Center operates as a cultural center. Art exhibits, art classes, workshops for children or adults, concerts, and films are offered to the public.

Reformed Church of Newtown (BY). – *85-15 Broadway Elmshurst. Open Tuesday through Saturday 9AM to noon.*

In 1731 the church was organized as a congregation of the Dutch Reformed Church. Because of its growing parish, the original structure (1732) was entirely rebuilt (1831) in the Greek Revival period with some reminders of the Georgian and Federal Styles.

Flushing (CX). – Best known today for the **World's Fairs** held here, Flushing has an old and honorable past. As early as 1643, a small settlement named Vlissingen was established here ; the Dutch name eventually was transformed into Flushing.

Beginning about 1655, local history was associated with the **Quakers,** or Society of Friends. The Quakers believe in simplicity of life and of religious practices, complete tolerance towards others and pacifism ; they were often persecuted. John Bowne, an Englishman who settled in Flushing, allowed Quakers to hold meetings in his home. His arrest and acquittal helped to establish religious freedom in America. The Society of Friends flourished in Flushing, which has one of the oldest **Friends Meeting House's** *(see p. 75)* in America *(on Northern Boulevard near Linden Place).* At 137-15 Northern Boulevard, is the old Flushing **Town Hall,** a 1862 Romanesque building which has been restored.

Bowne House (CX **A**). – *Open Tuesday, Saturday and Sunday from 2:30 to 4:30 PM. Admission free. Subway : IRT 7 line to Main Street.*

Located at 37-01 Bowne Street the house was built in 1661 ; these include the kitchen with its monumental chimney. Nine successive generations of the Bowne family lived in the house until 1946. There is a collection of 17th and 18th century furniture as well as pewter, paintings and documents.

Kingsland Homestead (CX **D**). – *Open Tuesday through Saturday 11AM to 2PM and Sunday from 2:30 to 4:30 PM. Closed Monday and holidays.*

Located in Weeping Beech Park at Parsons Boulevard and 37th Avenue, this old 3 story farmhouse built in 1774 is a mixture of Dutch and English traditions : notice its divided front door and central chimney. The house contains a number of period rooms and is now a musuem.

Flushing Meadow Park (BCY). – Once a swamp favored by ducks and then a sanitary landfill, this 1,275-acre park was developed in the 1930's to accommodate New York's World Fairs. From 1946 to 1949 the United Nations General Assembly also met here.

Meadow Lake, 3/4 of a mile long and 1/4 of a mile wide, was created for the 1939 World's Fair. Vestiges of the 1964-65 Fair include the **Hall of Science** (**B**) with its museum of science and technology and the **Unisphere** (**C**) (140 feet high) ; its stainless steel framework supports panels representing the parallels and meridians, as well as the continents.

To the north of Flushing Meadow Park, **Shea Stadium** (BX) also dates from the 1964-65 World's Fair. Home of the New York Mets baseball team and the New York Jets football team, it can hold 55,000 to 60,000 spectators. The 10,000 seats can be moved along rails in order to change the shape of the field. Restaurants which can seat 1,000 people and 45 acres of parking lots are available to fans.

John F. Kennedy International Airport★★ (CZ). – One of the busiest airports in the world Kennedy International Airport covers 4,900 acres in the southeast corner of Queens, along Jamaica Bay, an area the size of Manhattan Island from Midtown to the Battery. Construction, begun in 1942, was placed under the jurisdiction of the Port Authority of New York and New Jersey in 1947. Opened as Idlewild Airport a year later, the airport was renamed in 1963 to honor the late President.

To visit JFK an express coach service runs from Grand Central Station and the East Side Terminal ($4) ; helicopter flights from the World Trade Center Battery Park City Heliport $12.73 - $23.15) ; for flight information call 212-661-5100 for a bird's-eye view of New York.

Central Terminal Area. - This is the heart of the airport comprising passenger terminal buildings, a control tower, parking areas, three chapels and other structures and facilities.

International Arrivals Building★★ . – An arched pavilion forms the center of this 2,000 foot long building, designed by Skidmore, Owings and Merrill, which houses the arrival hall and in its wings a number of airline terminals.

From the observation platform there is an overall **view** of the airport. Next to the building rises the 11-story control tower.

Pan Am Terminal★★. – The Worldport a striking four-level building topped by a suspended roof, it is devised in such a way as "to bring the aircraft to the passengers rather than make the passengers walk to aircraft".

Visitors to the Worldport can obtain a bird's-eye-view of the jumbo jets from the rooftop parking.

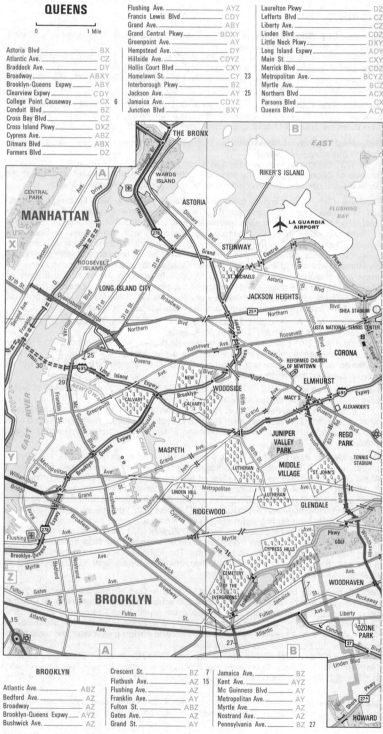

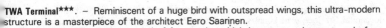

TWA Terminal★★★. – Reminiscent of a huge bird with outspread wings, this ultra-modern structure is a masterpiece of the architect Eero Saarinen.

The main building is composed of four vaults which intersect and rest on only four points. The walls are thick grass.

La Guardia Airport (BX). – Close to Manhattan (8 miles from 42nd Street), this major airport bordering on Flushing and Bowery Bays was established in 1939 and named after the city's Mayor Fiorello H. La Guardia, affectionately known as "The Little Flower" (mayor from 1934-1945).

Despite its relatively small size, which is 1/9 of Kennedy, La Guardia is capable of handling most of the domestic flights.

Rockaway Blvd	BDZ	Woodhaven Blvd	BCYZ	**MANHATTAN**	
Roosevelt Ave.	ACY	14 th Ave.	CX	Franklin D. Roosevelt Drive	AXY
Shore Pkwy	BZ	21 st St.	AX	Second Ave.	AXY
Southern Pkwy	CDZ	31 st St.	AX	57 th St.	AX
Springfield Blvd	DYZ	46 th Ave.	CX		
Sunrise Hway	DZ	63 rd Rd.	BY	**NASSAU COUNTY**	
Sutphin Blvd	CZ	69 th Rd.	BY	North Hempstead Turnpike	DX
Union Turnpike	CDY	94 th St.	BX		
Utopia Pkwy	CXY	122 nd St.	CX	**BRIDGES AND TUNNELS**	
Van Wyck Expwy	CYZ	164 th St.	CY	Bronx-Whitestone Bridge	CX	2
Vernon Blvd	AXY	168 th St.	CYZ	Kosciuszko Bridge	AY	
Whitestone Expwy	CX	212 th Pl.	DY	Pulaski Bridge	AY	29
Willets Point Blvd	CX	212 th St.	DY	Queensboro Bridge	AXY	
				Queens-Midtown Tunnel	AY	30
				Throgs Neck Bridge	CX	33
				Triborough Bridge	AX	
				Williamsburg Bridge	AY	

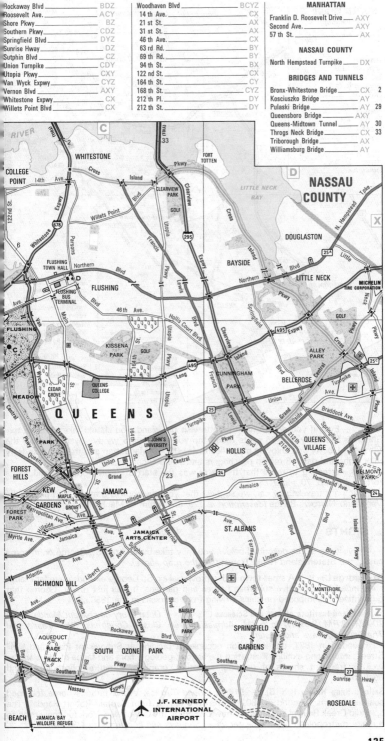

STATEN ISLAND (Richmond)

The fifth borough of New York City, Staten Island is still relatively rural with the exception of its capital, St. George. Its country air so close to Manhattan may surprise the visitor.

Most of the island is flat, although it boasts the highest point on the Atlantic coast, Todt Hill (410 feet above sea level). Formed by the terminal moraine of a Quaternary glacier, it is about 14 miles long and 8 miles wide. Large sandy beaches run along the southeastern shore. Still fairly uncrowded, the best known is South Beach ; and the recently created Gateway National Recreation Area includes Great Kills Park and Miller Field.

Named after the Dutch States General, Staten Island acquired its alternate name in honor of the Duke of Richmond, son of Charles II. The population is 336,000 and includes many Italians, as well as the descendants of some old families who have lived there since the 18th century.

STATEN ISLAND
(RICHMOND)

0   2 Miles

Amboy Rd	AZ
Arthur Kill Rd	AZ
Bay St.	BY
Bloomingdale Rd	AZ
Clarke Ave.	BZ 2
Clove Rd	BY 6
Forest Ave.	BY
Forest Hill Ave.	BY
Huguenot Ave.	AZ
Hylan Blvd	AZ
Jewett Ave.	BY 7
Lily Pond Ave.	BY 9
Manor Rd	BY
Midland Ave.	BZ

Seaside Blvd	BZ
Staten Island Expwy	BY
Todt Hill Rd	BY
Vanderbilt Ave.	BY 21
Victory Blvd	BY
West Shore Expwy	AZ
Willow Brook Pkwy	BY
Woodrow Rd	AZ

Page Ave.	AZ
Richmond Ave.	AY
Richmond Hill Rd	AY 13
Richmond Pkwy	AZ
Richmond Rd	BZ
Richmond Ter.	BY
School Rd	BY 19

BRIDGES

Bayonne Bridge	BY	25
Goethals Bridge	AY	27
Outerbridge Crossing	AZ	28
Verrazano-Narrows Bridge	BY	30

Visit. — Even if you do not have time to visit the island, you should take a trip on the Staten Island Ferry. For 25 cents round trip you will have a windy voyage, skirting the Statue of Liberty and enjoying magnificent **views★★★** of Manhattan and the Bay. The ferry runs night and day (18 million passengers and 700,000 cars in 1977).

It is interesting to recall that this ferry was the start of "Commodore" Vanderbilt's fortune *(see pp. 70 and 91).*

If you are traveling by car, we suggest that you drive out to Staten Island across the Verrazano-Narrows Bridge *(description p. 129)* and return to Manhattan by the ferry.

■ SIGHTS

To visit the sights described below, you may take buses from St. George or, in some cases, the Staten Island Rapid Transit *(see the map above).*

St. George (BY). — A small town with a provincial air, St. George extends quite far inland, surrounded by attractive suburban homes and gardens. It was just off St. George that quarantine was imposed on ships arriving from overseas in the 1850's.

Staten Island Institute of Arts and Sciences (BY **M**). — *Open every day except Monday from 10 AM (2 PM Sunday) to 5 PM. Admission free. Closed Christmas, New Year's and Thanksgiving Days and Easter.*

Founded in 1881, this institution occupies a building at Stuyvesant Place and Wall Street : interesting exhibits illustrating the history, geology, flora and fauna of the island as well as frequent shows of painting, sculpture, graphics, furniture, photography and costumes.

Sailor's Snug Harbor (BY **B**). — *914 Richmond Terrace.* World famous home for aged seamen, it was founded in 1801 thanks to a legacy from Captain Robert Randall. The splendid Greek Revival buildings are now owned by the City of New York for conversion to a major metropolitan cultural center *(open Sundays and holidays 1 to 4:30 PM).*

Staten Island Zoo★(BY). – *Open every day from 10 AM to 4:45 PM. Admission free Monday through Thursday ; 75 cents ; children 50 cents Friday through Sunday.*

Located in Barrett Park, this smallish zoo is not lacking in interest. It was opened in 1936 and possesses a collection of snakes and reptiles which enjoys a world-wide reputation, surpassing that of the Bronx Zoo in this field. There is also a Children's Center.

Fort Wadsworth (BY **A**). – *Open 1 (10 AM Saturdays) to 4 PM Sundays, Mondays, Thursdays and Fridays ; closed holidays. Admission free.*

Originally a small blockhouse in Dutch times to protect them against the Indians it was transformed by the English and by 1812 was a real bastion.

Today Fort Wadsworth is the oldest continuously manned military post in the United States. Situated in a pleasantly green site, there are splendid **views**★ from the fort of the entrance to the port of New York.

The museum traces the history of the fort from 1663 to the present and exhibits collections of insignia, uniforms, arms, etc.

Jacques Marchais Center of Tibetan Art (BZ **E**). – *338 Lighthouse Avenue. Open Thursday, Friday, Saturday and Sunday (June through August) from 1 to 5 PM. $1.00*

Laid out on Lighthouse Hill in enchanting gardens, the Center displays a collection of art covering the culture, religion and mythology of Tibet, China and India. The library, furnished with Chinese furniture, contains a number of books about Tibet, Buddhism, Asian art, perfumes, etc.

High Rock Park Conservation Center (BY **F**). – *Open every day from 9 AM to 5 PM. Admission free.*

This forest, at the end of Nevada Avenue, is being preserved in its natural state. A varied topography, a wide range of flora and fauna make the place very attractive. The Center provides self-guided tours and conducts special environmental educational programs, workshops and holds a variety of cultural programs.

Richmondtown Restoration★ (BZ). – Richmondtown the historic and geographic center of Staten Island county, is in the process of restoration. The village's evolution from the 17th to 19th century can be traced through the houses, furniture, gardens and implements on display from the different periods.

The houses are scattered in a bucolic setting near Latourette Park which also contains a golf course.

Voorlezer House (C). – *63 Arthur Kill Road.* Built at the end of the 17th century, this building served as a church and schoolhouse (the oldest known schoolhouse in America), as well as residence for the church clerk (voorlezer).

Museum of the Staten Island Historical Society (M). – *441 Clarke Avenue. Open 10 AM (2 PM on Sundays) to 5 PM ; closed on Mondays. Admission 50 cents or $1.50 for a combined ticket giving access to some of Richmondtown Restoration houses.*

Some parts of the building date back to the middle of the 19th century. Exhibits and documents relate the history of the island : costumes, ceramics, craftsmen's tools and a reconstructed old store. There is also a special children's section in nearby Bennett House.

Treasure House (C). – A former tannery, was established here at the beginning of the 18th century. A century later, a surprised new owner discovered $7,000 in gold hidden in a wall. *Closed : restoration in progress.*

Church of St. Andrew (G). – Founded in 1713, this church was rebuilt twice ; the present edifice is Gothic Revival.

Moravian Cemetery (BY **H**). – This peaceful, gardenlike cemetery is affiliated with a Moravian church. The denomination, founded in the 15th century as an evangelical communion in Bohemia (Moravia), accepted Protestantism in the 17th century. Ascetic in the early years, their main precept was strict observance of the teachings of the Holy Bible.

The church at the entrance was reconstructed and improved in 1845 by the Vanderbilt family ; one of their ancestors belonged to the sect in the 17th century. Some of the tombstones date from the 18th century ; a mausoleum which cost nearly a million dollars is dedicated to the memory of the Vanderbilts.

Conference House (AZ **J**). – *Open every day but Monday from 1 to 4 PM. Closed Christmas through New Year's. 50 cents.*

At the southwestern tip of Staten Island, Conference House is named after the negotiations between the British and the Americans, including John Adams and Benjamin Franklin, which took place here in September 1776, after the Battle of Long Island.

The 17th century manor house has been restored. The interior, furnished in Colonial style, also displays remembrances of Benjamin Franklin.

**RATING OF THE WALKS
AND SIGHTS**

★ ★ ★ Very highly recommended

★ ★ Recommended

★ Interesting

BEYOND THE CITY LIMITS

The fame of New York City has somewhat obscured the attractions of its outskirts. Nevertheless, not even the passing tourist should neglect the charms of country air, hills and forests, islands and beaches, forts and historic mansions which abound in this region. New Yorkers themselves are well aware of these advantages, as may be seen from the estates remaining on Long Island, as well as the more modest suburban homes both there and in Westchester.

Suburban and even « exurban », this area is also extremely well equipped for vacationers, with its extensive network of roads and parkways, its hotels and motels complete with swimming pools and other recreational facilities which make it ideal for weekends or vacations ; golf, tennis, boating and sailing, horseback riding (from foxhunting to dude ranches), fishing, skiing and fresh-and salt-water swimming. About one-third of the people who work in Manhattan live in the suburbs.

Since this guide is devoted essentially to New York City, we shall describe only three basic excursion trips which provide a pleasant change from the hustle and bustle of town. There are many other possibilities for trips further afield : Niagara Falls, the Catskills or the Adirondacks, Albany and Saratoga in New York State ; Tanglewood and Sturbridge in Massachusetts, or New Haven and Old Mystic Seaport in Connecticut among others.

■ THE HUDSON RIVER VALLEY★★★

The majestic Hudson, which leads the way toward the Saint Lawrence and the Great Lakes, flows between rocky crags and wooded peaks, a romantic and even grandiose setting. The river has often been celebrated in literature and art, especially by the painters of the Hudson River School, whose best known representatives were Cole and Kensett.

Originating high in the Adirondacks, the Hudson flows 315 miles to the sea. Navigable as far as Albany, it is linked to the Great Lakes by the **Erie Canal**, once a busy waterway between Albany and Buffalo.

A TWO DAYS' EXCURSION
(167 miles round trip)

This trip covers only the southern part of the Hudson. It is at its best in the fall, when indian summer gilds the forests along its banks. If you have only one day available, we recommend that you drive north on the east bank in the morning and return on the west bank in the afternoon, to avoid having the sun in your eyes.

Note : from late May until Labor Day, you may take a boat trip up the Hudson from New York City, which is highly recommended. Call the Hudson River Day Line (Pier 81, West 41st Street) at 279-5151 for information.

Towns and sites

Our description covers the main sights following the itinerary shown on the map adjoining. U.S. Route 9, going north, and U.S. Route 9W, for the return, afford frequent glimpses, and occasionally sweeping views, of the river.

THE HUDSON RIVER VALLEY

Leave Manhattan via the Henry Hudson Parkway, which leads into the Saw Mill River Parkway. You will pass Van Cortlandt Park and Yonkers : you are now in Westchester County.

After Yonkers, turn left *(on U. S. Route 9)* toward Dobbs Ferry, and then continue north. Beyond Irvington, a road to the left, West Sunnyside Lane, winds along a valley to Sunnyside, on the banks of the Hudson.

Sunnyside*. – *Open every day from 10 AM to 5 PM. Closed Thanksgiving Day, Christmas and 1 January, Admission : $2.25.*

Sunnyside was the home of the author-humorist and scholar **Washington Irving** (1783-1859), who lived here for many of the last 25 years of his life. Irving transformed the original stone cottage which he had bought in 1835 into his "snuggery" with a mixture of architectural styles.

Sunnyside lies along the east bank of the Hudson River and its 20 acres have been landscaped in the 19th century style.

The museum includes furniture and memorabilia of the author of *Diedrich Knickerbocker's History of New York* and the chronicler of Rip van Winkle and Sleepy Hollow *(see p. 31 : New York and Literature)*.

Philipsburg Manor*. – *Admission as at Sunnyside.*

Philipsburg Manor appears as it did in the early 1700's when it was an important gristmill trading site along the Hudson River.

It now has an operational water-powered gristmill and its stone Manor House, begun in the 1680's by Frederick Philipse I, founder of the family's land and trading empire, is outfitted with period furnishings. Philipsburg also has a 200-foot-long oak dam and a large 1750's barn.

Continue north on U.S. 9, passing through Ossining, site of the Ossining Correctional Facility formerly known as Sing Sing prison. You will then reach Croton-on-Hudson and the Van Cortlandt Manor.

Van Cortlandt Manor. – *Admission as at Sunnyside.*

The Manor House was home to the Van Cortlandt family for 260 years and now appears as it did during the American Revolutionary War period.

Its owner then was Pierre van Cortlandt, patriot and the first lieutenant governor of New York State, who presided over 86,000 acres. The House contains original family furniture, paintings and pewter. The Ferry House, Ferry House kitchen, fields and gardens recall 18th century Hudson River Valley life.

Benjamin Franklin, Marquis de Lafayette, Comte de Rochambeau and John Jay are all said to have visited the manor.

Route 9 north after leaving Putnam County next enters Dutchess County, an agricultural and aristocratic area, where many New Yorkers had, or still have, country places.

A French emigré, Févret de St-Mesmin, once tried to found an ideal city, Tivoli, between Poughkeepsie and the Hudson. We now reach Poughkeepsie, seat of Vassar College.

Vassar College. – Vassar is one of the best-known private liberal arts colleges in the United States. Founded as a women's college in 1861, it became coeducational in 1968 and now has 2,250 students.

The library possesses 500,000 volumes. The buildings reflect the history of American architecture styles of the last 100 years.

Six miles north of Poughkeepsie, Hyde Park is also on Route 9.

Hyde Park**. – Once a resort for wealthy New York families, and then for a time an occasional summer White House, Hyde Park has remained a rather quiet village.

Franklin D. Roosevelt Home National Historic Site. – *Open 31 May to 5 September 9 AM to 6 PM (5 PM the rest of the year) ; admission : $1.50 valid for the Vanderbilt Mansion.*

National Historic Site and last resting place of Franklin D. Roosevelt, the estate was acquired by the president's father, in 1867 ; Franklin D. was born here in 1882. The house dates back to 1826, but has been extensively remodelled and enlarged. The house, Library and Museum contain memorabilia of the late president and his family.

In the rose garden *(admission free)* is the simple slab of white Vermont marble which marks the final resting place of Franklin D. Roosevelt and his wife Eleanor.

Vanderbilt Mansion. – *Admission as at F.D.R.'s home.*

Just to the north of Hyde Park, Frederick W. Vanderbilt commissioned McKim, Mead and White to build this sumptuous residence in 1898. Now a National Historic Site, it bears witness to a bygone age of opulence. Before the Vanderbilts bought the property in the early 19th century, it belonged to Dr. Hosack *(see p. 34)*, who introduced exotic plants. The interior contains a collection of furniture of 16th to 18th century design and works of art.

Return to Poughkeepsie and cross the Hudson, take 9W south to West Point.

West Point**. – Renowned as the site of the United States Military Academy, West Point overlooks the Hudson River.

The Military Tradition. – Already serving as a military outpost dominating the Hudson in the 18th century, West Point was used during the late 1700's, as a training school for artillerists and engineers, under the tenure of General Henry Knox as Secretary of War.

It was not until 1802, however, that the US Military Academy, the oldest of the nation's service academies, was established by Congress, with West Point selected as its site.

In the Academy's first year 5 officers trained and instructed the 10 students ; there are now 4,417 men and women cadets. Among its graduates are Generals MacArthur (1903), Patton (1909) and Eisenhower (1915) as well as astronauts Borman (1950), Aldrin (1951), Collins and White (1952) and Scott (1954).

The buildings. — The chapels, monuments and museum are open to the public *(see the map)*. Of particular interest are the **museum** *(open 10:30 AM to 4:15 PM 15 May to 15 November, except Christmas and New Year's Days. Admission free)*, housed in a wing of the former indoor riding ring, Thayer Hall; among the exhibits are Napoleon's sword and Goering's marshal's jewel-encrusted baton; and an exceptional collection of arms which traces the development of automatic weapons from the Civil War to the present; the **Cadet Chapel**, an example of the "military Gothic" style, built in 1910; 18th century Fort Putnam, partially restored in 1907 with further restoration in 1976; Trophy

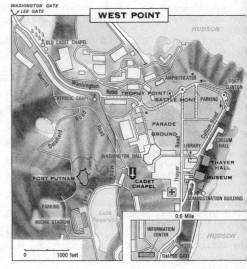

Point, where Revolutionary troops strung a great chain across the Hudson to prevent British ships from navigating it; and the Battle Monument, in memory of the Civil War dead.

The parades. — From early September until November, and in May, the famous reviews are held; they are known for their precision of movement and the particular stance of the cadets.

For schedules, inquire at the Visitors Information Center, or telephone West Point (914) 938-3507.

Continuing south along the Hudson valley, you will pass **Bear Mountain**, the highest point (1,305 feet) in Palisades Interstate Park. There are many recreation facilities for all seasons.

Stony Point Battlefield. — *Open daily mid-April to 31 October.* This marks the site of a former English fortified position, they controlled Kings Ferry on the Hudson, a vital line in the American east-west line of communication. Stony Point was taken by General Wayne's troops in July 1779. Signs indicate where the fiercest fighting — often hand to hand — took place. The battlefield area is now a park with picnic places and affords a fine view over the Hudson.

Drive south on **Palisades Interstate Parkway**, high above the Hudson (superb **views**★★ of Yonkers, the Bronx and Manhattan) to the George Washington Bridge and Manhattan.

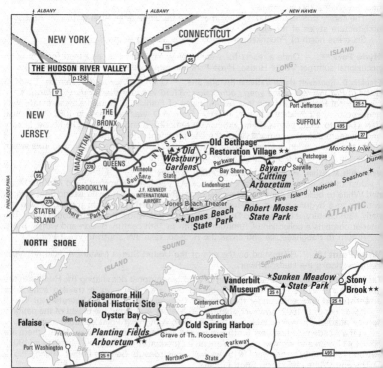

▪ LONG ISLAND★

Long Island, covering an area of 1,723 square miles has a population of approximately 2,800,000 and measures 125 miles long and 20 miles at its widest point. Although Long Island is often misleadingly said to include only Nassau and Suffolk counties, it actually comprises 4 counties, the other two being Queens (Queens County) and Brooklyn (Kings County), boroughs of New York City.

The western part of the island has developed into a suburban area due to its proximity to the city, whereas the eastern part is more rural. The North Shore because of the wealthy landowners searching the calm away from the city became known as the "Gold Coast" whereas the South Shore with its miles of white sandy beaches developed into a vacation spot for New Yorkers. The attractions are unlimited : small quiet lanes, a countryside flecked with golf courses and tennis courts, a walk in one of the many wildlife refuges, a visit to a "Gold Coast" palatial mansion or the rustic charm of a small village.

The economy is quite diversified, encompassing light manufacturing, service industries and agriculture. There are a number of farms – Suffolk County being the largest producer of agricultural products in the state of New York – engaged in truck farming (fruits and vegetables), dairy farming, raising those delicious Long Island ducklings or producing those famous Long Island potatoes.

Seafood is to be found especially on the Eastern coast : oysters, clams, scallops and lobsters have a well-deserved reputation.

Commercial and chartered deep-sea fishing boats leave daily from South Shore communities.

EXCURSIONS

North Shore

The North Shore faces Long Island Sound – there are rocky necks and beaches, thick woodlands, hilly coves, bays, inlets and steep bluffs ; the northern peninsula extends 25 miles culminating at Orient Point.

Falaise. – *Sands Point Park and Preserve, Port Washington. Visit by appointment only, call 516-883-1612.*

Home of the late Captain Harry F. Guggenheim, Falaise, located amidst 209 acres, is one of the last remaining estates of the "Gold Coast". A courtyard leads to the Normandy-style manor house with an arcaded loggia, overlooking the Sound. Inside is a collection of 16th and 17th century French and Spanish decorative accessories.

Planting Fields★★. – *Planting Fields Road. Oyster Bay. Open daily 10AM to 5PM, adults $1.50 ; children free (off-season no admission fee during the week).*

Formerly the private estate of William Robertson Coe, a financier, the Planting Fields Arboretum, under the administration of the Long Island State Parks and Recreation Commission, comprises 409 acres of planting fields and 160 acres are developed as an arboretum ; the remainder have been kept as a natural habitat of woods and fields.

The plant collections include over 600 rhododendron and azalea species *(blooming period : mid-April through May) ;* the camelia collection, the oldest and largest of its kind under glass *(blooming period : February, March)* the Synoptic Garden, approximately 5 acres of selected ornamental shrubs for Long Island gardens ; and greenhouses filled with orchids, hibiscus, begonias and cacti, etc.

Amidst these landscaped gardens and spacious lawns stands Coe Hall, a fine example of Elizabethan architecture.

Oyster Bay. – Vacation spot, port for pleasure craft and suburban residential town, Oyster Bay a hamlet, has slightly more than 6,000 inhabitants. In Young's Cemetery you will find the grave of **Theodore Roosevelt** *(details p. 75).*

Raynham Hall. – *20 West Main Street. Open weekdays except Tuesdays, 10AM to noon and 1 to 5PM ; Sundays, 1 to 5PM. 50 cents.* This old farmhouse played an important role during the American Revolution. It was the home of Samuel Townsend, whose son, Robert, was Washington's chief intelligence agent in New York City. The interior is complete with period furniture and memorabilia.

Sagamore Hill National Historic Site. – *Open daily from 9:30AM to 6PM (4:30PM the rest of the year), July 1 through Labor Day. Closed Thanksgiving, Christmas, New Year's Day. 50 cents.*

Located east of Oyster Bay, the Theodore Roosevelt Home is maintained as it was during his Presidency (1901-1909). Exhibits depicting his publc and private life are located in the Old Orchard Museum, where the visitor may also see a biographical film.

LONG ISLAND

0   20 Miles

Cold Spring Harbor. – From 1836 through 1862 the Cold Spring Harbor whaling fleet of nine ships sailed to every ocean navigeable in search of whale oil and bone. The masters of the Cold Spring vessels were from established whaling centers such as New Bedford and Sag Harbor.

The Whaling Museum★. – *Open daily 11 AM to 5 PM mid-June to mid-September. Adults 75 cents ; children : 25 cents.*

The most outstanding exhibit is the fully equipped whaleboat just as it was aboard the whaling brig *Daisy* on her 1912-13 voyage out of New Bedford ; nearby is the diorama of Cold Spring Harbor – representing in detail : village houses, whaling company buildings, wharves – as it was in the 1840's, the zenith of the whaling period.

Dispersed throughout the museum are examples of whalecraft : harpoons, navigation instruments, whaleship models, old prints and maps. Note especially the extensive collection of scrimshaw demonstrating practically every form of the whaleman's folkart as well as a collection of sailors knots.

Vanderbilt Museum★. – *Little Neck Road, Centerport. Open every weekday except Monday, May through October, 10 AM to 4 PM Sundays and holidays, noon to 5 PM. $1.00.*

This museum occupies a former country house richly decorated for William K. Vanderbilt Jr., great-grandson of "Commodore" Cornelius *(see pp. 70 and 91),* and set in a 25-acre estate overlooking Northport Bay.

The collections gathered by William during his travels include : curiosities of natural history, ship models, arms and armor and mummified heads. On the grounds there is also a **Planetarium.** *(There are changing one-hour shows all year round, held frequently during July and August.) For programs and schedule call 516-757-7500 ; adults : $1.75, children : $1.00.*

Sunken Meadow State Park★★. – Sunken Meadow, is a large beach with fine sand bordering a bay on Long Island Sound which is almost always calm. The recreational facilities are outstanding.

Stony Brook★★. – A typical colonial village of the 18th century, Stony Brook shelters a number of reconstructed buildings in a charming rural setting ; the complex comprises such buildings as an art museum, a carriage museum, and several period buildings (i.e. blacksmith shop, school house, a barn and a museum store).

Carriage Museum★★. – This museum houses an exceptional collection of horse-drawn carriages from gigs to commercial vehicles. A gallery is reserved for fire fighting apparatus.

Fine Arts Museum. – Displayed here is a permanent display of the **paintings by William Sidney Mount★★** (1807-1868). Mount settled at Stony Brook and painted anecdotes of his rural surroundings, becoming the first major genre painter in America. Among the works displayed are : *Farmer Whetting his Scythe, Dancing on the Barn Floor,* and *The Banjo Players.*

South Shore

The shoreline's surfside fronts the Atlantic Ocean and the bayside faces the Great South Bay. The beaches are vast, smooth expanses of sand attracting vacationers and weekenders all along the coast.

Jones Beach State Park★★. – A series of beaches, 6 1/2 miles long, make up this bathing resort, with its double exposure (ocean and bay). New Yorkers flock here in summer.

Extremely well equipped, Jones Beach includes the well-known **Jones Beach Theater,** a nautical stadium, heated pools, sports fields and play areas. The Water Tower, inspired after the Campanile of St. Mark Church in Venice, rises above a freshwater well, 1,000 feet deep.

Old Westbury Gardens★. – *Old Westbury Road. Open May through October Wednesdays through Sundays, 10 AM to 5 PM. Gardens and house $3.00.*

Old Westbury Gardens is the former estate of the late John S. Phipps, sportsman and financier. The stately Georgian mansion is set in an 18th century park ; its interior is preserved as it was during the family's occupancy with antique furnishings, and English paintings and adorned with gilded mirrors and objets d'art.

The estate (100 acres) containing flowers, shrubs and trees (linden, beech) presents a continually changing picture with the seasons.

Old Bethpage Restoration Village★★. – *Round Swamp Road. Open 10 AM to 5 PM (4 PM November through February). Adults $2.00 ; children $1.00.*

Nestled in a 200-acre valley, Old Bethpage is an active farm community which recreates the lifestyle of a pre-Civil War American village. Over 25 historic buildings saved from destruction, caused by suburban development, have been moved to the site of the former Powell Farm.

Strolling leisurely through the village you will see the blacksmith hammering at his anvil, the cobbler making shoes, the tailor sewing and the farmers working their fields.

Bayard Cutting Arboretum. – *Entrance by Route 27 A. Open Wednesdays through Sundays 10 AM to 5:30 PM (4:30 PM in winter) $1.00.*

Started in 1887 by William Cutting in accordance with plans by Olmsted, the Arboretum covers 690 acres of woodlands and planted areas. Many of the specimens in the Pinetum date back to the original planting of fir, spruce, pine and other evergreens. Rhododendrons and azaleas *(blooming period : May, June)* border the walks and drives ; wild flowers are also featured.

Fire Island. – The island is 32 miles long and one-half mile to less than 200 yards wide and is 1,400 miles of **National Seashore★**. A relaxed informality prevails in parts of the island which has no roads for automobile traffic. Ferry service from Patchogue, Sayville and Bay Shore connects with the Fire Island communities *(Fire Islands Ferries : 665-5045 or Zee Line : 665-2115).*

Robert Moses State Park. – The western part of Fire Island is named for Robert Moses, the former superintendent of Long Island parks. Its dunes are a refuge for waterfowl. The Atlantic coast is excellent for surf casting.

The Hamptons★. – A chain of seafaring towns dominating a 35-mile stretch of Long Island's South Shore, which have now become vacation colonies ; starting at Westhampton Beach rimming Shinnecock Bay and subsiding at Amagansett.

Westhampton Beach. – Formerly a seafaring community, Westhampton is a lively resort where many New Yorkers among them musicians, writers, artists, etc., like to spend their weekends or take up summer residence. During the first weekend in August is the annual Westhampton Beach Outdoor Art Show.

A drive along Dune Road on the narrow barrier beach passes by everything from the New England type home, brown shingled and trimmed with white, to the bungalow ; a 15 mile long beach from Moriches Inlet to Shinnecock Inlet.

Southampton. – This famous shore resort is the largest of the Hampton communities and the home of many fine estates. To the northwest of town is one of the largest museums devoted to the automobile, **The Long Island Automative Museum★** *(open daily June through September 9 AM to 5 PM ; late May and October weekends only. Adults $2.00 ; children $1.00).*

East Hampton. – A charming little town whose **Main Street★** is lined on both sides by magnificent elm trees. Its village green with a central pond flanked by fine old houses gives it the appearance of an English country town. East Hampton's quaint charm has attracted writers and artists.

Sag Harbor. – This sea town with its deep water-harbor, nestled in a sheltered cove, docks and Custom's House (the first custom's house established in New York State ; *open Memorial Day to Labor Day 9 AM to 5 PM ; 50.cents),* was named Port of Entry for the United States by George Washington. With its fine colonial homes, Sag Harbor, still preserves the salty flavor and nostalgia of yesteryear *(mid-June : Old Whaler's Festival).* Stop at the **Suffolk County Whaling Museum** *(open 15 May to 30 September 10 AM (1 PM Sundays) to 5 PM. 75 cents),* a Greek Revival edifice containing exhibits of the whaling days, set in the atmosphere of a whaling captain's home.

Montauk. – A ten mile strip jutting into the ocean composed of thousands of acres of natural woodlands, stark cliffs, dunes and white beaches. It is one of the favorite centers among sports fishermen (deep-sea-fishing). Built in 1795, at the point of the peninsula, is the Montauk Lighthouse located in the Montauk State Park.

▬ PRINCETON UNIVERSITY★★

In the western part of New Jersey, Princeton University is the center of a residential town which has remained calm and verdant.

Access. – *119 miles round trip.* A bus line connects Princeton to New York : information at the Port Authority Bus Terminal. If you drive, leave Manhattan by the Lincoln Tunnel. Take the New Jersey Turnpike south to exit 9 ; turn right and cross the Lawrence River ; take Route 1 toward Penns Neck. Princeton can also be reached by the Pennsylvania Railroad.

A BIT OF HISTORY

It was in 1746 that a small group of Presbyterian ministers decided to found a college for the middle eastern colonies, and named it the College of New Jersey.

First established at Elizabeth, and then at Newark, it moved to the present site in 1756, after Nassau Hall was finished.

Nassau Hall was then the largest educational building in North America, and had room enough to house all of the college.

During the Revolution, it served as barracks and hospitals, successively, for British and American troops. Its capture by Washington on January 3, 1777 marked the end of the Battle of Princeton and a victory for the colonists. The Continental Congress sat here for six months in 1783, and the final treaty of peace was signed here.

On its 150th anniversary, the College of New Jersey (already called Princeton College) became Princeton University.

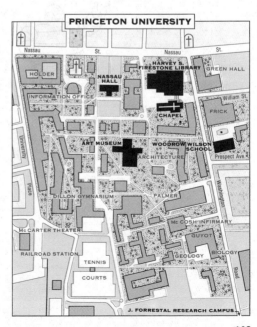

PRINCETON UNIVERSITY

Studies. – Princeton is one of the Ivy League colleges. Formerly all-male, it became coeducational in 1969. Women now make up over one-third of the undergraduate population.

Since the 18th century, Princeton has been noted for its men of science and for its teaching of the arts of government ; the first chair of chemistry in the United States was created here in 1795. Since Woodrow Wilson's presidency of the University, from 1902 to 1910, Princeton has emphasized individual research and small seminars. An honor system prevails for examinations.

Princeton University has a full-time faculty of about 750 and about 5900 students ; 45 per cent of the undergraduates hold scholarships or receive special loans.

> *Albert Einstein, J. Robert Oppenheimer and former ambassador George Kennan have been among the distinguished scholars associated with the Institute for Advanced Study located in Princeton but not affiliated with the University.*

Visit. – *Free guide service is offered by the students all the year round ; it is preferable to request a visit three days in advance. Information available at the Orange Key Guide Service, Stanhope Hall (telephone : (609) 452-3603).* The 144 buildings of the University are scattered over the 2,600 acre campus : we describe here only the most important ones.

Nassau Hall. – This majestic edifice is named for the Nassau dynasty of Orange which reigned in England at the time of the founding of the college. Around Nassau Hall stretches the shady green campus. Nassau Hall is now used as an administration building.

Harvey S. Firestone Library. – Containing almost 3,000,000 volumes, it also provides 500 individual carrels for students and lecture rooms for 12 different disciplines.

Chapel. – A congregation of 2000 can worship here. There is a 16th century wooden pulpit from the north of France.

Art Museum. – Particularly strong in Italian drawings from the 16th, 17th and 18th centuries : works by Guerchin, Salvator Rosa and Tiepolo, among others.

Woodrow Wilson School. – A noted school of public administration and international affairs.

James Forrestal Research Campus. – To the east of Princeton proper, beyond Lake Carnegie, this Campus was opened in 1951 for research in applied mathematics, physics and chemistry. It houses the Plasma Physics Laboratory, the University's center for fusion research.

INDEX

|---|---|
West Point, Bryant Park	Cities, picturesque sites, points of interest.
Lincoln	Historical or famous figures.
Brownstones	Terms explained in the text of the guide ; practical information.

A

Abigail Adams Smith House. 120
Abyssinian Baptist Church 115
Action Painting 30
Airport : See proper name and pages. 14, 17
Algonquin (Hotel) 31, 42
Alice Tully Hall 103
Amagansett (Long Island) . 143
American Academy. . . . 120.
American Bicentennial Celebration 23
Americana (Hotel) . . . 36
American Crafts Council . 37
American Folk Art (Museum of) 37
American Indian (Museum of the) 120
American Numismatic Society 120
Americas (Avenue of the). . 34
Ammann (Othmar H.) . 129
Antiques Center of America. 121
Armory Show. 23, 29
Arsenal (Former) . . 50, 101
Ascension (Church of the). . 77
Asia House 50
Astor (Caroline) . . 43, 49
Astor (Hotel) 41
Astor Library 80
Astor Place 80
Audubon (John J.) . . . 105, 119
Audubon Terrace. . . . 119
Avenue : See proper name
Avery Fisher Hall 102

B

Barnard College 108
Barnard (George Grey) . 110
Barnum 118
Bartholdi (F.-Auguste) . 95
Battery Park. 93
Bayard Cutting Arboretum (Long Island) 142
Bear Mountain 140
Béchet de Rochefontaine . . 86
Bellevue Hospital 118
Bernstein (Leonard) . . 103
Biltmore (Hotel) 74
Bleecker Street 79
Blind (Library for the). . . 46
Bloomingdale's 120
Booth (Edwin) 75
Bowery (The). 81
Bowling Green. 90
Bowne House 133
Bradford (William) . 22, 87
Bridge : See proper name
British Building 34
Broadcasting (Museum of) . 74
Broad Street. 90
Broadway 41
Bronx (The) 20, 123
Bronx Community College 126
Bronx Museum of the Arts. 126
Bronx Zoo 123

Brooklyn 20, 127, 141
Brooklyn Academy of Music. 132
Brooklyn-Battery Tunnel . 93
Brooklyn Botanic Garden. 132
Brooklyn Bridge . . 23, 86
Brooklyn Children's Museum 132
Brooklyn Heights 127
Brooklyn Museum . . . 130
Brooklyn Public Library . 132
Brooks Brothers 74
Brownstones (The) 28
Bryant Park 47
Bryant (William Cullen) . 47, 99
Building : See proper name
Burlington House 37
Burr (Aaron) 92, 115
Butler Library 108

C

Canal Street 82, 84
Carl Schurz Park. . . . 121
Carnegie Hall 121
Carriage Museum (Long Island) 142
Cast iron 82
Castle Clinton. 93
Cathedral : See proper name
CBS Building 36
Celanese Building 36
Central Park. 99
Central Park Zoo. . . . 101
Central Terminal Area (Kennedy Airport). . . . 133
Chanin Building 69
Channel Gardens (The). . . 35
Chase National Bank . . 92
Chase Manhattan Bank Building 92
Chase (Salmon P.) . . . 92
Chatham Square. . . . 83
Chemical Bank Building . 71
Cherry Lane Theater . . 79
Chinatown 83
Chinese Museum. . . . 83
Christie's 72
Christopher Columbus (Statue of) 98
Chrysler Building 69
Church : See proper name
Citibank 91
Citibank Building 72
Citicorp. 72
City Hall 84
City of New York (Museum of the) 114
Civic Center. 84
Cleveland (President) . . 95
Clinton (De Witt) . . . 107
Cloisters (The) 110
Coe (William Robertson) . 141
Cold Spring Harbor (Long Island) 142
Collens (Charles). . . . 110
Colgate Palmolive Bldg . 72
Colonial architecture . . . 28
Colonnade Row 80
Columbia University . . . 107

Columbus Circle 98
Coney Island 130
Conference House . . . 137
Conservatory Gardens . . 114
Consolidated Edison Building. 122
Constitution (The). . . . 23
Contemporary Crafts (Museum of) 37
Cooper-Hewitt Museum, The Smithsonian Institution's National Museum of Design 114
Cooper Union Foundation Building. 80
Corbin (Margaret) . . . 109
Corning Glass Building . 48
Cortlandt Street 121
Croton Distribution Reservoir 46
Crystal Palace. 46

D

Daily News Building . . . 68
Dauphine (The) 93
Declaration of Independence . . . 23, 85
Delancey Street 82
Department Stores. . . . 120
Diamond Row 47
Dickens (Charles) . . . 81
Donnell Library Center. . 37
Duchamp (Marcel) . . 29
Duke House (The James B.) . 50
Dune Road (Long Island) . 143
Dutchess County (Hudson River Valley) . . . 139
Dyckman House 122

E

East Coast Memorial. . . 94
East Forty-Second Street 68
East Hampton (Long Island) 143
East Village 79, 80
Eden Theater 80
Eighth Avenue 97
El (The) 23, 81
Ellis Island 94
Empire State Building . . 44
Entertainment 15
Equitable Life Building. . 36
Erie Canal 23, 138
Essex Street Market . . . 82
European-American Bank and Trust Company . . 72
Events (A Tourist Calendar of) 32
Exxon Building. 36

F

Falaise (Long Island). . . . 141
Federal Hall National Memorial 87, 91
Fifth Avenue. 43
Fifth Avenue Presbyterian Church . . 48
Fifty-Five Water Street. . 96
Fifty-Seventh Street . . . 121
Financial District 87

145

MANUFACTURE FRANÇAISE DES PNEUMATIQUES MICHELIN
© Michelin et Cie, propriétaires-éditeurs, 1978
Société en commandite par actions au capital de 700 millions de francs
R.C. Clermond-Fd B 855 200 507 (55 B 50) Siège - Social Clermont-Fd (France)
ISBN 2 06 015 510 - X

Photocomposition : P.C.R.A. Villeurbanne — Impression TARDY QUERCY S.A., Bourges
Printed in France. 11.78.40 — Dépôt légal : 4e trim. 1978 (9095)

PIONEERS FOR PROGRESS

In less than 200 years, Americans have carved their way through the wilderness, spanned a continent, perfected countless machines, mastered the mysteries of flight and set foot on the moon.

Our magnificent system of transportation is a lasting tribute to this pioneering spirit that has made America a great nation.

Airplanes, trains, buses and especially trucks and automobiles have helped this country grow and prosper.

This same pioneering spirit in the complex field of transportation has enabled Michelin to maintain its worldwide leadership in tire technology since 1891.

EASTSIDE/WESTSIDE...MICHELIN AROUND THE TOWN! Everyone knows that New York City, one of the largest and most visited cities in the world, has a lot to offer to both tourists and native New Yorkers alike. From museums to theaters, from skyscrapers to historical sites, New York City is a great place to visit any time of the year. If you visit New York City by car, Michelin recommends that you check the condition of your tires before you make the trip. Stop-and-go city traffic and rough city streets can be very hard on tires.

If you think that your tires might not stand up to the rigors of city driving, your authorized Michelin dealer offers a wide range of quality steel-belted radials. You can depend on more than thirty years of Michelin radial tire experience to help you get all the performance your car was designed to deliver.

Don't let the possibility of tire trouble spoil your visit to the "Big Apple"! If you need tires, equip your car with a new set of Michelin 'X' steel-belted radial tires.

THINK MICHELIN FIRST!

At Michelin, over 100,000 employees worldwide are dedicated to the research, manufacture and sale of tires of the highest quality. At Michelin quality means:

LONGER MILEAGE: It's a proven fact. Under the same driving conditions (same car, same driver) Michelin 'X' Radials give at least twice the tread mileage of bias-ply tires.

FUEL SAVINGS: Because Michelin 'X' Radial tires roll "easy", your car will use less energy from the engine. The result can be a substantial fuel savings over bias-ply tires.

TRACTION: Tests have proven Michelin's performance on dry as well as rain-soaked roads.

BRAKING: Distortion-free, steel-cord braced tread helps to provide stopping power when you need it most.

STEERING PRECISION: Your driving will require less effort because Michelin 'X' runs true to course...does not wander on straightaways.

PUNCTURE PROTECTION: Steel-cord belts beneath the tread help to shield against most punctures.

RIDING COMFORT: Michelin 'X' Radial cushions shocks and jolts because the radial plies in its body flex in the same direction.

XWW Specially engineered for American cars, this tubeless whitewall radial tire assures a smooth ride, predictable, responsive handling and proven fuel economy over conventional bias-ply tires. The Michelin 'X' radial tire is available in millimetric and alpha-numeric sizes. Alpha-numeric sizes have varying widths of whitewall stripe depending on the wheel diameter.

XM+S With an aggressive mud and snow tread pattern on the outside and Michelin's belted radial construction on the inside, the Michelin XM+S is specially designed to meet the driving needs of winter. All Michelin XM+S radials are pre-drilled for studs, to be used in states where studs are legal.

XZX Designed for most imports and American compact cars, XZX radial tires offer the feature of a wrap-around shoulder design for exceptional handling and traction. In addition, these tires run at a low noise level.

TRX The Michelin TRX is a new low-profile radial designed for high cornering stability, excellent traction on wet and dry roads, improved riding comfort and long tread life. The TRX must be mounted on a TR or JM rim.

At Michelin, satisfying your specific tire needs is our goal. For passenger cars, imported cars, imported sports cars, recreational vehicles, light commercial vehicles, trucks, and earthmoving equipment, ask for Michelin 'X' steel-belted radial tires.